THE LOST
MATRIARCH

UNIVERSITY OF NEBRASKA PRESS
LINCOLN

THE LOST MATRIARCH

Finding Leah in the Bible and Midrash

JERRY RABOW

THE JEWISH PUBLICATION SOCIETY

PHILADELPHIA

Library of Congress Cataloging-in-Publication Data
Rabow, Jerry, 1937–
The lost matriarch: finding Leah in the Bible and
Midrash / Jerry Rabow.
  pages   cm
"Published by the University of Nebraska Press as a
Jewish Publication Society book."
Includes bibliographical references and index.
ISBN 978-0-8276-1207-5 (pbk.: alk. paper)
ISBN 978-0-8276-1180-1 (epub)
ISBN 978-0-8276-1181-8 (mobi)
ISBN 978-0-8276-1179-5 (pdf)
1. Leah (Biblical matriarch) 2. Leah (Biblical
matriarch)—In rabbinical literature. 3. Jacob
(Biblical patriarch) I. Title.
BS580.L43R33 2014   222'.11092—dc23
2014011422

Set in Minion Pro by Renni Johnson.
Designed by Karla Johnson.

The greatness of a teacher can be measured by how much you learn; the greatness of a rabbi can be measured by how much you change. This book is dedicated with deepest affection and gratitude to my great teacher and rabbi of more than forty years, Harold M. Schulweis, who taught me so much more than I thought I was searching for, and who changed me so much more than I imagined possible.

And this book about Leah is also dedicated to my Leah—my wife Lola (*Leah bat Yitzhak u'Peninah*), who will always be my "Leah the Loved."

CONTENTS

PREFACE

Why a book about Leah? Other biblical heroines perform more impressive deeds and deliver more memorable speeches than Leah. After Deborah leads the Israelites in a grand battle against the Canaanites, she commemorates her victory in a song of praise to God (Judg. 4:4–5:31). Hannah resolutely corrects the mistaken accusations of the priest and later expresses her thanks for the birth of Samuel in a song of prayer (1 Sam. 1:1–2:10). And in the Apocrypha, Judith saves the Israelites by killing the Assyrian general Holophernes, memorializing her victory in a song of glory to God (Jdt. 8:1–16:25). But the Bible does not describe any great victories for Leah, and she doesn't deliver any impressive prayer-songs.

It is true that Leah is a member of that exclusive club of biblical heroines whom we remember as our Matriarchs. In contrast with how the Bible describes the other Matriarchs, however, the text remains stubbornly mute about Leah's words and deeds. Those other Matriarchs are shown living brave and memorable lives of action and initiative, performing acts that change their families as well as the destiny of the Jewish people: Sarah protects her son by demanding the removal of his half brother Ishmael, a proposal expressly ratified by God (Gen. 21:9–13). Rebekah in turn intervenes for Jacob, her favorite son, by orchestrating Isaac's blessing ceremony so that it will be for the benefit of Jacob and ultimately for the Children of Israel (Gen. 27:5–17). And Leah's sister, Rachel, forcefully assumes responsibility over her own life and her posterity when she resolutely seeks to bear the children initially denied to her (Gen. 30:1–8, 14–15, 24).

But the Bible describes very few of Leah's qualities, recounts very few of her actions, and quotes even fewer of her statements. As a consequence, her position in the remembrance and affection of people throughout history seems slight in comparison with the popular regard for other biblical Matriarchs and heroines. To the extent that Leah *is* remembered by the people, this seems attributable more to reverence for her illustrious descendants than any appreciation or even awareness of her personal qualities. Leah has become our Lost Matriarch.

All these points certainly seem to present an impressive list of reasons for not devoting an entire book to Leah. But those very reasons are what compelled me to search for her—the silent woman who essentially lost her place as a great Matriarch. Because so little about her appears in the biblical text, I felt I had to seek out the fuller story of her life elsewhere.

We have all heard that the Bible is the best-read book in history. But that is not so. It may be the most *widely* read book in Western civilization, but it is probably also the *worst*-read book in the history of literature. The principal reason it is so hard to read the Bible as literature, I believe, is because of our culture's widespread reverence for the book. Many people view it as a God-written or God-inspired work, and this presumption makes it difficult to read the Bible critically in the same manner that we read other books.

And unlike the way we were introduced to other great world literature, many of us first learned to read the Bible as young children, instructed by religious-school teachers or our parents. Once a child has been introduced to the Bible via simplified Bible stories that are presented by an authority figure as being historically, literally, (and, for some, divinely) true, it is very difficult to return to it later and read it with fresh adult eyes.

As I began this search for Leah, it soon became obvious that I was far from the first to seek her. Fascinating clues to the concealed story of her life can be found throughout that great body of inventive and thought-provoking traditional Jewish rabbinic and literary commentary on the biblical narrative called midrash (from the Hebrew root for "search out," "seek," "investigate").

The term "midrash" means different things in different contexts. It can refer to a literary form of explanation or elaboration of specific verses of the Hebrew Bible (*exegesis*) using a traditional process of close textual examination. But it can also refer to a written product of that process (a "midrash" or *pl.* "midrashim"), or sometimes to formal compilations of such writings.[1] Some scholars restrict the term to only early rabbinic commentaries from approximately the fifth through the thirteenth centuries; others use a broader period from the third through the sixteenth centuries. For some purposes, midrash is distinguished from similar commentary found within the Talmud. But in nonacademic settings, the term is commonly used to encompass all Hebrew Bible commentaries, regardless of date, including contemporary interpretations written by lay scholars and literary critics. For convenience, this book will adopt the latter common usage, and will use the terms "midrash" and "commentary" interchangeably.

But the most valuable treasure I found in pursuing Leah through the midrashic commentaries was not in the answers I discovered there. The real benefit of delving into these commentaries comes from absorbing the *process* of midrash, not just its conclusions. Midrash can show us how to read the Bible as literature by providing a model for developing our own interpretations of the biblical text. Biblical scholars are of course very familiar with the role midrash can play in interpreting the biblical text. However, many lay readers have not yet experienced reading the Bible as literature, including using the content and method of midrash to illuminate and expand the text. For me, approaching the Bible through midrash has been crucial in my search to uncover the secrets of Leah's life.

Midrash is an attempt to solve a basic problem in reading

the Bible: What do we do when an important Bible story seems incomplete? How do we proceed when vital background information or a major character's motivations and emotions are either ambiguous or totally absent? The Rabbis who first created midrash did exactly what we do today when we read contemporary literature. They imagined and speculated about what the unexpressed parts of the narrative might have said. And like modern readers and writers of midrash today, the Rabbis seldom agreed on interpreting the Bible. They were often influenced by the circumstances of their times, the moral lessons they wanted to share, or their underlying religious and philosophical beliefs.[2]

Reading midrash is not like reading accepted truths, but more like sitting in on lively conversation among spirited debaters—often with those debaters speaking with each other across the centuries. Reading midrash calls for honoring what has been called the principle of "indeterminacy"—accepting multiple interpretations, even inconsistent interpretations, as different yet possible aspects of the truth contained in the underlying text. Each commentary may be true for a different reader, in a different time, or under a different circumstance.[3]

In a sense, the rabbinic interpretations of midrash become no less than a second Torah (from the word for "teaching"). Jewish tradition developed the concept that there are indeed two Torahs: (1) the Written Torah that God delivered or dictated to Moses atop Mount Sinai, and (2) the Oral Torah, which is also seen as God's Torah, but revealed through rabbinic explanations and elaborations on the sacred text. The Oral Torah was continuously passed on and developed in oral tradition from the elders to the Rabbis, to their disciples, and then to those disciples' students, and so forth, until it was eventually written down. For the past two millennia, later generations of commentators have continued the tradition by adding their interpretations.

According to this traditional view, both the Oral Torah and the Written Torah constitute the holy word of God, with equal power and authority. But, as the contemporary Bible scholar

James Kugel notes, since the rabbinic explanations and elaborations of the Oral Torah were eventually accepted as *what the Torah means*, we could say that, in some sense, the Oral Torah of rabbinic midrash has become even more authoritative than the Written Torah.[4]

The Bible is a poorly read book because many people read the Written Torah without the aid of midrashic commentaries. In our attempt to understand the Bible as literature, of course, it is not necessary to personally believe that the commentaries constitute revelation of God's Oral Torah. It is not even necessary to believe that there is divinity at the source of the Written Torah. It is enough that the early Rabbis of the talmudic era and the great commentators of the Middle Ages believed that they were engaged in the holy enterprise of developing the Oral Torah. We can take them and their literature seriously because they took their task seriously. (This is not to say that the seriousness of the task of midrash dictated a serious form of prose. Quite to the contrary, we will soon see that midrash can be deliberately playful and irreverent, often adding mundane, earthy details to reverential Bible stories about our great heroines and heroes.)

Understanding midrash requires understanding what "truth" is for the Bible. Although Bible stories tell histories, the Bible is not history. The Bible does not attempt to tell historical or scientific or archeological truths. Instead, Bible and midrash tell other important truths: truths about human nature, how the world works, and how we should try to live our lives. From this perspective, it is not at all troublesome that the commentators often offer such conflicting interpretations of the biblical text. Midrash is an exploration of the possibilities in the text rather than a revelation of a single underlying truth. Conflicting interpretations may simply be proposing different possibilities, each carrying its own measure of truth.

All the foregoing explains the construction of this book. *The Lost Matriarch* tells Leah's story in familiar biblical-chronological order, highlighting it against the background of the other major biblical figures who share and help shape her life. Biblical passages and midrashic tales and interpretations are integrated into Leah's story through quotations or summaries at appropriate points.

Because many important questions about Leah and her family have received more interpretations than we have room for in this book, I have included some alternative and additional commentaries in supplemental materials on my website at www .jerryrabow.com. I have also posted there some additional explanatory points in the form of extra chapter notes.

Finally, I want to make clear that this is a book about reading the Bible as literature. It is a book of interpretive techniques and possibilities, not an attempt to transmit any particular religious truth. The only truth I hope you will arrive at is that you can find your own meanings of the biblical text with the help of two thousand years of commentary—and most importantly, with your own insights as reader/interpreter/partner in the transmission of the Bible's great stories.

If you have any questions, comments, or personal interpretations of Leah's story that you want to share, I would welcome hearing from you. Please e-mail me at jerry@jerryrabow.com. I hope to post e-mails and my responses on my website, www .jerryrabow.com.

NOTE ON THE SOURCES

The classical or "biblical" Hebrew originally used for the Bible is an ancient language. As a result, the Bible presents several special problems for reading in translation. The language of the time possessed only limited grammar and vocabulary. And the Bible in its original Hebrew text lacks capitalization, vowels, and punctuation (no commas or periods). There isn't even a word for the present tense of the verb "to be" (the basic "is," in English). Furthermore, the Bible's literary style is often laconic and ambiguous. We have also lost some word meanings over time. All these problems have left us with biblical words and phrases—some of them crucial to understanding the story being told—that defy any agreed-upon translation.[1]

As a foundation for the English translations of Genesis (*B'reishit*), I have relied upon the New Jewish Publication Society (NJPS) translation (1962) for its high level of contemporary language and modern scholarship. However, some of the early commentaries or my own interpretations of the text are easier to understand when read with older, sometimes more literal translations, especially to appreciate the rabbinic wordplay often used in classical midrash. And so I have modified many of the Bible translations by using some words or phrases either from the first JPS translation (1917) or my personal translation.

While the JPS translations are the most widely read, there are other fine ones as well, so for your personal use and study I hope you will consider sampling the many available translations and commentaries, which reflect a broad range of contemporary scholarship and viewpoints, such as the several listed in the bibliography: JPS's *Torah: The Five Books of Moses* and *Etz Hayim: Torah and Commentary*; Oxford's *The Jewish Study Bible*; Harvey A. Fields, *A Torah Commentary for Our Times*; Robert Alter, *Genesis: Translation and Commentary*; Richard Elliott Friedman, *Commentary on the Torah: With a New English Translation*; Everett Fox, *The Five Books of Moses*; Stephen Mitchell, *Genesis: A New Translation of the Classic Biblical Stories*; and W. Gunther Plaut, *The Torah: A Modern Commentary*.

I have also substantially adapted passages from the Midrash Rabbah and the Talmud, based on the translations of contemporary commentator Jacob Neusner.[2] The capitalized text in the Midrash Rabbah and the Talmud refers to passages from the Bible, which either appear in the original translations or have been added by me for clarification.

Use and adaptation of the selections from the Torah and from Ginzberg, *Legends of the Jews*, are with permission of the Jewish Publication Society. Use and adaptation of the Neusner/Scholars Press selections from midrash and Talmud is with permission of University Press of America (Rowman & Littlefield Publishing Group).

THE FAMILY OF JACOB AND LEAH

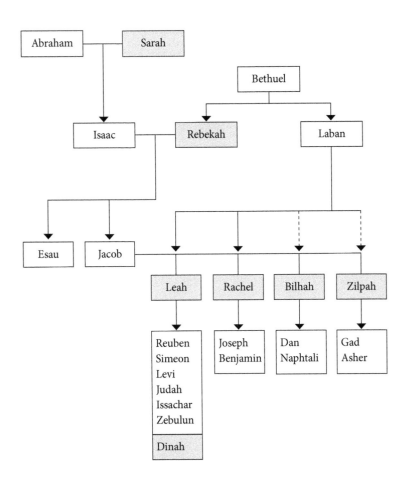

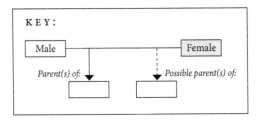

KEY:

Male — Female

Parent(s) of:

Possible parent(s) of:

THE LOST
MATRIARCH

INTRODUCTION
We Meet Leah

Why Leah Is Important to Us

Ordinarily, we expect that the relative amount of text devoted to a character in a book gives us an indication of the character's importance in the story being told. But the Bible doesn't work that way with Leah. Her life story receives only skimpy treatment, while if we consider Leah's role in the Bible's grand story of the Jewish people, she surely qualifies as one of its major figures.

Leah is one of the four Matriarchs of the Bible. She gives birth to six of the twelve sons of Jacob (the original twelve "Children of Israel"). From her sons come the two great dynasties of Judaism that developed in the early nation of Israel—the priesthood through her son Levi's descendant Aaron and the monarchy through her son Judah's descendant David. And the Bible promises us that at the end of history, it will be Leah's descendant (through the Davidic line) who will finally appear as the Messiah.[1] Furthermore, the tribes of Judah and Levi, descended from Leah, are the only ones surviving today. The other ten tribes of Israel have been lost through foreign conquest or assimilation into Judah. Thus, all present-day Jews who claim ancestry back to Abraham count themselves as descendants of Leah through the tribes of Judah or Levi.[2]

And while it is true that Leah has to share her husband, Jacob, with his three other wives, Leah can claim a unique status there as well. Leah is not only Jacob's first wife, she may have been his only legal wife, as we will explore later. Leah appears to have had the longest marriage to Jacob of all his wives, and she is the only wife buried with Jacob in the holy Patriarchal/Matriarchal burial cave at Machpelah, along with Abraham, Sarah, Isaac, and Rebekah.

But these undeniable markers in the biblical text that establish Leah's formal status as a great Matriarch don't point to the most significant basis for her claim to greatness: her unique relationship with God. This relationship can be seen in the special ways the Bible depicts God perceiving Leah's travails and responding to them by intervening to help her. In reading the Bible as literature, it is important that we read the text through the lens of those who wrote and compiled the book, as well as those for whom the book was initially written. The Bible is not just a history of humankind or a story of how families work, but a story of how God works in the world, how God intervenes in history.[3] Although some modern readers may not feel comfortable with biblical stories about God, we should not dismiss the Bible's God-talk as a separate or extraneous religious add-on. As a matter of literary interpretation, God is central to what the Bible is trying to express. The problem here, however, is that it takes some work for us to recognize and understand the often veiled biblical descriptions of what God's actions indicate about Leah's character.

Our challenge is that, despite Leah's exalted position and unique achievements, she has only two short lines of direct dialogue, and the text expresses only brief and indirect indications of her thoughts and feelings about just a few of the most momentous events in her life. Leah has a rich story; it is only that she has not been permitted to tell it in the Bible.

Fortunately, even those few words from or about Leah in the Bible are enough to reveal that her life encompasses a magnificent struggle against the most daunting confluence of challenges. We see Leah trapped in the entanglements of family relationships, communal expectations, cultural standards, and the forces of history (or in biblical terms, divine intervention). She continually wrestles with opportunities for good and evil. Moreover, her life is defined by a seemingly unending sibling rivalry over love, power, and status. The Bible presents Leah to us as love driven, love obsessed, and always, always, love denied. Leah our Lost Matriarch is Leah the Unloved.

And although we might initially see Leah solely in terms of being the unloved wife of Jacob, a closer reading of the text points to other aspects of love that go beyond romantic love or its absence. Leah also struggles, as we all do, with issues of love and the lack of it in her other relationships, including at times being unloved by her sister, her father, her children, the community at large, and, in a sense, by history. Moreover, Leah sometimes seems to struggle with how to love herself.

Reading about Leah in the Bible presents more than just the challenge of putting the few puzzle pieces of her life together; it also compels us to find within the meager hints about her life important lessons about the struggles we all face. Leah appears to be living a life of continual conflict, which, on the surface at least, she often seems unable to overcome. And yet if we dig deeper, she does seem to achieve a significant measure of victory. She eventually becomes, if not the beloved of her husband, then the beloved of God. She manages to triumph over the lack of love to become a much different person than she was at the beginning of her story.

Leah struggles with the challenges of love, disappointment, and the need to persevere to the limits of human endurance—all challenges that can confront us today. Most importantly, Leah manages to accomplish all that she does without sacrificing her essential moral standards. Indeed, she appears to have attained her life's real victories as a direct consequence of heroically maintaining her ethical concerns in dealing with others despite her daunting struggles. Even the Bible's few terse lines about Leah's life are enough to convince us of the universality of the themes she battles over. But we are also left convinced that we need more than those limited words of the text to fully grasp Leah's experiences.

When we moderns approach a book, film, or play that withholds crucial information, we understand that the author has made it our job to work at filling in the gaps—to figure out the inner life of the main character, detecting underlying motivations and feelings so that we can better understand her and perhaps apply the lessons of her life to our own. While much has changed during the two thousand years of rabbinic commentary swirling around Leah's story, one element has remained constant: the Rabbis share our compelling curiosity about Leah, the Lost Matriarch. Like us, they are not content to read Leah's story only through the Bible's handful of words about her. Instead, the biblical commentators struggle to grasp what must have been the fuller reality of this character's physical, emotional, and moral life, and how she coped with the crushing conditions of a life without love.

If we open ourselves to midrash—this second Torah of rabbinic interpretations—we can deepen and transform our understanding of Leah's story. With the help of classical and contemporary midrashic commentaries we can learn some of the timeless lessons of our Lost Matriarch.

The Background of Leah's Story

The stories of Genesis comprise a grand family saga. The major characters are part of a genealogical history stretching back to the sixth day of Creation. But historical context in the Bible does not only look backward; the lives of these heroes are also illuminated by what will happen to their descendants. More than a literary device, the setting of Bible stories in the context of both preceding and future generations reflects the Bible's underlying religious-philosophical view of how God works in history.

In particular, one of the principal literary devices used by the Bible to tell the family story of humankind is the central concept of "measure for measure" (*middah k'neged middah*)—the notion that God rewards or punishes a person in ways that reflect and repeat the essence of his or her previous good or evil deeds, or sometimes the deeds of his or her ancestors. The later event commonly resounds with a specific, ironic echo of the prior act. Today the expectation of fairness pervades much of our contemporary culture. In the Bible, however, extreme punishments or rewards readily attach to later generations who are wholly innocent of their ancestors' actions.

It is not important whether we personally believe that history unfolds in accordance with this premise that individuals or their descendants reap what has previously been sown. What is important for reading the Bible as literature is that the Bible appears to have been written—and frequently interpreted—by people who believed in such a view of how the world works. Understanding this is one key to reading midrash, for in the classical midrashic commentaries, the Rabbis often pursue their biblical analysis by searching for antecedent behaviors that might explain a character's present actions or circumstances.

In addition to that essential philosophical approach, the Rabbis' interpretations often reflect their practical knowledge of human nature, gained in their roles as teachers and confidants in their communities and in their personal life experience as sons, brothers, husbands, and fathers. And this knowledge of human affairs must have convinced the Rabbis that the meager outline of Leah's life expressed in the Bible conceals a far richer and more meaningful story, replete with valuable lessons for us all.

The Lost Matriarch is the story I found deep within the midrashic commentaries that have interpreted, expanded, and, to put it bluntly, *created*, a fuller story of the biblical Leah. But although we're about to explore the Leah story that speaks to me, you may find other insights in the classical texts that speak more convincingly to you. That is how you can personally participate in the midrashic process. Such participation is encouraged by the central Jewish texts of commentary and interpretation, such as the Talmud and the Midrash Rabbah, which traditionally handle divergent interpretations by including and discussing alternative approaches rather than presenting only a single authoritative conclusion. *The Lost Matriarch* will likewise often include alternative possibilities, and more will be available online at www.jerryrabow.com if you wish to delve deeper.

So now, because the creators of Leah's story believed that past actions influence present developments measure for measure, we begin our search for Leah in the same manner they did. We start by recalling the Genesis story of her husband, Jacob, leading up to the point when our heroine first appears for her brief turn upon the Bible's main stage to meet him.

A modern psychological profile of Jacob's character might begin by examining the influence that his parents have had on him. His father, Isaac, is the son of Abraham and Sarah, and Isaac's life has been affected by two critical childhood events: First, his parents exile his older half brother, Ishmael, from the family to protect Isaac from sibling rivalry and Ishmael's bad influences (Gen. 21:9–14). Then Isaac suffers the extraordinary near-sacrifice by his father (Gen. 22:1–13).

Isaac's traumatic last-minute escape from sacrifice seems to transform him from a potentially heroic Patriarch like his father, Abraham, into a tragically passive character. He suffers major alienation and isolation from his family. He never lives with or speaks again with his parents after that episode. Later, he so deeply mourns his mother's death that he can only be comforted when a bride is selected for him and brought to him, and he takes her to his mother's tent. His family life with that wife, Rebekah, and their children will be marked by a continuing lack of communication, and worse. Isaac will suffer deceit and manipulation at the hands of each of his family members.

Before Jacob meets Leah, his life as a son of Rebekah and Isaac is marked by a fierce and pervasive sibling rivalry with his older twin brother, Esau. Their rivalry bears the unmistakable mark of their father's own rivalry with his older brother Ishmael—parental preference. For Jacob and Esau, moreover, the parental preference issue is heightened by the competing preferences of both parents: "Isaac loved Esau . . . but Rebekah loved Jacob" (Gen. 25:28). As a result, Jacob's early character is forged by his rivalry with Esau. The Bible opens the story of Jacob and Esau by relating how these apparently diametrically opposite character types begin their struggles, literally, in the womb. Their subsequent conflict as young men in their parents' home is presented to us in two crucial episodes that raise deeply troubling questions about Jacob's integrity.

In the first episode, the birthright story, Esau the hunter comes back from his day in the fields to find Jacob cooking a pot of red lentils. The famished Esau demands some of the food. Jacob demands in exchange that Esau cede to him the birthright of the firstborn. Esau agrees to the bargain, dramatically declaring that he is about to starve to death (Gen. 25:29–34).

On the basis of this biblical text about Jacob's actions, we have to wonder just what kind of Patriarch would take such advantage of a starving brother. The Rabbis wonder too. One possible response might be to admit that young Jacob indeed acts unfairly in obtaining the birthright, just as he will next act deceitfully in obtaining the firstborn's blessing. Acknowledging Jacob's deceit could still be consistent with his ultimate patriarchal character if we were to attribute Jacob's early behavior to youthful inexperience. Then, by virtue of his later life experiences, Jacob could still be transformed into a great moral Patriarch.

The later well-known scene of the mature Jacob wrestling with the stranger/angel could symbolize such a transformation. Jacob's wrestling victory results in God changing Jacob's name in recognition of his new character. As we shall soon see with Leah's children, names are often extremely important in the early Bible stories. At birth, Jacob had grabbed the heel of his twin brother, Esau, in order to emerge from the womb, perhaps in a struggle to be born first. Jacob's birth name, *Ya'akov*, refers to this grasping (the name is apparently derived from the word for "heel," *ekev*) (Gen. 25:26). But after his wrestling episode, the Bible will explain that his new name, Israel (*Yisra'el*), proclaims that he has wrestled (*sarita*) with God (*El*) and man, and prevailed (Gen. 32:29; 35:10).

However, most classical rabbinic commentaries do not see Jacob's life as a gradual development of ethical character. The Rabbis prefer their biblical heroes to be pure from birth, even if this requires extrabiblical stories to make the point. So midrash works hard in an attempt to show that Jacob always acts ethically, despite apparent contradictions in the Bible itself. To achieve this, the commentators expend much effort in closely examining the text of the birthright episode for the slightest clues that might salvage Jacob's character from the implication of wrongdoing.[4]

The second major episode in Jacob's rivalry with Esau—the blessing story—is even more troubling. At the urging of his mother, Rebekah, Jacob tricks his blind father, Isaac, into performing a powerful, permanent ceremony. Jacob poses as his older twin, Esau, in order to have Isaac give to Jacob the special blessing reserved for the firstborn son. The Bible presents an uncharacteristically detailed narrative of this episode, replete with direct quotations of the participants' conversations. The biblical record of the event suggests that Jacob is expressly lying to his father, deceiving him by taking advantage of his blindness. This is hardly behavior we expect to observe in a Patriarch. The episode concludes when Rebekah arranges for Jacob to flee from Esau's anger and seek refuge (and find an appropriate bride) with her brother Laban's family in Haran, the Mesopotamian city of Rebekah's family home.

For the blessing story, as for the earlier birthright episode, many of the commentators labor hard attempting to justify Jacob's participation in what seems to be monumental unfairness. But some commentators are forced to concede that Jacob's actions are simply inexplicable. These interpreters accept that Jacob's moral character must have subsequently developed through time and experience, or else that, in appropriating the blessing, he simply exhibits some of the inevitable human imperfections found in all biblical heroes and Patriarchs.[5]

Leah's Life with Jacob

Thus, before Jacob meets Leah, the Bible recites his personal history, including the two dramatic episodes of the birthright and the blessing. Regrettably, the text fails to relate any corresponding backstory for Leah. Those few details that the Bible does reveal concerning Leah's background and life leading up to Jacob's arrival in Haran are so minimal that they scarcely require compression in order to be briefly summarized. The text abruptly presents Leah with neither background nor history. She is simply introduced as Laban's older daughter—implying, perhaps, that she is not worthy of more description.

Where is Leah's history? Female characters in the Bible (even the Matriarchs) are not nearly as developed as their male counterparts. This is especially true for Leah, who must share her life story not only with her husband, Jacob, but also with Jacob's three other wives. These co-wives crowd Leah off the biblical stage. She is rendered strangely silent and invisible even at key points in her own life. Consistent with this, the immediate background leading up to Leah's story is largely not about her but about her husband, Jacob.

When Jacob first arrives at Leah's home in Haran, he immediately falls in love. Unfortunately for Leah, it is not she, but her younger, beautiful sister, Rachel, who becomes Jacob's beloved. Jacob agrees to work for their father, Laban, for seven years as the bride-price for Rachel. But as we shall soon examine in detail, on the wedding night, in a momentous event that will echo throughout and beyond Leah's lifetime, Laban tricks Jacob by substituting Leah as the bride. After the deception is revealed the next morning, Jacob obtains the right to marry Rachel also, but only by promising to work for yet another seven years.

Leah and Rachel then engage in a battle to produce sons for Jacob, even providing their respective handmaidens, Zilpah and Bilhah, as proxy wives to bear them more children. The final third of Genesis is devoted to the story of Jacob's twelve sons, centering on the conflict between Rachel's son Joseph and his ten half brothers. The conflict is sharpened when Joseph is appointed viceroy of Egypt and Leah's Judah becomes the leader of the brothers who had remained in Canaan. But the sisters' competition over producing Jacob's sons seems ultimately resolved later in the Bible when we learn that the hereditary kings and priests of the Jewish people will descend from Leah's sons.

Because of the paucity of biblical text about Leah's life, her story as related in the Bible is easily misinterpreted. Some of the rabbinic commentaries read Leah's life primarily in terms of the apparent contrasts with her younger, attractive sister, Rachel. Since the Bible goes out of its way to describe Rachel's beauty while remaining ambiguous and essentially silent about Leah's, it is easy for us to presume that Leah was plain or perhaps even ugly. And since the Bible repeatedly emphasizes Jacob's immediate and lifelong romantic love for Rachel, it is easy for us to presume that Leah was unloved to the point of being hated (which is the literal meaning of the Hebrew word *s'nuah* actually used to describe her husband's feeling for her in Gen. 29:31). Finally, since the last narrative segment of Genesis focuses on the extraordinary triumph of Rachel's son Joseph, who saves Jacob and all his descendants from disaster, it is tempting to conclude that Leah's life is not especially important for the grand history of humankind or of the Jewish people.

The magnificence of midrash, however, is its many voices. If we search them out, we find a broad range of interpretations of these biblical texts. Many commentators see Leah in her own right and not merely as "not-Rachel." Accordingly, some are able to conclude that Leah shares physical beauty and moral dignity with her sister, that she feels romantic love for Jacob and eventually comes to be loved by him in return, that God has a unique relationship with Leah, and that in the Bible as well as in Jewish history as a whole, it is Leah who becomes the more important and more rewarded of the two sisters.

Midrash holds the full, dramatic story of Leah's life and the lessons it can teach us, which we're about to explore in some detail. The often-divergent rabbinic commentaries fill in many of the gaps in Leah's story with approaches ranging from respectful to audacious, traditional to groundbreaking, and ancient to contemporary. Listening closely to the frequently discordant chorus of commentators' voices, we can finally hear the powerful themes of this life—lessons from Leah, the Lost Matriarch.

1

WAITING FOR LEAH

Where Was Leah When Jacob First Sees Rachel?

As we view Leah's life unfolding in the Bible, we will observe various expressions of the powerful theme of how she struggles with being unloved. We might naturally expect that the most important aspect of her story about the consequences of love or the lack of love would relate to romantic love. After all, our contemporary culture is steeped in it, driving much of what we experience today in literature, film, theater, opera, popular music, television drama, advertising, and social traditions.

Scholars don't agree on when romantic love became such a major cultural expectation in Western society. Depending on definitions, some argue that the concept had its genesis in twelfth- or thirteenth-century notions of chivalry (perhaps due to influences from Arab cultures). Others believe that the modern Western cultural concept of romantic love was not fully developed in life or literature until the nineteenth century.[1] Under either understanding, we shouldn't be surprised if discussion about Western-style romantic love were largely absent from the ancient biblical story of Leah. But the real surprise is that the very opposite turns out to be true. Even the limited description of the Matriarch Leah that seems grudgingly expressed in the Bible leaves no doubt that the major issue in her life is what we think of as romantic love—or, rather, the lack of romantic love in her marital relationship with Jacob.

At the outset, nothing could speak louder about Leah, her future romantic relationship with Jacob, and the resulting rivalry with her sister, Rachel (who will also become Jacob's wife), than the Bible's delay in introducing Leah. The contrasts are evident: We first read at length about Jacob's early life beginning from even before the time he emerges from the womb. When Jacob arrives at Haran to seek a wife, the Bible immediately details his emotional meeting with Rachel at the well, a meeting that we are about to examine.

Paradoxically, although the other party in this familiar scene of Jacob at the well is Rachel, the scene nevertheless will serve as our first exercise as literary detectives attempting to uncover the hidden story of Leah. Leah is not only absent from this meeting, she is not even referred to in Jacob's dialogue with the local shepherds or his statements to Rachel. However, the Rabbis know, as we readers know, what will be the eventual outcome of the sisters' marriages to Jacob. Although Rachel will be Jacob's beloved, Leah will nevertheless be the first wife. Jacob may have preferred to spend his nights in Rachel's tent, but it will turn out that Leah will be the one lying next to Jacob for eternity, buried with him in Machpelah. In light of these measures of Leah's ultimate triumph over her sister, the commentators feel impelled to account for Leah's absence from the Bible's opening story of Jacob's sojourn in Haran. Indeed, the Rabbis use Leah's initial absence from the biblical narrative to help us understand what awaits Jacob in Haran.

> [And Jacob said to the shepherds of Haran:] "Water the flock and take them to pasture." But they said, "We cannot, until all the flocks are rounded up; then the stone is rolled off the mouth of the well and we water the sheep." While he was still speaking with them, Rachel came with her father's flock; for she was a shepherdess. (Gen. 29:7–9)

So we start Leah's story with a close reading of the Bible's introduction of Leah's sister, Rachel (several passages before the first express mention of Leah). If we stopped with a straightforward reading of the biblical text according to its plain meaning (a method of interpretation called *peshat*, discussed below), we would read the text as a simple descriptive introduction of Rachel coming to the well. But the midrashic process goes beyond the surface, peering into even the most incidental words to search for significance. The first question that midrash asks about this seemingly simple description of Rachel's appearance at the well actually serves as our first encounter with Leah. The Rabbis ask: How is it that Rachel is serving as the sole shepherdess for her father's flock? From the fact that Rachel can handle the herd alone, the Rabbis deduce that Laban's flock must be a small one. Laban, apparently once prosperous, must have fallen on hard times.

But even if Laban's flock is small enough for one girl to manage, midrash persists in its examination: Why is Rachel, and not Leah, caring for it? The Bible soon tells us that Rachel is the younger sister (Gen. 29:16), but it doesn't directly state the ages of Leah and Rachel. The commentaries are in conflict about the sisters' ages. However, the text seems to offer abundant clues that Rachel is not a young child when she meets Jacob at the well. It would be highly surprising if Laban sent a young child to handle the herd alone, especially with an older sister available to help. And it certainly becomes difficult to visualize Rachel as a young child once we read the Bible's description of her as having a beautiful face and a shapely figure (Gen. 29:17). It seems more logical to presume, as most commentators do, that Rachel is already a young woman by the time she meets Jacob at the well. This certainly is more consistent with the romance that appears to develop between them.

But analyzing Rachel's age still gives no direct clue as to Leah's age. We just know that she is older. And while it may be tempting to imagine Leah as an older spinster sister, the many close parallels in this story between the twin brothers Jacob and Esau and the sisters Rachel and Leah suggest an interesting possibility. Since Esau is slightly older than his twin, then perhaps the sisters are also twins, and Leah is likewise only moments older. Note that even if the sisters were both young women at that time, the fact that Leah is the older sister could explain why Rachel is herding alone: Perhaps their father fears that Leah will be at risk of romantic entanglements or worse if she goes out in the fields with the shepherds of Haran.[2] As for Rachel, even if she is the equally mature but technically younger twin, this status may be enough to protect her from similar romantic involvement with the locals because of the community custom her father later expresses to Jacob: that in Haran everyone understands that the older sister has to marry first (Gen. 29:26).[3]

Without the benefit of more helpful clues in the text, midrash offers a range of other answers to the question of why Rachel is tending the flock alone. One commentary offers a provocative suggestion: Rachel may have volunteered for the burdensome and perhaps undignified task of tending to the flock among the town's shepherds out of respect and honor for her older sister.[4] Under this insight, Rachel serving as sole shepherdess in place of Leah would mark the beginning of a lifelong pattern of unexpectedly generous behavior between these competitive sisters. We will see how the Rabbis depict both sisters—even while in the grip of intense rivalry and mutual jealousy—performing selfless acts of kindness out of concern for the reputation and feelings of the other.

Before leaving our first examination of the midrashic process, perhaps it should be our turn to raise a question: The Bible hasn't yet mentioned Leah, but the Rabbis nevertheless use a statement in the text about Rachel to begin their speculations about Leah and the relationship between the sisters in the context of both their family's economic and social background and what the Bible will reveal later about their lives. Is this a valid method of interpretation? We will be better able to wrestle with this issue later, after we have had the opportunity to work with a broad range of midrashic interpretations. But for now, perhaps we should simply note that midrash is not limited only to restating the interpretations found in a simple, direct reading of the text (the *peshat* method). Midrash may propose possible alternative interpretations with deeper meanings, often related to other biblical passages (the *derash* method)—understandings or possible understandings that we, as intelligent readers, can accept, modify, or reject.

Jacob and Rachel Meet

> *Then Jacob kissed Rachel, and broke into tears. Jacob told Rachel that he was her father's brother, that he was Rebekah's son; and she ran and told her father. (Gen. 29:11–12)*

The opening scene of this family drama is not an auspicious one for Leah. Jacob's arrival in Haran is immortalized by the text's marvelous description of his meeting Rachel at the well. Here, in two brief verses, we read the dramatic story of the first romantic meeting described in the Bible.[5] Jacob meets Rachel, kisses her, cries, and speaks to her. There is no room for even a mention of Leah in this text. But we readers know that Leah will soon become Jacob's first wife. In order for us to understand her marriage, we need to know whether Leah ever had the possibility of being loved by Jacob. Was all hope for love immediately lost because Jacob had already met and fallen in love with Rachel? To answer this, midrash goes all out to understand not just what the Bible says but what must have happened when Jacob met Rachel. The Rabbis trust their knowledge of human nature. Their commentaries begin by dissecting each word of this text.

Jacob's Kiss

Jacob kisses Rachel. While biblical Hebrew may not have had a sufficiently sophisticated vocabulary to express all the possible nuances lurking in such a powerful word as "kiss" (*va-yishak*), the Rabbis are not constrained by the limitations of vocabulary, and they certainly don't suffer from lack of curiosity. Much like modern readers of Hollywood gossip, they want to know: was this just a kiss or was this a KISS? It might appeal to our modern sensibilities to agree with the few commentators who suggest that this may have been an ecstatic kiss of romantic first love. However, even on the theory that this meeting at the well was an occasion of love at first sight, it seems contrary to the Bible's general literary style to read this as a kiss of passion.

So the great majority of the Rabbis agree that this must have been a socially acceptable kiss. From analyzing the Hebrew grammar, some conclude that this was not a kiss on the lips or even on the face, but only a kiss on the forehead or shoulder. Others point out that Jacob and Rachel were first cousins, and that kissing between relatives is permissible.

Of course, according to the text, at this point Jacob is still a stranger to Rachel. Only Jacob recognizes their relationship, and therefore only in his eyes would the kiss be proper. For Rachel, the kiss may have signified more, but she accepts it without comment, perhaps because she too regards it as innocent. However, one modern commentator speculates that Rachel's silent acceptance of Jacob's kiss is a sign that Rachel might not fully reciprocate what already was Jacob's romantic interest. This could be the first warning to us that their marriage might not prove to be a mutually ideal one.[6]

Jacob's Tears

Immediately after Jacob kisses Rachel, he breaks into tears. Some commentaries claim that these are the emotional tears of a romantic lover. It will become clear in the subsequent biblical text that Jacob is permanently infatuated with a deep and abiding romantic love for Rachel. Since there are no particular later events described that suggest a separate basis for such a love, it makes sense to presume that this first meeting at the well is indeed "love at first sight."

One commentary offers the midrashic speculation that Jacob's instant romantic attraction at the well may have been due to

Rachel's natural physical resemblance to her aunt Rebekah, Jacob's mother (a surprisingly modern Freudian/Oedipal observation despite its origin in the thirteenth century).[7] As part of the dramatic narrative, this interpretation would fit in well with some earlier textual suggestions that Jacob grew up as something of a "Momma's boy": He spent his time in the (women's?) tents rather than hunting in the fields; he was his mother's favorite; and his role in the birthright episode started with his performing what the Bible seems to consider a woman's task (cooking a stew, a chore similar both to the task that Rebekah undertook in the blessing episode and to the one that Abraham assigned to Sarah when he was visited by the three strangers). Jacob's special relationship with his mother continues into his adulthood, ranging from her initial favoring of him to her orchestrating and commanding his reluctant participation in the blessing episode and its aftermath.[8]

Some commentators agree that Jacob's tears at the well are indeed tears of joy but avoid attributing the Patriarch's joy to romantic ecstasy. Instead, they strive to come up with other, more dignified reasons for that joy that are not related to love. Conversely, many other commentators see Jacob's tears as tears of distress, although they likewise offer a variety of explanations as to the cause for this distress. One noteworthy midrashic analysis of Jacob's tears as being tears of distress presumes that the source of that distress is Jacob's concern that the shepherds and other local townspeople might misunderstand what he intended as an innocent kiss of kinship. They might gossip against Rachel's character.[9] Under this explanation, Jacob's tears express the previously mentioned motif of heightened sensitivity for another's reputation, embarrassment, and shame—a motif that can help explain many of the most powerful turning points in this family's complex story.

Several commentaries attribute Jacob's tears to his prophetic foreknowledge that he and his beloved Rachel will not be together forever—that she will die young and moreover will not be buried next to him in the family burial cave at Machpelah.[10] With this analysis, the commentators interject a foreshadowing of what will turn out to be one of the key consequences of Leah's upcoming marriage to Jacob: Leah will be the only one of Jacob's four wives to be buried next to him at Machpelah (Gen. 49:31). In contrast, Rachel will be buried alone, on the road to Bethlehem (Gen. 35:19).

In our eyes, having Leah lie in eternal sleep next to Jacob in Machpelah may not seem to fully compensate her for the nightly conjugal sleeping arrangements that she so ardently but apparently unsuccessfully pursues at times during her married life. Nevertheless, her interment in Judaism's most revered burial place will provide one mark of ultimate victory for Leah. Even if romantic love eludes her during life, her perseverance in pursuit of her husband's affection eventually secures her this place of honor in the history of the Jewish people.

It is one thing, however, to recognize the literary device of measure for measure—the presumption that God works though history by imposing consequences of past actions on individuals or their descendants. It is a much less palatable literary device to create convenient motivations by selectively imputing to a character occasional prophetic knowledge of future events, such as attributing Jacob's distress at the well to his awareness of Rachel's destiny. In examining Leah's story, we will find it impossible to totally avoid discussing some of the many classical interpretations that rely on reading back future events as the basis for a character's present actions. But even without relying on this handy midrashic device of presuming that a character acted from prophetic foreknowledge, we can still consider the possibility that the character may have acted out of a more general motivation, such as a concern for others, a desire to share in a greater destiny, and so forth.

The Lovers' Missing Conversation

When the Bible describes Jacob and Rachel meeting at the well, we can't help being disappointed: this first meeting of the Bible's first lovers tells us almost nothing of what was said. We learn only that Jacob tells Rachel he is her father's "brother" and Rebekah's son (Gen. 29:12). Rachel says nothing, and Jacob says nothing more. But just as we immediately recognize a narrative lack here, the Rabbis likewise recognize that this is not the real stuff of lovers' talk. Midrash therefore imagines what Jacob and Rachel might have said to each other. And the Rabbis begin by dealing with something puzzling in the biblical text.

The Rabbis first want to know what Jacob means when he tells Rachel that he is the "brother" (*ahi*) of her father, Laban. Perhaps Jacob was simply saying that he was "kin." Indeed the most prominent early Aramaic translation (*Targum*) of the text, by Onqelos, ignores this awkward word, "brother." Instead, Onqelos combines it with the immediately following reference to Rebekah, changing the verse to have Jacob say that he is "the son of her father's sister."[11]

But classical midrash takes this word "brother" seriously (as it does every word in the Bible) and asks what *could* it mean for Jacob to say he was the brother of Laban. Laban is an Aramean, a pagan people known later in the Bible for their repeated attacks against the Israelites. More important here for the Rabbis is the play on words hiding in the Hebrew name for that nation. *Ha-arami* is "the Aramean"—*ha-aramai* (related to *ramah*, "deceive") is "the swindler."[12] So every time the Bible refers to Laban the Aramean, the Rabbis read a caution: "Watch out for the swindler!"

As the contemporary commentator James Kugel points out, many midrashic interpretations of biblical words seek meanings from other words that sound similar, even if they are spelled differently or derived from different roots.[13] Listening for such auditory clues is a valid and appropriate technique for reading Bible stories since, according to modern analysis, parts of the written text are based on stories that had been told and retold in earlier oral tradition.

And here the Rabbis' warning turns out to be right. As Jacob's life in Haran unfolds, Laban will amply prove himself to be a swindler—indeed, a master of deceit. He is a lying trickster who continually takes unfair advantage of Jacob, as will be epitomized in the remarkable night of Jacob's unintentional wedding to Leah.

But then why would Jacob declare that he is a brother to this trickster? When midrash deals with the earlier stories of Jacob's actions as a younger brother to Esau in the purchase of the birthright and the taking of the blessing, the commentaries struggle over the Patriarch's morality. If the Rabbis are willing to work so hard to defend Jacob's character from the implication of trickery and deceit in those previous episodes, you can be sure that they won't let his statement that he is Laban's brother turn into a confession that Jacob too is a deceiver. Instead, Jacob's use of this single word "brother" sparks the midrashic invention of a substantial new and intimate conversation between the lovers, Jacob and Rachel—a conversation fabricated in the Talmud but wholly absent from the biblical text. This imagined conversation goes far beyond merely explaining the use of the term "brother." It goes on to set the stage for a powerful midrashic explanation later of how Leah becomes Jacob's first bride.

> As is written, AND JACOB TOLD RACHEL THAT HE WAS HER FATHER'S BROTHER (Gen. 29:12). Now was he really her father's brother? He was actually the son of her father's sister [Rebekah]. Rather he said to her, "Marry me." She said to him, "Yes; but my father is a deceiver, and you will not be able to outwit him." He said to her, "I am his brother in deceit." She said to him, "And is a righteous man permitted to act deceitfully?" He said to her, "Yes, [it is written:] WITH THE PURE BE PURE, BUT WITH THE CROOKED BE SLY (2 Sam. 22:27)." He said to her, "And what is the deceit [that your father will attempt]?" She said to him, "I have an older sister, and he will not marry me off before her." He [Jacob] gave her [Rachel] signs [to identify herself]. When the [wedding] night came, she [Rachel] said, "Now my sister will be disgraced." She gave her [Leah] the signs. (Talmud *Megillah* 13b)

The Rabbis create this conversation because they know that Jacob and Rachel must have done more than merely share a surprise kiss at the well. They are in love, and lovers talk to each other. So according to classical midrash, Jacob immediately goes on to propose marriage to Rachel at the well, and she as quickly accepts. But in the midrashic tale, Rachel also warns her betrothed that her father will be scheming to first marry off her older sister, Leah, even if that requires tricking Jacob into marrying Leah. Jacob and Rachel will have to be very clever to bring about their pledged marriage in the face of Laban's expected deceit. It is in response to this warning that Jacob assures Rachel that he is the brother (the equal) of her father when it comes to deceit.[14]

By this point in the biblical story, the reader might be ready to accept that, Patriarch or not, Jacob certainly seems to have at least begun his life as a deceiver. The two episodes in his life so far that the Bible recounts in detail are the birthright and the blessing stories. If we look at only the text, it is easy to conclude that Jacob acquires the birthright by tricking a starving Esau into selling it for a quick pot of lentils. And Jacob's deceptiveness seems uncomfortably clear in the blessing story, where he appears in Isaac's tent with his neck and arms covered in goatskins, and then twice tells his blind father that he is Esau returning for the firstborn's blessing. As already pointed out, however, many of the commentators seem driven to exalt the morality of the Patriarchs. This leads to some extremely inventive commentaries seeking to exonerate Jacob through creative interpretation of the birthright and blessing episodes.[15]

Similarly for the present situation, midrash strongly insists that Jacob's declaration to Rachel that he and her father are brothers in deception is not an admission of culpability by Jacob. The Rabbis have Rachel immediately challenge Jacob's statement by asking him if deception is appropriate for the pious. Jacob responds that it is appropriate to act according to the behavior of others: the pious should answer righteousness with righteousness, but they may use deception to defend against deception.[16]

Midrash goes on to outline the plan that Jacob devises to frustrate any potential trickery Laban might use to get him to marry Leah instead of Rachel. Jacob gives Rachel secret signs that can serve as passwords to positively identify Rachel regardless of what scheme Laban might attempt.[17]

Some commentators conclude that these signs were special words—in particular, the intimate passages of Jewish law governing marital relationships that the scholarly Jacob learned in his prior years of study.[18] Others propose that the signs were not words, but a very specific touch—Rachel was to touch Jacob's right toe, right thumb, and right earlobe.[19] Perhaps this is meant as a reference to the priestly ritual later specified in Lev. 14:14–17 for the guilt offering of the leper, calling for blood and oil to be touched at these same places in order to purify the leper.[20] Is the sign from Rachel supposed to purify Jacob from the stain of his having obtained the blessing in place of Esau? For if these touches, rather than words, are to serve as the lovers' secret sign, this procedure would mirror how Jacob had previously obtained the blessing from Isaac. Jacob fooled his blind father through Isaac's sense of touch (with the animal skins Jacob wore on his neck and arms), rather than by imitating Esau's voice (Isaac states in the text that he recognizes Jacob's voice, Gen. 27:22–23).

Thus, one of the midrashic versions—that the secret signs were physical ones—suggests a direct linkage between the hoax Jacob previously perpetrated by appearing in the darkness of his father's blindness and the hoax Laban will be working on Jacob by having Leah appear in the darkness of the wedding tent. Finding such a linkage between the two episodes in the biblical narrative confirms the Rabbis' underlying philosophy that God exacts justice in the world measure for measure. For modern readers approaching the Bible as literature, such linkages serve as important literary elements, heightening the dramatic, ironic tension in the unfolding story.

Leah Still Waits: Jacob and Laban Meet

If a modern romance novelist had crafted this story, we might accept the temporary delay in introducing Leah as a dramatic device intended to heighten the impact of her eventual appearance and the start of her rivalry with Rachel. But the scene following the lovers' meeting at the well still does not introduce Leah. Instead, we meet the sisters' father, Laban. The biblical text telling how Laban greets Jacob is deceptively simple. Laban runs out to meet Jacob, embraces him, kisses him, and brings him into his home.

> On hearing the news of his sister's son Jacob, Laban ran to greet him; he embraced him and kissed him, and took him into his house. He [Jacob] told Laban all these things. And Laban said to him, "You are truly my bone and flesh." When he had stayed with him a month's time, Laban said to Jacob, "Just because you are my brother, should you serve me for nothing? Tell me, what shall your wages be?" (Gen. 29:13–15)

If we were to read these few lines without the inventiveness (and bias) of midrash, we might take the surface words to describe nothing more than basic hospitality and family relationship. A kindly Uncle Laban is merely expressing ancient desert hospitality, similar to that of his great-uncle Abraham in earlier days.[21] But midrash knows better.

AND IT CAME TO PASS, WHEN LABAN HEARD [the news of his sister's son Jacob, he ran to greet him] (Gen. 29:13–14). He [Laban] thought, "Eliezer [the servant Abraham had previously sent to Haran to find a bride for Isaac] was only a servant of the household, but about him it is written: AND THE SERVANT TOOK TEN CAMELS (Gen. 24:10). This one [Jacob], who is the favorite of the household, how much the more so!" When he did not see a wallet, HE EMBRACED HIM, thinking, "Perhaps he has his money in his girdle." When he did not find money, HE KISSED HIM, thinking, "Perhaps he has pearls and conceals them in his mouth." [Jacob] said to him, "What are you thinking? That I came carrying money? I have come carrying nothing but words." [Thus:] HE TOLD LABAN ALL THESE THINGS (Gen. 29:13). (Midrash Rabbah, Genesis 70.13)

The Rabbis do not see family hospitality here. Instead, midrash portrays a desperate Laban who had lost most of his wealth to drought and who is now consumed with how he can profit from Jacob's arrival. Laban remembers the rich caravan of gifts that Abraham's servant brought when he came and chose Laban's sister, Rebekah, as a bride for Isaac. Naturally presuming that Isaac's son would be bringing similar or greater gifts, Laban can't contain himself and runs to greet Jacob. Laban embraces, and then kisses, Jacob. Midrash sees this embrace as a subterfuge to allow Laban to pat down Jacob's clothing—such is Laban's eagerness to find the jewels or coins his nephew must have on his person. Discovering nothing, Laban goes on to kiss Jacob, this time to probe his mouth in hope of finding a precious gem secreted there.[22]

The Bible tells us that Jacob lives in Laban's house for a month. Midrash infers that Laban waits that month in hope that a caravan of wealth would soon be following his nephew's arrival.[23] An alternative interpretation of the month of residence fails to view Laban in any kinder light: Some commentators conclude that when Jacob "told Laban all these things" (Gen. 29:13), his tale included how he had arrived penniless (either because he fled from Esau's wrath in such a hurry that he took nothing with him, or because a vindictive Esau sent his son in pursuit, and this son caught up with Jacob on the road to Haran and robbed him of all his possessions).[24] When Laban is told about this, he therefore gives up expecting wealth from Jacob. Laban then immediately puts Jacob to work to see if he can be a valuable shepherd worth keeping in the household, or if Laban should instead expel him after what may have been a customary one-month term of hospitality for relatives.[25]

The concept that Jacob had been laboring, unpaid, during this first month (when we might expect Laban to exhibit more generosity for a relative) is based on reading Laban's question to Jacob at the end of the month as: "Just because you are my brother, should you [continue to] serve me for nothing? Tell me, what shall your wages be?" (Gen. 29:15)

And we also see that Laban calls Jacob his "brother," the word Jacob had used earlier in the text when meeting Rachel. The word here may simply signify "kin," but even if so, midrash is not necessarily wrong to read Jacob's earlier statement as intended to reassure Rachel that he was her father's equal in trickery. Thus the repetition here might be a signal to Jacob (as well as to readers) to expect some trickery in the coming labor negotiations. Words in the Bible can have double meanings (a quality that academics call "polysemous").

Other commentaries, perhaps less charitable to Jacob, assume that when Jacob "told Laban all these things," his revelations included not just his journey to Haran, but also the details of the previous birthright and blessing episodes. Therefore, when Laban hears these stories of connivance and deceit, he recognizes Jacob as truly his "bone and flesh" (Gen. 29:14)—not just a relative who is entitled to hospitality, but also a fellow trickster and deceiver, like Laban.[26] Indeed, in light of the parallels between Jacob's trickery in Isaac's blessing tent and Laban's trickery in Jacob's wedding tent, which we will soon see played out, it might be that the very story revealed to Laban by a brash (or simply love-struck) Jacob is enough to give Laban the idea for the wedding-night switch.

We also hear a strong echo behind Laban's effusive words that Jacob is his bone and flesh. Laban's statement recalls the majestic phrase previously proclaimed by Adam in the Bible's second telling of the creation of mankind. Adam could find no suitable companion among all the animals, so God created Eve from Adam's side while he slept. When Adam awoke and saw Eve he declared, "This one at last is bone of my bones and flesh of my flesh" (Gen. 2:23). There is ironic contrast between Adam's words and those of Laban. Adam speaks in awestruck recognition of his miraculous unity with Eve, while Laban's words hint at his approaching swindle of Jacob that will culminate in Jacob's unexpected and unwanted union with Leah.

All this midrashic interpretation uniformly casts Laban as an immoral, evil character. Just as they do with Esau, the Rabbis seem determined to read all Laban's actions and words in the worst possible light. Indeed, the classical commentators often exhibit considerable interpretive ingenuity to accomplish this.

The midrashic treatments of both characters, Esau and Laban, seem related. As a literary device, making these characters into antagonists and moral opposites of the Patriarch Jacob heightens the dramatic qualities of these episodes. This outcome is especially evident in Jacob's struggles with Esau, his twin, his other half. Jacob appears more virtuous when he must contend against evil—some of Jacob's own ethically questionable actions are minimized or justified as a result.

And in each case, the Rabbis identify Jacob's antagonists with militarily strong nations that had come to oppress the people Israel by the time the midrashic commentaries were written. Esau is Edom and Rome; Laban is the Aramean.[27] So by painting these characters as personifications of evil that are eventually overcome by Jacob (who is later renamed "Israel," and thus a symbol of the entire people Israel), classical midrash is delivering a message of hope and a promise of ultimate triumph that was especially relevant to its contemporary audience.

We Finally Meet Leah

When the Bible at last introduces Leah, it does so with only a few simple words, even though Leah's appearance marks a pivotal shift in the course of Jacob's life and in the story of the Jewish people. The Bible has already told tales of other sibling struggles: Cain and Abel, Isaac and Ishmael, and Jacob and Esau. The styles of those stories focus with equal intensity on the two brothers involved. But it is a very different story with these two sisters. We have just read the Bible's brief but intense description of Jacob and Rachel meeting at the well, complete with fast action (kissing and crying and running) and dialogue (Jacob speaking with the shepherds and with Rachel, as recorded in the text, together with the lovers' additional, intimate exchange of betrothal pledges and secret signs as imagined in midrash). Given the equal focus placed on both siblings in the previous Bible stories, and especially in light of the dramatic treatment of Jacob meeting Rachel at the well, we might expect next a comparably detailed scene depicting Jacob meeting Rachel's sister and rival, Leah.

But as is true for almost everything we come to know about Leah, we are actually introduced to her and her relationship with her sister primarily through a few enigmatic words. It remains up to us to supplement those words by pondering what is surprisingly absent from the meager text.

> *Now Laban had two daughters; the name of the older one was Leah, and the name of the younger was Rachel. (Gen. 29:16)*

Everything about this seemingly straightforward sentence invites our close inspection.

Two Daughters

To begin with, although the text is specific that Laban has two daughters, midrash reads the Bible's later description of Laban's ultimate farewell to Jacob as indicating that Laban has four daughters, not two. When Laban provides first Leah and then Rachel as wives to Jacob, the Bible interrupts its narrative with what seem to be two extraneous interjections: Laban gives a handmaiden to each bride, Zilpah to Leah, and Bilhah to Rachel (Gen. 29:24, 29). Bilhah and Zilpah are eventually given in turn by their mistresses to Jacob as additional wives. The biblical story clearly grants these handmaidens significantly higher status than servants. Some midrashic interpretations conclude that Bilhah and Zilpah are also Laban's daughters but initially served as handmaidens to their sisters because Leah and Rachel were daughters of Laban by his wife, while Bilhah and Zilpah were the lesser-status daughters of Laban by his concubine.[28]

The matter of Bilhah and Zilpah aside, from a literary perspective, by ignoring the handmaidens and introducing Leah and Rachel as Laban's two daughters—the older and younger—the Bible makes a much more powerful statement about what awaits Jacob. We remember that he had been forced to flee for his life from his family home because of how he triumphed over his older brother by obtaining the birthright and then the blessing. In both those episodes, Jacob reversed the tradition that such benefits were the entitlements of the older son. Now, the text signals that Jacob is about to learn the hard way to respect the prerogatives of the older child. He will soon receive a most extraordinary lesson: the people of Haran can go to extremes to fulfill the local custom that the older daughter must marry first.

And as previously mentioned, some Rabbis push even further in comparing Jacob and Esau with Rachel and Leah. If the older and younger brothers are twins, perhaps the sisters are also twins.[29] And if Leah and Rachel are twins, then no matter how much they differ in appearance or character, their twinship could heighten their rivalry and increase the dramatic parallelism with the story of Esau and Jacob.

Older and Younger

The Bible's initial description of the sisters states only that Leah is the older and Rachel the younger. Thus initially they are defined not in terms of their individual qualities, but in a comparative, perhaps competitive, relationship with one another. Suggesting such competition, the text again offers a glimpse into the future. The Bible will come to define and describe much of Leah's and

Rachel's lives in terms of their overarching rivalry—what each of them has that the other covets. It is a rivalry that will continue even beyond their lifetimes.

Midrash underscores their rivalry by playing with the words of the text. The Hebrew used here for older (*g'dolah*) and younger (*k'tannah*) are words commonly used to denote greater and smaller size, not age. And so the Rabbis interpret these descriptions to show how God would write the final outcome of their rivalry: Although Jacob won't love Leah as much as he will love Rachel, Leah will ultimately be given the greater gifts in the history of the Jewish people. The tribes from two of Leah's sons, Judah and Levi, will receive Israel's permanent kingship and priesthood. In contrast, Rachel's two sons, Joseph and Benjamin, will receive only temporary ascendancy over Jacob's other descendants (during the reigns of Joseph as viceroy of Egypt, and Saul, from the tribe of Benjamin, as the first king of Israel).[30]

Leah's Eyes and Rachel's Beauty

In one of the most enigmatic lines in the Bible, the text concludes its brief introduction of Leah with the Bible's only description of a physical difference between Leah and Rachel.

Leah had tender [rakhot] eyes; Rachel was shapely and beautiful. Jacob loved Rachel. (Gen. 29:17–18)

Leah has *rakhot* eyes, but Rachel is beautiful in face and figure. The definition and implications of that Hebrew word, *rakhot*, are the subject of vast discussion and dispute among the commentators. I believe that this is one of the translation challenges where the King James Version of the Bible gets it right (as do other translations, such as the modern ArtScroll editions) by describing Leah's eyes as "tender." It is helpful to translate the Hebrew word *rakhot* as "tender" because like that English word, *rakhot* could be read here in the sense of either eyes that are soft and beautiful, or eyes that are weak, dull, poor sighted, or sensitive.[31]

Some commentators see *rakhot* here as a positive adjective, presuming that the description of Leah's eyes is juxtaposed in the text to the mention of Rachel's beauty not by way of contrast but to show Leah's corresponding best point. While Rachel possesses overall physical beauty, Leah has her own singular beauty—her soft, attractive eyes, which are perhaps light in color (such as blue), contrasting with Rachel's dark eyes.[32] Most commentators, however, feel no obligation to presume that the Bible says only complimentary things about the Matriarchs and Patriarchs. Leah's eyes are "weak"[33]—unattractive because they are worn, dull, lusterless, or even of poor vision.[34]

So why do most commentators choose to read the description of Leah's eyes in a negative light? I believe that choice is motivated by the desire for an image that would best fit in with the rest of the narrative, as a matter of literary style. Many modern novels are designed to lead the first-time reader along a path of discovery in order to understand the author's intent. But the Bible uses a different process. There's no attempt to channel the reading experience in chronological order. The Bible is instead written for readers (or, earlier, listeners) who are already familiar both with what has happened before and what will happen in the future in the overall biblical narrative's timeframe.

Here I agree with a contemporary commentator who notes that if the biblical text were telling us that Leah had poor vision, this would resonate with an echo of the central literary motif of blindness in the story of Jacob's life.[35] At the beginning of Jacob's life, the Bible details how he obtains the blessing from his father because Isaac is blind (Gen. 27:11–29). Later we read that Jacob is fooled on his wedding night because his vision fails—from darkness, drunkenness, or love-blindness for Rachel (Gen. 29:23, 25). And eventually, Jacob will suffer failing vision at the end of his life when he blesses Joseph's sons and extends to yet another generation (or perhaps finally resolves) the dispute over the prerogatives of the firstborn (Gen. 48:10, 14). And of course, this strong theme of physical blindness carries a forceful metaphoric reference to the actor's moral blindness and loss of prophetic vision and understanding.

But even those commentators who agree that Leah's eyes suffered from some type of defect quarrel about that defect's impact on her overall beauty. Some strive to read only positive things about the Matriarchs. These commentators defend a weak-eyed Leah by insisting that the two sisters are nevertheless equally beautiful,[36] or that the sisters share the same general beauty, but Leah's weak eyes mean Rachel has a slight advantage in beauty due to this single attribute.[37]

I choose to see the weakness of Leah's eyes as significant enough to render her unattractive, certainly when contrasted with the beautiful Rachel. This assumption moves the story forward in several respects that paradoxically could benefit Leah. Leah's unattractiveness might dissuade the fearsome Esau from forcing her to marry him (a midrashic invention discussed next below), and it might also motivate her father, Laban, to do whatever is necessary to get his unattractive older daughter married to Jacob—the only available (and blissfully unaware) new prospect in town. Moreover, as a plot device, the description of Leah as so physically different from Rachel means that Laban cannot easily substitute the older for the younger as bride for Jacob. Thus if Leah were unattractive, there would be literary justification for the later elaborate wedding hoax in order to have Jacob marry Leah before Rachel, a hoax that will require the closely orchestrated cooperation of Laban, Leah, Rachel, and the townspeople of Haran.[38]

Midrash, always uncomfortable with gaps in the biblical narrative, goes further and asks why Leah's eyes would be weak.

AND LEAH'S EYES WERE WEAK [*rakhot*] (Gen. 29:17). R. Yohanan's *amora* [a teacher who expounded on the earlier statements of a sage] explained the matter before him: AND LEAH'S EYES WERE [naturally] WEAK. He said to him, "Your mother's eyes could be weak. But what is the meaning [in this verse] of 'weak'? They had become weak from weeping, for people had said: This is the agreement [between Laban and Rebekah]—the older daughter [Leah] will be married to the older son [Esau], and the younger daughter [Rachel] to the younger son [Jacob]. So she [Leah] wept, saying, 'May it be God's will that I do not fall into the hands of that wicked Esau.'" Said R. Huna, "Great is prayer, for it nullified the decree, and not only that, but she [Leah] came [to be married] before her sister." (Midrash Rabbah, Genesis 70.16)

This midrashic invention transforms Leah's physical defect into a moral virtue. The Rabbis return to the basic parallelism that aligns Leah and Rachel with their cousins Esau and Jacob. Building upon this foundation, midrash weaves a tale of how Laban and Rebekah had previously pledged that their children would be married to each other when they grew up. Naturally, such a pairing would match the older with the older (Leah to be Esau's bride) and the younger with the younger (Rachel to Jacob). Leah becomes heartsick when she learns from the townspeople of Haran that she has been promised to Esau, for she has heard of her cousin's evil character.[39] Leah's deep distress at her fate results in her crying so much that she makes her eyes weak from tears. According to some, she cries until her eyelashes drop from her lids.[40] (Perhaps to some of these male commentators, Leah's eyes are "weak" not just in their appearance but also in their inability to withhold that flood of emotional, feminine tears.)[41]

This searching midrashic examination of the implications of the sisters' physical descriptions is unusual because the Bible rarely describes people's appearance, and generally does not emphasize the beauty of its heroines.[42] And the statement in the text immediately following the mention of Leah's eyes only highlights the potential difficulties that can follow when the Bible does provide such physical descriptions. We're abruptly told, "Jacob loved Rachel." Is it proper to think of the righteous Patriarch Jacob measuring a beautiful face and figure against beautiful or weak eyes in order to select the woman whom he believes should bear the twelve sons promised by God?

In this instance, the Rabbis seem not to be embarrassed by the idea that Jacob may have fallen in love with Rachel because of her superior physical beauty. They believe they understand how romantic relationships work (at least from their culture-bound view of gender roles), and they see a wife's beauty as important because it arouses her husband's desire, and this ensures children and contentment. Beauty creates the attraction needed to sustain the marital bond. And seeing beauty brings joy, which is necessary to better serve God. Finally (in what must be one of the most self-interested declarations in the Talmud), the Rabbis conclude that it is especially appropriate for a Torah scholar to have a beautiful wife because that will help avoid temptations, bring peace, and maximize attention to scholarship.[43]

Some classical commentaries go beyond this male-oriented construct of the role of feminine beauty by attributing Jacob's love for Rachel to something more than physical beauty: Jacob loves Rachel for her character and because she is his destined partner. Rachel's outward physical beauty is enhanced by the emanation of her inner spiritual beauty.[44]

But acknowledging Rachel's inner beauty of character doesn't imply that Leah's character is comparatively lacking in moral excellence. Midrash is clear about Leah's equal if not superior righteousness. If Leah's eyes were flawed, the Rabbis can conclude that her beauty, like her sister's, was internal.[45] The midrashic story of Leah ruining her eyes by weeping over the prospect of marriage to evil Esau evidences her moral sensitivity. In midrash, even God recognizes this: Leah's tears are accompanied by her prayers imploring God to save her from marrying her villainous cousin, and God is so moved by her sincerity that God intervenes to change her destiny so that she will marry Jacob before Rachel does.[46]

To the classical commentators, this affirms that God intervened in history to reward Leah for her moral superiority.

Indeed, midrash counts three specific occasions when God responded to Leah's righteous prayers by changing her destiny: making Jacob her husband instead of Esau, granting her fertility so that her marriage to Jacob would be permanent, and changing the gender of her unborn seventh child.[47]

Does Leah Have Any Chance for Jacob's Love?

Immediately after the Bible recites its few lines introducing and describing Leah, she is shunted off the stage and the spotlight shifts again to Jacob's love for Rachel. It is difficult to tell what Leah might be feeling at this point. Later in the narrative, we will see how Leah's explanations for the names she chooses for her children with Jacob reveal her deep longing for his love. But we're not told when her romantic yearnings for Jacob began. Because of the very limited description of her, we're not sure if she is Rachel's unattractive, older spinster sister who might see Jacob as her last, best chance at marriage, or if she is Rachel's twin sister, a close or equal rival in beauty, who might see herself as a realistic or even favored candidate for his love. Perhaps under either scenario, we could conclude that Leah would have been devastated when, immediately after she is introduced, we read that Jacob loves Rachel and that he promptly arranges with Laban to marry his beloved.

> *Jacob loved Rachel; and so he said, "I will serve you seven years for Rachel your younger daughter." And Laban said, "It is better that I give her to you than that I should give her to another man. Stay with me." (Gen. 29:18–19)*

The marriage negotiations are strictly between Laban and Jacob. Although they are covered in only a few lines in the Bible, midrash adds ample analysis and commentary: First, why did Jacob offer to work for seven years, rather than some other period, in order to marry Rachel? Perhaps seven years was simply the standard term in that society for a general labor contract. Or since Rachel is introduced as the younger sister, perhaps she is so young that a seven-year term would be an appropriate waiting time before marriage.

The more interesting question, however, is not why it was precisely seven years (especially since "seven" is such a basic, stock number used throughout the Bible), but rather why did Jacob have to perform any unpaid labor for his uncle Laban to marry his cousin Rachel? Here the Rabbis' answer is based on a midrashic tale that Jacob arrives at Laban's home penniless because Esau's son, Eliphaz, robbed him on his journey to Haran. Since apparently even a related suitor is expected to bring money or property to the marriage as a bride-price, Jacob had nothing left to offer except his labor.[48]

Some midrashim even challenge what the majority of commentators think is obvious from the text—that Jacob offers his labor specifically for Rachel because he already loves her. Based on the earlier midrashic story that Rebekah and Laban had betrothed Leah to Esau at infancy, some Rabbis read the text as indicating that Jacob initially offers to work for Rachel not out of love but because he is afraid that Esau will become further enraged if, on top of all that Jacob has already taken from his brother, Jacob now steals Esau's pledged bride, Leah.[49] In this interpretation, the Bible's previous statement that Jacob loved Rachel is shifted in time to mean that Jacob comes to love Rachel. At the beginning, there was not yet a love match, and Jacob only develops a preference for Rachel gradually during the seven years' delay, or perhaps only after they are married.[50] But I suspect this minority view that Jacob develops a later and gradual affection for Rachel is a rabbinic attempt to rehabilitate what some feared to be the unseemly emotional text of Jacob's immediate, passionate love. While many instances of midrashic invention add provocative insights that propose ways to read the text, the attempt to diminish the force of the lovers' dramatic meeting at the well seems more driven by doctrinaire bias than by literary inventiveness.

Other commentaries read these two text lines reporting the wedding negotiations differently to reach a different interpretation, perhaps driven by a different sort of bias. The Patriarch Jacob can't be left as the "brother" (moral equal) of the Aramean Laban. So midrash reads Jacob's labor negotiations with Laban as the start of differentiating between the scoundrel Laban and the pious Jacob. We have previously considered the midrashic story of Rachel warning Jacob that Laban could attempt to use trickery to marry off his older daughter first. Midrash now observes that, in the actual text of the proposal, Jacob expresses his offer of marriage to Rachel in precise, lawyerlike terms, which he believes will leave Laban no ambiguities or loopholes.

> BUT RACHEL WAS SHAPELY AND BEAUTIFUL. AND JACOB LOVED RACHEL (Gen. 29:17–18). [Jacob] said to [Laban], "Since I know that people in your town are deceivers, I am going to make my offer perfectly clear." AND HE SAID, "I WILL SERVE YOU SEVEN YEARS FOR RACHEL YOUR YOUNGER DAUGHTER (Gen. 29:18). FOR RACHEL, not for Leah. YOUR DAUGHTER, so you cannot bring someone else named Rachel from the marketplace. THE YOUNGER ONE, so you may not exchange your daughters' names for one another." But even if you put a wicked person in a carpenter's vice, you won't accomplish anything. AND LABAN SAID, "IT IS BETTER THAT I GIVE HER TO YOU THAN THAT I SHOULD GIVE HER TO ANOTHER MAN" (Gen. 29:19). (Midrash Rabbah, Genesis 70.17)

Jacob will work for Rachel (not Leah), Laban's daughter (and not someone else named Rachel), and she must be Laban's younger daughter (and not his older daughter, Leah, even if Laban were to change Leah's name to Rachel).[51] Of course, as readers already familiar with the rest of the story, we immediately appreciate the comic irony of the trickster Jacob's futile effort to avoid being tricked. Jacob can no more rely on words to assure his bride choice than could his father, Isaac, rely on Jacob's words ("I am Esau," Gen. 27:19, 24) to assure that the blessing was going to its intended recipient.

Indeed, if there is anything in the text of the Bible that should amply defend Jacob from the accusation that he is by nature a wily trickster, it is this negotiation. Once Jacob makes his carefully worded offer, he seems utterly oblivious to any hint of trouble to come from Laban, although we readers can clearly hear the warning reverberating in the words of Laban's reply. Instead of clear-cut agreement to the proposed marriage contract, Laban responds with only a noncommittal observation that "it is better that I give her to you, than that I should give her to another man" (Gen. 29:19). Not only does this statement fail to provide a yes or no response to Jacob's offer, but it also works to deceive Jacob in the manner of the most effective deceptions—by telling a version of the truth. Laban's observation is true, of course. There is no man better suited to marry Rachel than Jacob, who will become a man of righteousness, who is a man who already loves Rachel, and whose destiny it is to marry her. And we see that Laban is also telling another version of the truth: he will indeed give Rachel to Jacob in marriage after his first seven years of labor—just not under the circumstances that Jacob envisions. Jacob the trickster has more than met his match in Laban. This seemingly simple marriage contract will prove to be the first step in Jacob's path from swindler to a man of righteousness.

The seven years that Jacob works for the family are a long time for Leah to be absent from the story. But in fact neither the neglected Leah nor the beloved Rachel is an active character during this time. Unfortunately for Leah, what the text reveals about the sisters during this period relates exclusively to Jacob's feelings for his beloved Rachel.

> So Jacob served seven years for Rachel and they seemed to him [lit., "and they were in his eyes"] but a few days because of his love for her. (Gen. 29:20)

When he thought he was laboring to obtain Rachel as his bride, the years "seemed to him but a few days, because of his love for her" (Gen. 29:20). Without the insights of midrash, most contemporary readers would see in these few glorious words simply an extraordinary expression of pure romantic sentiment that needs no commentary. And of course the commentators themselves are not blind to the poetry and power of this eloquent expression of the Bible's first romance.[52] But even romance and poetry don't escape rabbinic analysis.

One commentary sees this statement as referring not to how quickly the time passed for Jacob, but how he felt about the bargain he had made: He saw Rachel as a woman of inestimable value, so worthy that, in comparison, the seven years of labor and postponement seemed negligible.[53] Or perhaps these years were as but days *in his eyes* (the literal meaning of the Hebrew words for "seemed," *va-yih'yu v'einav*) because he was blinded by love—another reference to the blindness motif in Jacob's life.[54] Earlier, when Rebekah urged Jacob to flee to avoid Esau's revenge, she used the same phrase, "a few days" (*yamim ahadim*), to describe how long Jacob would have to remain in Haran until Esau got over his rage (Gen. 27:44). What Rebekah said to Jacob (a few days that in fact turn into many years) now echoes in reverse in what Jacob experiences (many years that in his eyes turn into a few days).

> *Then Jacob said to Laban, "Give me my wife, for my time is fulfilled, that I may go in to her." (Gen. 29:21)*

How can it be that one of the most sublimely romantic lines in the Bible (that the seven years of labor "seemed to him but a few days because of his love for her," Gen. 29:20) could immediately be followed by what sounds like an expression of urgent animalistic lust ("Give me my wife . . . that I may go in to her," Gen. 29:21)? Midrash recognizes that the Hebrew term Jacob uses for "going in to" a woman (*avoah eileha*) is crude and inappropriate for a learned, pious person. The great eleventh-century commentator Rashi leaves no doubt about this when he notes that even the most vulgar person would not stoop to use such language.[55]

But the Rabbis—including Rashi himself—rally to rescue Jacob from criticism. The principal defense, which is repeated by many commentators, is that Jacob is expressing a divine impatience. He is not impatient with lust for sexual gratification, but impatient to begin the holy task of producing the twelve sons God had promised him (according to another midrash) at Bethel.[56] Such impatience would seem quite justified if we were to accept, as the Rabbis did, the talmudic calculation that Jacob is eighty-four years old by the time he completes this initial seven-year term of labor![57]

Midrash also points out that by the technical terms of Jacob's agreement with Laban, Jacob and Rachel were (at least with the conclusion of the seven years) legally betrothed, a status that was at that time essentially equivalent to marriage. Jacob even refers to Rachel in this demand as "my wife" (*ishti*). Therefore Jacob should not be condemned for being impatient merely because he demands what he is entitled to, or perhaps even obligated as a husband to provide to his wife—immediate cohabitation.[58]

We should emphasize that Jacob here demands simply his "wife," while seven years earlier he was very lawyerlike with Laban by specifically referring to "Rachel." Perhaps we are meant to hear a reference to the earlier misidentification by which Jacob induced Isaac to give him Esau's blessing.[59] Or perhaps the current phrasing is simply an ironic literary device, setting us up for the rest of the wedding story, where Jacob indeed gets what he asks for—immediate cohabitation with his wife, although not the wife he is expecting to sleep with.

The Rabbis elaborate on the idea that his completed performance of the terms of the wedding agreement justified Jacob's crude language. Midrash imagines that Jacob had already made several polite requests to Laban for the formal wedding ceremony, but Laban ignored him. Thus, the language in the biblical text appears coarse and extreme only because we have not explicitly heard Jacob's earlier, more diplomatically worded requests. Laban's refusal to listen to the prior requests excuses

Jacob's using the rough language that becomes necessary to get Laban to respond.[60]

In the end, it is up to the reader to decide whether these pious justifications work. At least one modern scholar is not convinced. Robert Alter prefers to ignore the programmed midrashic attempts at rehabilitating the Patriarch, and instead accepts that Jacob's language frankly expresses sexual impatience (certainly justifiable for a lover who has had to wait seven years—and until age eighty-four, if you accept the rabbinic calculations—to consummate his first marriage).[61]

Leah's Lessons from Her Introduction

Here in the Bible's introduction of Leah, she has been rendered almost invisible by the dazzling glow of the spotlight focused on her sister, Rachel, and Jacob. Perhaps the best that we can say from Leah's point of view is that her story begins by laying the literary foundation for the great conflict to come: the rivalry between Leah and Rachel.

But this introduction does more than merely justify Leah's later participation in the sibling rivalry. Leah's victory will be that she will not allow the struggle to escalate beyond what is appropriate. She will put limits on her competitiveness in the rivalry, in accordance with her personal ethics. And Leah's adherence to her moral standards despite her existential difficulties will be enough to enlist God as her champion in the coming struggle.

All this is presaged by the midrashic analysis of Leah's "tender" (i.e., "weak") eyes. The Rabbis are willing to explore possible resolutions for the Bible's ambiguity about Leah's age, appearance, and sexual attractiveness. In the Bible itself it seems clear that, in Jacob's eyes at least, Rachel is the more beautiful sister. On the other hand, the midrashic story that Leah injured her eyes with tears of distress at being pledged as bride to the evil Esau allows her moral character to become the basis of how God reacts to her. We're about to see how, in response to Leah's despair over the prospect of marrying an immoral man, God will initiate the first in what will become a series of remarkable divine interventions, all seemingly compelled by God's recognition of Leah's goodness.

So the Bible's introduction to Leah provides more than just a general background for the rivalry about to be waged. In that single word, *rakhot*, describing Leah's eyes, the reader can read, as the Rabbis do, the initial episode in a story of Leah that will be centered on her ability to maintain ethical standards as part of her response to life's struggles. And she will remain faithful to her character despite facing cruel disadvantages (such as her husband's indifference toward her and his abiding love-preference for her sister). Even in an introduction from which she is primarily absent, Leah begins to teach us that one mark of heroism is maintaining personal standards of moral behavior despite the stakes.

2

WHAT REALLY HAPPENED ON LEAH'S WEDDING NIGHT?

The Wedding Feast

Jacob's wedding is the signal event of Leah's lifetime; it will shape the lives of Jacob's family and launch Leah's fierce rivalry with her younger sister. But we're told only that Laban gathers together all his neighbors and makes a feast. Of course, every reader who is familiar with the rest of the wedding story knows this will be no ordinary wedding feast. (Indeed, it seems that, like us, every character in the story is in on the surprise except for Jacob.) It is the prelude to the most amazing wedding night in the Bible—an event that will, no less than Abraham's covenant or Isaac's near-sacrifice, permanently alter the course of history for the Jewish people. Given the importance of the wedding and the paucity of description in the text, the Rabbis are driven to create midrash expanding each phrase of the narrow text into stories that satisfy their (and our) hunger for drama, details, and significance.

And Laban gathered together all the men of the place and made a feast. (Gen. 29:22)

Having learned that "Laban gathered together the men of the place," we can read this in several ways:[1] We can interpret it in accordance with the simple, plain meaning of the words, perhaps informed by any special usages applied to the words due to historical conditions at the time the Bible was written or according to biblical literary conventions. This is the *peshat* (plain meaning) method of biblical interpretation. According to the *peshat*, then, we would understand the text to be stating simply that the wedding feast begins when Laban convenes the men of Haran. We might conclude that the literary function of this biblical sentence is to describe what happens, revealing a custom of that time and place—that weddings were not just private family matters but communal celebrations.

We can also closely examine the text and look for latent connections to other words or events in the Bible that might deepen our understanding. This is the *derash* (deep reading) method of biblical interpretation. Using *derash*, we might read the verb "gather together" in its alternative sense of unifying—Laban consolidates the divergent opinions of the townsmen so that they agree on a joint conclusion. Similarly, we could apply the *derash* method when we notice that the text seems to go out of its way to refer to "the men of the place" rather than use more direct phrases that we might expect, such as "the men of Haran" or "his neighbors." Perhaps the men are of the same place (situation) in life.

Midrash (note that the word is related to *derash*) often extends the technique of *derash* to a further level of imaginative elaboration and even speculative invention that can create a supplemental or sometimes alternate version of the biblical story.

AND LABAN GATHERED TOGETHER ALL THE MEN OF THE PLACE AND MADE A FEAST (Gen. 29:22). He brought together all the men of the place. He said to them, "You know that we needed water. But since this righteous man came, the water has been blessed." They said to him, "Do as you wish." He said to them, "Do you want me to deceive him and give him Leah, and, because he loves Rachel more, he will stay and work here with you for another seven years?" They said to him, "Do as you wish." He said to them, "Give me your pledges [monetary guaranties] that none of you will tell him of this." They gave him their pledges. Then he went and with their pledges he got wine, oil, and meat [for the wedding feast]. So this is why he was called Laban the Arami [the Aramean]: Since he deceived [*rimmah*] even his own townspeople.

All that day the people . . . sang his [Jacob's] praises saying, "Hi-leah! Hi-leah!" In the evening they came to bring her in [to the wedding tent] and they put out the lamps. He [Jacob] said to them, "Why are you doing this?" They said to him, "Do you think we're indecent, like you? [In Haran, marital relations only take place in darkness.]" (Midrash Rabbah, Genesis 70.19)

In the midrashic interpretation of the biblical text about the wedding feast, the Rabbis (who generally see Laban as the epitome of trickery and deceit) attribute a very sinister meaning to his "[gathering] together all the men of the place." Laban has a plan in mind to marry off his older daughter, Leah, but he needs the assistance of his neighbors. So midrash creates this new scene in which Laban gathers together (unifies the opinion of) his fellow farmers and herders by reminding them that they are all in the same place (economic circumstances). Before Jacob's arrival, Haran's flocks had been devastated by drought, but since he appeared seven years ago, the local wells have been continuously full and pure.[2] (This story element of Jacob bringing plentiful water to a drought-stricken Haran is not directly expressed in the text. It is a midrashic extension, perhaps suggested by the Bible's description in Gen. 29:2–3 of the primitive rationing device of a large stone that had to be rolled off the well by several cooperating herders.) Laban gets his neighbors to assist him in the coming wedding hoax by convincing them that if Jacob is allowed to marry Rachel, the lovers will go away together, the wells will once again dry up, and Haran's prosperity will abruptly end.[3]

Laban proposes that his neighbors could take advantage of Jacob's great love for Rachel to keep the Patriarch in Haran.[4] If

Jacob could be tricked into marrying Leah in exchange for the seven years of labor just completed, Laban is sure that Jacob would agree to work an additional seven years for Rachel. The neighbors' job will be to dull Jacob's senses with revelry and wine. (The word for "feast" [*mishteh*] in the text is derived from the verb "drink" [*shatah*], and thus suggests a drinking feast.)[5] In order to switch the brides, the townsmen need to convince Jacob that according to local custom, the marriage ceremony and subsequent act of consummation must occur in darkness. The men agree to go along with the charade.

The Rabbis assert that Laban even persuades the men of the town to furnish money for purchase of the wine and food for the wedding feast. (In the midrash quoted above, Laban obtains the supplies "with their [money] pledges.") This is presented as another devious motivation for Laban to invite the townspeople and bring them into his plan.

Describing the feast, midrash imagines the men rejoicing and singing their drinking refrain to the increasingly befuddled bridegroom: "Hi-leah! Hi-leah!" Jacob assumes this is just a local drinking song. Only the next morning would he realize that the guests were warning (or perhaps mocking) him: "*Hi Leah! Hi Leah!*" ("She's Leah! She's Leah!").[6] One commentary suggests that Laban may have even arranged for this drinking song so that if Jacob tries to claim the next morning that the wedding was invalid because of the deception, Laban can respond that Jacob had been warned by the guests and so must have voluntarily entered into the marriage with Leah.[7]

The Wedding Night

Suddenly the heart of Laban's audacious plan is revealed to us (but not yet to Jacob) in a few sharp words suggesting a continuous and swift chain of events.

When evening came, he took his daughter Leah and brought her to him; and he went in to her. (Gen. 29:23)

The rhythm of the text conveys a sense of haste and unstoppable momentum. Midrash delves into almost every word of this densely packed sentence to uncover what happened.

"When Evening Came"

The only descriptive, passive phrase here tells us that it is evening. However, midrash doesn't dismiss this as mere background detail. To the Rabbis, no word of this holy text lacks importance. (The modern literary style of reading the Bible relies on a similar approach, although it is based on an assumption of human literary brilliance rather than necessarily a belief in divine authorship.)[8] The basic midrashic expansion of the Bible's reference to "evening" explains that when the bride (Leah) was led into the wedding tent, presumably veiled, the guests extinguished the candles, explaining to Jacob that, in respect for the modesty of the bride, it was the local custom to have the rest of the wedding night in darkness.[9]

If the wedding feast for Jacob described in the immediately prior verse (Gen. 29:22) had begun in the evening darkness, we would expect that the reference to evening in Gen. 29:23 would instead have been made in that prior verse. This implies that the feast started during daylight, but that Laban waited until darkness to produce Leah in place of Rachel.[10] And the significance of delaying Jacob's wedding until darkness fell elicits further commentary: Jacob ends up being deceived in darkness, just as he previously deceived his father in darkness (Isaac's blindness) to obtain the blessing.[11] This interpretation marks one of multiple key occasions in the story of Leah and Jacob when the text shows Jacob receiving poetic justice (*middah k'neged middah*—measure for measure) for his prior dealings with Esau.

This traditional view of how God works justice through history seems to be solely a two-party transaction between God and Jacob. Leah becomes a mere stage prop in Jacob's drama. But reading the story of Leah's wedding as if it were no more than the occasion for Jacob's divine chastisement and moral instruction deeply disturbs our modern sensibilities. To their credit, the authors of the classical midrash were also uncomfortable with such objectification of Leah. We will see later how the Rabbis deal with this through some creative midrashim.

"And He Took Leah His Daughter"

Laban "took" (*yikach*) Leah. Some midrashim read this as Laban physically dragging Leah so he can thrust her into the nuptial tent.[12] Alternatively, perhaps Leah is not physically coerced to engage in the wedding-night deception, but is persuaded to do so as a dutiful daughter obeying her father's command. Such an interpretation would further enhance the dramatic parallelism between the blessing and the wedding episodes. According to midrash, when Jacob impersonated his brother in order to receive Isaac's blessing, he acted not out of personal deceptiveness, but out of reluctant obedience to his mother's command.[13] Now Leah can be seen to impersonate her sister in order to marry Jacob out of reluctant obedience to her father's command. And just as some commentators absolve Jacob of moral blame for his earlier deception because he acted from filial duty, they likewise absolve Leah here.

"And He Brought Her to Him"

Because traditional midrash presumes that every word of the Bible is significant, the Rabbis find additional meaning in the text if the same word is repeated in two places or if different words are used to describe the same thing. First Laban "took" Leah; now he "brought" her to Jacob. The new word should carry a different meaning. One answer, obscured by the English translation, is suggested by the Hebrew word in the text: "brought" is *va-yaveh*, from the root for "come" (*bo*), and means "caused to come."[14] In the final phrase of this sentence, the same root in an almost identical form but with a single vowel change is used to describe how Jacob went in (*va-yavo*) to Leah that night. Jacob's Haran sojourn started with his declaring to Rachel that he was her father's brother—that he could be a brother in cunning and deception if necessary. Now the text seems to reinforce that pairing of Jacob with Laban. They each play a role (expressed in pointedly similar verbs, "bringing to" and "coming in to") that depends on the other's participation to make the wedding-night deception possible. Jacob's initial conflicts in life were with his twin brother. This pattern continues in the Haran episodes, but here Jacob's adversary is a different kind of twinned brother—the arch-deceiver, Laban.

"And He Went In to Her"

As just noted, the final clause of this sentence states that when Laban brought Leah to him, Jacob "went in" to her. But this word is noteworthy for more than just its linguistic similarity to the word used to describe how Laban brings Leah. Just two verses earlier, midrash defended Jacob against apparent crudeness for using the future tense of this same verb (*avoah*, "I will come into") in demanding marital intercourse with Rachel. Now the text repeats the same coarse term to describe Jacob's actions with Leah. This repetition sounds the note of literary irony: Jacob is getting what he asked for. He is impatient for marital intercourse (whether to satisfy physical lust or to begin procreation of his promised twelve sons), so he gets marital intercourse—but not with the woman he intends. The irony is further reinforced when we remember that in his prior demand for this, Jacob failed to mention Rachel by name. He referred only to having relations with his "wife." After the just-concluded wedding ceremony with Leah, that is exactly what happens.

What Really Happened on the Wedding Night

We can't help but wonder whether Jacob knows it is Leah in the marriage bed that night. Indeed, how is it possible that this first romantic lover in the Bible, a prophet and Patriarch, is unaware that his mate in the wedding tent is not his beloved Rachel? But in the biblical text, any such speculation about

Jacob possibly knowing his bride's true identity ends two lines later, when the remarkable "morning-after" scene begins with a description of Jacob's shock and amazement at finding Leah sharing his marital bed.[15]

> *And it came to pass in the morning that, behold, it was Leah! (Gen. 29:25)*

But while the unambiguous (for once) biblical text compels almost all the commentators to accept that Jacob was genuinely surprised, the Rabbis certainly have much left to explore, using the standard midrashic methodology of following subtle clues in the text to imagine what must have happened during that extraordinary wedding night.

> [It] is written, AND IT CAME TO PASS IN THE MORNING THAT, BEHOLD, IT WAS LEAH! (Gen. 29:25). Does this mean that until now it was not Leah? Rather, because of the signs that Rachel passed on to Leah, he [Jacob] did not know until now [the morning]. (Talmud *Megillah* 13b)

In a sense, all the commentaries strive to answer the critical question posed by the classical midrash: the text says that she is Leah in the morning; does this mean that at night she wasn't Leah?[16]

Rachel Gives Leah the Secret Signs

So how could it be that Jacob, who had lived with the family for seven years, didn't discover the substitution during the wedding night? The Rabbis' answer reverts to the earlier midrashic tale of the secret betrothal conversation between Jacob and Rachel at the well. After being warned by Rachel at the outset that her father might use deception to get Leah married first, Jacob gives Rachel a secret word or touch to be used as a sign for identification. The Rabbis conclude that when Rachel sees Laban taking Leah to Jacob, Rachel fears that Leah will be humiliated before Jacob on her wedding night. So to spare Leah from shame, Rachel discloses to her sister the secret signs.[17]

It is also possible that Rachel cooperates throughout the entire wedding hoax, motivated by a concern for sparing Leah from perhaps the greater public humiliation of having the community see her remain unmarried while her younger sister is wed (in contravention of the local custom that Laban is about to recite to Jacob).

The power and importance of community humiliation as an instrument of social control in primitive Haran may not be apparent to those of us living in modern society. But the Bible and its early commentators understood it well. We have already seen that one explanation for Jacob weeping after he kisses Rachel at their first meeting at the well is his distress that his innocent kiss of kinship could be misinterpreted by the townspeople and damage Rachel's reputation. The act of sacrificing self-interest in order to shelter the other from public scorn and feelings of humiliation is a strong continuing theme that motivates the actions of both Leah and Rachel throughout their rivalry.

Most classical commentators therefore adopt the midrashic invention that Rachel gives the secret identification codes to Leah to spare her sister humiliation. But even if this were true, it would only explain how Jacob could have been fooled initially into accepting Leah as being Rachel when they are first brought together in the wedding tent. To explain the rest, the Rabbis must search deeper, trying to understand how the entire first night of intimacy could have failed to alert Jacob to the bridal switch.

If the secret codes were a matter of touch rather than words, we could perhaps imagine a first night of silent touching without Jacob realizing the truth. Maybe Jacob is deceived by Leah touching his skin in the darkness of the wedding tent in the same way that blind Isaac had been deceived by touching the animal skins on Jacob's neck in the tent of the blessing. But Isaac had only a moment to make his identification; Jacob has the entire night. The Rabbis know enough about marriage to wonder how Jacob could not have noticed during their sexual intimacies.

According to those Rabbis who are determined to defend the Patriarch's character, Jacob is fooled because he is so pious that he uses intercourse that night solely for the purpose of procreation. Thus, Jacob keeps the tent in modest darkness and does not engage in any preliminary caressing or other activities that might have revealed his bride's identity.[18] Of course, a more realistic and less programmed analysis could reach the same general conclusion (Jacob and Leah experience a night of marital relations without romantic caressing or foreplay) but assume a very different motivation (Jacob's impatient lust, due either to his desperate love for Rachel or to the long delay in having sexual relations).

On the other hand, if the codes were secret words rather than touch, the Rabbis must grapple with the issue of vocal impersonation. In the blessing episode, they asked the same question: did Jacob speak in Esau's voice? The commentators are divided on that.[19]

In the wedding episode, however, many think Leah may have said the secret code words in the voice of Rachel. Either she was actively impersonating her sister or, since they were sisters, their voices naturally sounded similar. Or perhaps (like Esau and Jacob), the sisters were twins, and twins often sound alike.[20]

But surely the most arresting midrashic tale of what happened in the wedding tent places Rachel there too. One well-known midrash concludes that, to prevent Jacob from recognizing Leah's voice, Rachel hides beneath the wedding bed and responds to Jacob's questions and conversation throughout his night of lovemaking with a silent Leah.[21] This midrash goes on to imagine that it was the extremity of Rachel's self-sacrifice in Leah's wedding tent that later empowers the spirit of Rachel to cause God to relent from permanently punishing the exiled tribes of Israel.

Then [when God refused to temper His anger at the exiled Israelites], Rachel, our mother, leapt into the fray and said to the Holy One, blessed be He, "Lord of the world! It is perfectly self-evident to you that your servant, Jacob, loved me with a mighty love, and worked for me for my father for seven years, but when those seven years were fulfilled, and the time came for my wedding to my husband, my father planned to substitute my sister for me in the marriage to my husband. Now that matter was very hard for me, for I knew the deceit, and I told my husband and gave him a sign by which he would know the difference between me and my sister, so that my father would not be able to trade me off. But then I regretted it and I bore my passion, and I had mercy for my sister, so that she should not be shamed. So in the evening for my husband they substituted my sister for me, and I gave my sister all the signs that I had given to my husband, so that he would think that she was Rachel. And not only so, but I crawled under the bed on which he was lying with my sister, while she remained silent, and I made all the replies so that he would not discern the voice of my sister. I paid my sister only kindness, and I was not jealous of her and I did not allow her to be shamed."

Forthwith the mercy of the Holy One, blessed be He, welled up, and He said, "For your sake, Rachel, I will bring the Israelites back to their land." [See Jer. 31:15–16] (Midrash Rabbah, Lamentations, Prologue 24)

This midrash relates that when the Jewish people break their covenant with God, God withdraws His presence from them and from the First Temple. The Temple is then destroyed and the people are exiled to Babylonia. In the midrash, God resists the heavenly pleas of Abraham, Isaac, Jacob, and Moses to spare the people. But finally Rachel appears and reminds God of her act of extraordinary selflessness. When she contrasts her sacrifice with God's punishment of the Jewish people (her "children" in Jer. 31:14, 16), God finally relents. He promises Rachel that, on the strength of her wedding-night sacrifice, God will someday restore all the Jewish people to their position in the Promised Land and in the world.[22]

This midrashic invention paints for us a strikingly vivid picture of Rachel's sacrifice and what she must have felt that night. We see Rachel spending the entire night in the tent with her intended husband. But what an extraordinarily different night than the one she would have envisioned during their seven-year betrothal! We can imagine Rachel crouching beneath the nuptial bed on which she should have been lying, answering for Leah the lover's words that should have been directed to her, all while unable to shut out the sounds of Jacob making love to her sister.

And we must not forget about Leah. According to this midrash, Rachel saves Leah from public humiliation and postpones (but just for one night) Leah's humiliation in Jacob's eyes. But surely Leah also suffers deeply from this bizarre plan that, while allowing consummation of her marriage, requires her sister to be there, only inches away. What joy is possible for Leah, knowing that the marital intimacy is false, the love expressed by Jacob is false, and even the words of love that Leah is supposed to be saying are false? After her wedding night, can Leah ever lie in bed again with her husband, Jacob, without somehow feeling that Rachel is there too? Indeed, even if we disregard the midrashic tale of Rachel hiding under the bed that night, perhaps just the fact of substituting Leah for Jacob's beloved Rachel in the wedding would have been enough to spoil the remainder of Leah's marriage; Rachel would forever be the third person in Leah's marital bed.

But as terrible as the wedding-night deception is for Leah, the lesson of Rachel's sacrifice is not lost on her. Rachel's remarkable actions in permitting Leah's wedding night to proceed demonstrate that loving acts of self-sacrifice for one's rival can be an appropriate, if paradoxical, response to frustration in love. We will examine later how Leah applies this lesson through her own magnificent act of sacrifice for Rachel's dignity at the time of Dinah's birth.

The imaginative range of midrashic interpretation generally means that we are offered many provocative questions and suggestions, but no clear answers. For Leah's wedding night, however, a penetrating modern commentary may provide a satisfying answer to the question posed by the midrash: If the text says that she is Leah in the morning, who was she the night before?

One answer to this question is that, indeed, Leah was not Leah in the night. She was Rachel. Midrash agrees that Leah was at least passing herself off as Rachel in the wedding bed by using the lovers' secret signs. The contemporary commentator Avivah Zornberg goes further. She suggests that during the wedding night, just as Jacob had done in the blessing episode, Leah does more than merely impersonate a sibling in order to fool another person. When Jacob earlier receives the blessing in Isaac's tent, what is perhaps more important than the blessing itself is that Jacob finally knows what it feels like to receive his father's unreserved love as the favored son. This temporary psychological transformation of identity imparts a kind of transitory truth to Jacob's problematic declaration to his father, "I am Esau" (Gen. 27:19, 24). In a similar sense, Leah becomes her sister in the wedding tent. For that one night, at least, Leah is permitted to feel what will be denied to her for the rest of her life: being Jacob's primary wife, his beloved—his Rachel.[23]

Jacob's Morning-after Talk with Laban

In the text, Jacob's reaction to discovering the bridal substitution the next morning is to confront Laban, angrily accusing him of deceit. Although Jacob appears oblivious to the obvious parallels between Laban's wedding-tent deception and Jacob's previous deception of Isaac in the tent of blessing, the Rabbis are quick to draw the connections to illuminate what has happened to Jacob. In the earlier blessing story, dramatic impact is heightened by the Bible's description of what happens directly after Isaac gives the firstborn's blessing to Jacob. Perhaps still fearful of being found out, Jacob rushes out of Isaac's tent immediately after receiving the blessing. The Bible notes that, as soon as Jacob leaves the tent, Esau appears with the food from his hunt, in order to begin what he expects to be the firstborn's blessing ceremony (Gen. 27:30). When Esau learns that Jacob has tricked Isaac into bestowing the blessing on him, Esau "cried with a very great and bitter cry" (Gen. 27:34) and complains to Isaac that Jacob has taken Esau's blessing just as he had previously taken the birthright Esau deserved as the firstborn (Gen. 27:36).[24] And now in the wedding, Jacob the deceiver has in turn been deceived by a similar sibling substitution.

> So he said to Laban, "What is this you have done to me? I was in your service for Rachel! Why did you deceive me?" Laban said, "It is not the practice in our place to marry off the younger before the older. Fulfill the bridal week of this one and we will give you the other one too, provided you serve me another seven years." Jacob did so; he fulfilled the bridal week of the one, and then he gave him his daughter Rachel for his wife. (Gen. 29:25–28)

Jacob's cry of complaint to Laban immediately after the wedding switch can be seen as a direct counterpart to Esau's cry to Isaac immediately after the blessing switch. But while Isaac's response to Esau was an attempt to soothe his pain and indignation, Laban's response to Jacob is cool and smooth—more "smooth talk" for Jacob, the man who was born smooth (Gen. 27:11). Laban makes no attempt at denial, but instead delivers a withering justification by invoking the rights of the firstborn. As a literary device, the villainous Laban here becomes the instrument of God's punishment for Jacob taking the blessing. Indeed, the very crux of this incident is that the parallel birthright/blessing and wedding episodes that occur in Canaan and Haran, respectively, are linked by the central and oft-repeated biblical literary trope of *middah k'neged middah* (measure for measure). Jacob's trickery in obtaining the birthright from a famished, or at least impulsive, brother, and obtaining the blessing from a blind—in several senses of that word—father, are met with God delivering a deliciously ironic comeuppance to Jacob, the trickster, through the agency of Laban, a fellow trickster. As if the readers of this story could possibly miss this connection, Laban pointedly expresses his pious self-justification for the wedding-night deception when he tells Jacob that in Haran (unlike where Jacob comes from), they wouldn't think of doing improper things like ignoring the privileges of the firstborn.

And all this occurs in the biblical text itself. Without having to rely on retrospective rabbinic midrash (although the Rabbis do offer many comments about the linkage of the birthright/blessing episodes and the wedding-hoax episode), this "morning-after" text alone is enough to establish that in the Bible's philosophical-theological view, God works in history to punish evil (and by implication, to reward righteousness) measure for measure. Divine justice takes the form of poetic justice. From a literary aspect, moreover, we get to enjoy a demonstration of how divine justice can be delivered with a dramatically creative, ironic twist.

Midrash presumes that Laban knows about Jacob obtaining the birthright and the blessing because when Jacob first arrived in Haran, "he told Laban all these things" (Gen. 29:13), including the story of the birthright, the blessing, and fleeing from Esau's wrath.[25] In a further note of irony, it may have been that very story from Jacob that first planted in Laban's mind the seeds of his plan for the wedding switch. So Laban's response to Jacob on the morning after the wedding, which refers to the rule against taking precedence away from the firstborn, becomes a most effective kind of defense. Laban's justification for his own deception takes the form of a pointed attack on the morality of his accuser.

And Laban's attack seems to have been quite effective. Jacob's protests are immediately stifled; he says not a single word more in this exchange with his father-in-law. Jacob doesn't even make a verbal response to Laban's proposal that he can also marry

Rachel as soon as Leah's wedding celebration week is concluded, provided Jacob agrees to work for yet another seven years as a second bride-price. We only learn that Jacob agreed when we are told, "Jacob did so" (Gen. 29:28).

Jacob's Morning-after Talk with Leah

In the Bible, this dialogue between Jacob and Laban is the only express mention of the previous night's wedding hoax. But midrash is really interested in another "morning-after" talk. This is the conversation that appears nowhere in the biblical text, but which the Rabbis nonetheless are certain must have happened: the inevitable confrontation between the newly-weds, Jacob and Leah. Previous midrashic commentaries had scripted a detailed scene of Jacob and Rachel's private lovers' conversation when they met at the well. Now, the Rabbis once more draw on their knowledge of life (and perhaps lessons from their personal experience as husbands) to imagine a very different tone of conversation between Jacob and Leah when Jacob finally wakes up—figuratively and literally—to his eventual realization of the bridal switch.

> All that night he would call her "Rachel" and she answered him. AND IN THE MORNING, BEHOLD, IT WAS LEAH (Gen. 29:25). He said, "How could you have deceived me, you daughter of a deceiver?" She said to him, "Is there a teacher without faithful students? Didn't your father call you 'Esau,' and you answered him accordingly? So you called me by another name, and I answered you." (Midrash Rabbah, Genesis 70.19)

The conversation that this midrash envisions begins with Jacob angrily berating Leah for deceiving him by answering to the name "Rachel" when he spoke to her in the darkness of the wedding tent. Leah's defense in the midrashic story proves to be even more withering than Laban's defense. Leah answers Jacob that every teacher has his pupils—in some versions, that every book has its faithful readers, or that even a bad barber (a person not worthy of emulation) has his disciples. When she answered to her sister's name in the darkness of the wedding night, Leah was merely following Jacob's own example in the blessing episode when he deceived Isaac in his blind darkness by answering to the name of Esau. In one variation, Leah adds a further justification, arguing that, just as Jacob had gone along with the blessing deception in obedience to his mother's commands, Leah had likewise only reluctantly joined in the wedding deception in order to obey her father.[26]

All these retorts attributed to Leah highlight the unfolding of divine justice in Jacob's life. In fact, the contemporary commentator Robert Alter notes that what he calls the "symmetrical poetic justice" implicit in the wedding switch is especially important because it constitutes the Bible's moral commentary on Jacob's deceptive taking of the blessing.[27]

Since little occurs in the stories of Bible or midrash without far-reaching consequences, some commentaries on the subsequent marital life of Leah and Jacob will return to Jacob's bitterness over Leah's verbal attack imagined in this scene. Some Rabbis make the point that Jacob felt wounded not just by Leah's deception during the wedding night, but also by her harsh words the next morning. Jacob's reactions could explain why he continues to disfavor Leah and her children during the marriage despite what should have been her privileged status as his first and most fertile wife.[28]

Leah's hurtful words in the morning can be seen as contrasting sharply with the noble concerns that Rachel and, later, Leah herself display for saving each other from humiliation and embarrassment.[29] Perhaps the Rabbis invent such sharp words for Leah to justify Jacob's indifference to her. Perhaps they feel that Jacob has to learn to accept the wedding hoax as no more than what he deserves for having appropriated the blessing. But in a very early example of a gender-based judgment that blames the victim, the Rabbis appear to be assigning to Leah some personal measure of responsibility for Jacob's life-long coolness toward her, on the grounds of her sharp retorts in this imagined conversation—a conversation that the Rabbis themselves create.

Legitimacy of Leah's First Night of Marital Relations

Throughout this book we generally approach the Bible as literature—focusing on the aspect of Scripture called *aggadah* (story), rather than on *halakhah* (law). Nevertheless, at this point we can't help but ask a legal question: Were Leah's marital relations with Jacob on their wedding night legitimate despite the hoax perpetrated on the groom? The biblical text itself (Gen. 29:28) raises the issue when it reports that after the seven days of celebrating Leah's wedding, Laban gives Jacob his daughter Rachel "for [or as] his wife" (*l'ishah*), a term that was not used in describing Jacob's first night with Leah. So could the text be suggesting that Leah was not Jacob's legal wife on that first night?

Most of the specific laws of Judaism had not yet been revealed at the time of Jacob. However, midrash frequently presumes that the Patriarchs and Matriarchs have prophetic access to the laws, study them (as Jacob is supposed to have done in the tents of his youth), and are bound to observe them. Under this assumption, Leah's wedding night could be subject to the basic Jewish law insisting that lawful marital intercourse requires mutual specific intent; each party must be thinking about the other party during the physical act. Since Jacob believed he was with Rachel in the wedding tent, there could be no valid consummation of the marriage with Leah that night.[30]

This presents more than a technicality that could be subsequently cured by Jacob intentionally fulfilling his wedding obligations to Leah for the remainder of the first seven nights. The Rabbis deduce that Jacob's firstborn son, Reuben, is born as a result of Jacob's initial intercourse with Leah on their wedding night.[31] Thus, the validity of that act on that night becomes critical to the legitimacy of Reuben and his tribe. Midrash certainly finds itself in a delicate situation. As a practical matter the Rabbis can't invalidate Jacob and Leah's initial night of marital relations since that could question the legitimacy of one of the tribes of Israel. On the other hand, the Rabbis cannot restrict their efforts to only the literary task of interpreting the story. They are also responsible for interpreting the law.

As uncomfortable as they might be with this issue, the commentators are willing to wade in and answer it. Reading Jacob's protest to Laban on the morning after the wedding night, midrash notes that Jacob actually voices two complaints: What is this you have done to me? . . . Why did you deceive me? (Gen. 29:25). For the Rabbis, such a repetition implies two separate grievances against Laban. If the first is for tricking Jacob into marrying Leah at the ceremony, then the second must be for another act—deceiving Jacob into having marital relations with Leah while he thinks she is Rachel.[32] Thus, midrash ignores Jacob's impatience as a factor that possibly contributes to improper sexual relations and shifts all moral condemnation from Jacob to Laban.

Even if Jacob could be seen as blameless, the Rabbis recognize that his mistaken state of mind meant that his relations with Leah on their wedding night were not entirely pure. Their presumption is that this was sufficient to cause important and permanent consequences for the institution of the birthright, which should have belonged to Jacob's firstborn, Reuben.[33] The Bible previously set the stage for challenging the priority rights of the firstborn in the stories of Isaac supplanting his older half brother Ishmael and of Jacob acquiring Esau's birthright and obtaining the firstborn's blessing. Then Laban asserted the local tradition of the firstborn's marriage rights to justify substituting Leah for Rachel at the wedding ceremony.[34] Now, according to the Rabbis, it seems that Reuben's conception has indeed been tainted with some measure of impurity. The priesthood and kingship that would have gone to the tribe of Reuben, the firstborn, will instead be reassigned to the tribes of his younger brothers Levi and Judah. This momentous outcome seems finally to determine that the prerogatives of birthright are not automatically awarded to the eldest.

Putting these legal matters aside, we can return to Leah's story. Jacob has two brides and two wedding nights a week apart. His second marriage, to Rachel, begins a lifetime of events that will have an enormous impact on Leah. The text, however, says nothing about Leah's reaction. For some later events, midrash will play its frequent and valuable role of interpreting the text with speculative embellishments. But in this instance, we are left to imagine for ourselves just how much joy Leah could have felt in those seven days of her wedding celebration. Was she haunted by the knowledge that her victory over her sister would be only a momentary triumph? Perhaps Leah's seven days of wedding celebration felt to her more like an ominous countdown to the inevitable time when her stunned and angry husband would finally achieve his real desire—Rachel. Indeed, one midrash does go further and imagines that as soon as Laban promised that Jacob could also marry Rachel, Rachel began making Leah miserable with mean and hurtful statements of how Jacob truly loved only her.[35] If this is what happened, it surely couldn't have been much of a honeymoon week for Leah. In the end, we are left to ponder how the echoes of Jacob's initial morning-after complaint to Leah and her biting retort will resound throughout their marriage.

Leah's Lessons from Her Wedding Night

The story of Laban's bridal switch is one of the most dramatic episodes in the Bible. So it is a tribute to the bold inventiveness of midrash that the Rabbis are able to surpass it with their own fantastic tale of Rachel hiding under the nuptial bed and answering for Leah throughout the wedding night. As a literary element in Leah's story, however, this tale can be read as an extension of the Bible's insistent focus, not on Leah, but on Rachel. Indeed, the contrast here seems worse for Leah. Rachel is not only the younger, beautiful, beloved sister, but in this version she performs a stunning act of self-sacrifice and grace toward Leah.

So Leah is not even allowed to be the heroine of her own wedding-night story. To find a midrash that focuses directly on Leah, we must turn to the Rabbis' equally inventive tale of the conversation between Jacob and Leah on the morning after the wedding. The Rabbis imagine that Jacob's angry reproach is answered with sharp, strong justification from Leah. I can accept Leah's outburst in the conversation created in this midrash as a natural and understandable lashing out by a deeply hurt victim, but I cannot accept the conclusion by some commentators that Leah's comments somehow justify blaming her for becoming the victim of Jacob's subsequent hurtful behavior.

As a literary matter, this invented conversation entices us to continue reading the story of Leah's life to learn whether she can somehow overcome Jacob's angry reaction to the wedding switch. We can imagine a range of possible outcomes—a lifetime of continuing, fruitless bickering between Jacob and Leah, or perhaps a lifetime of bitterness and unlimited hostility between Leah and her sister and rival, Rachel. However, with a lesson that remains meaningful for our own lives, we will see how Leah manages to persevere and adapt. She comes to accept that she is unable to rewrite the core tragedy that has already occurred at the very outset of her married life. But while she can't alter the past, Leah will remain true to her character and thereby transform the consequences of Jacob's love preference for her sister. As a practical matter, Leah cannot avoid rivalry with a sister who shares her husband. The Hebrew Bible recognizes that the Matriarchs are human beings, not saints. But Leah is about to show us how persons of good character can impose limits on unavoidable conflict by staying true to their better nature.

3

LEAH BEGINS MARRIED LIFE IN CONFLICT

Jacob's Greater Love for Rachel

According to midrash, Leah and Rachel have just concluded an unprecedented act of cooperation to execute their father's plan. Leah spent the entire wedding night posing as Rachel and engaging in marital intimacy with Jacob. This, in turn, depended on Rachel selflessly giving the secret identification signs to Leah, and even hiding under the wedding bed to answer for her sister so that Jacob would not realize the bridal switch. Then Jacob's moral outrage was promptly squelched when Leah and Laban each answer his angry complaints about the deception by reminding him of his own deception of Isaac in obtaining the blessing intended for Esau. Jacob does not respond to either of them, and he passively agrees to Laban's proposal that he can promptly marry Rachel as well if he agrees to serve Laban for yet another seven years.

But it would be naïve to expect that these developments should in any way indicate a resolution of the tensions between the competing sisters and their now-shared husband. To the contrary, what we have just read marks the launching of a life-long rivalry between Rachel and Leah. In fact, even "lifelong" fails to fully describe the scope of the sisters' struggle. Their sibling rivalry will soon grow to entangle their husband, Jacob, their handmaidens, Zilpah and Bilhah, and all their respective children in a complex web of conflict that will stamp its indelible mark on the political and religious life of the Jewish people right up to today, four thousand years later.

> And Jacob went in to Rachel also; and he loved also Rachel more than Leah. And he served him another seven years. (Gen. 29:30)

The trouble for Leah starts immediately. "And Jacob went in to Rachel also, and he loved also Rachel more than Leah." The morning after Jacob's wedding night with Leah was marked by shock and anger, but the morning after Jacob's wedding night with Rachel one week later marks the establishment of Jacob's lifelong preference for Rachel over Leah. Midrash closely examines this text to try to read the exact temperature of the emotions running between Jacob and his two wives.

The Rabbis note that the word "also" (*gam*) is used twice in this brief phrase describing Jacob's marital intercourse with Rachel and his love for her. Midrash presumes that the Bible's repetition of words generally provides an emphatic pointer to something important. Here, if Jacob *also* loved Rachel more, the implication may be that he loved Leah too, just not as much.[1] The Rabbis speculate that perhaps for Jacob's first and only week of monogamy, previously described in the text, he simply loved Leah the way a new husband loves his wife. It is only once Jacob commences his marriage with Rachel that he is able to compare his two wives.[2] Avivah Zornberg likewise notices the repeated "also," but suggests it is a signal that Jacob will never have exclusivity with Rachel. Because of his marriage with Leah, his love and his marital relations with Rachel will always be marred for him by an inescapable sense of relativity, comparison, and competitiveness. Jacob's marital relations will always be qualified by the "also" in his life.[3]

And when we view from Leah's perspective the inevitable competitiveness that is inherent in polygamy, we can imagine the crushing burden that Jacob's second marriage must hold for her. With touching empathy for Leah's predicament, midrash proposes that Rachel's marriage is a major turning point for Leah as well as for Jacob. Until Jacob begins his second marriage, Leah similarly has no basis of comparison to measure Jacob's love for her. So midrash presumes that for the first week of her marriage, Leah clings to the hope that, despite Jacob's anger over the wedding deception, he might grow to love her fully.[4] But that hope ends with Jacob's new feelings upon his marriage to Rachel at the end of that first week.

One commentary suggests that Jacob's preference for Rachel causes him to move his bed into her tent, noting that this is not a case where Jacob's subsequent absence from Leah makes Leah more attractive to him. Perhaps absence can sometimes make the heart grow fonder, as appears to be the case for Jacob when he has to wait seven years for Rachel. But one week after his wedding to Leah, Jacob's new physical closeness to Rachel only deepens his love for his second wife.[5] He loves Rachel more.

The same Bible verse declaring that Jacob loved Rachel more also says that he worked another seven years for her. To the Rabbis, this indicates that Jacob's love is not diminished by his labors. Her greater "price" (Jacob's continued labor is presumed to be his second substitute bride-price) simply increases her value in his eyes rather than causing him regret or resentment.[6]

But Jacob's new marriage triangle also raises some legal questions. As noted above, the Rabbis enjoy a sweet literary conceit by presuming that the Patriarchs know and obey Jewish law even though the law would not be revealed to the Jewish people until a half millennium later. Of course, midrash sees no legal problem merely from the fact that Jacob has multiple wives, since biblical law never prohibited polygamy.[7]

Nevertheless, Jacob's second marriage does present a very serious problem for the Rabbis. Jacob's marriage to Rachel would violate the Bible's later express prohibition against marrying a wife's sister during the wife's lifetime (Lev. 18:18).[8] Midrash defends Jacob's righteousness on this point by asserting that, because the marriage to Rachel takes place outside the Promised Land, the future biblical prohibition would not technically apply. This argument leads to a somber speculation later, however. When Jacob eventually leaves Haran and brings his entire family back to the Holy Land, Rachel will die "on the road" at the border of the Promised Land (Gen. 35:19). Midrash concludes that her early death is explainable in part because she has to die to avoid violating the prohibition against Jacob being married to two sisters concurrently—a prohibition that would have become applicable once the family resides in the Promised Land (or at least once Rachel recovers from childbirth and is able to resume marital relations with Jacob).[9]

Besides these legal issues, there are also ethical issues as to whether Jacob acts properly in loving Rachel more than Leah. Nachmanides (Ramban), one of the great classical commentators of the Middle Ages, reads the text as suggesting that Jacob's greater love for Rachel is unnaturally excessive. Ramban believes that it is natural for a man to feel his greatest love for the "first love" of his life.[10] However, his critique of Jacob on this point only seems justifiable if his concept of "first love" refers to sexual initiation (which Jacob has with Leah) rather than romantic infatuation (which Jacob first, or perhaps only, has with Rachel).

From another point of view, we could consider Jacob's favoritism for Rachel over Leah as the divinely engineered consequence of the favoritism previously shown by Isaac toward Esau and Rebekah toward Jacob. But if this is God's measure-for-measure justice, we should once again feel troubled by the morality of God's biblical world. It is difficult to accept the righteousness of using Jacob's wives as objects of correction, moral instruction, or punishment for Jacob or his parents. Modern readers might suspect that this treatment of the wives has much more to do with the Bible's typical gender bias.

Finally, we could each write our own midrash speculating about what the course of biblical history would have been without the wedding deception—if Jacob had gotten his wish to marry Rachel and not Leah. If Rachel's destiny was to have only two children, would they still be Joseph and Benjamin (as midrash suggests), or would they be Jacob's first and second sons, Reuben and Simeon?[11] Without a Levi and a Judah, would there be a Moses or a David? And without David would the Jews have received the promise of Messiah? If there had been no wedding hoax, would we see not only a greatly changed Bible, but also an almost unimaginably changed (or perhaps even totally disappeared) Judaism? With stakes such as these, perhaps we should set aside our modern sensibilities and simply acknowledge (without necessarily agreeing or approving its moral implications) that in the view of the Bible and its early commentators, God acts in history by involving Jacob's wives in the wedding deception and its aftermath in order to advance God's divine plan for the Jewish people.

Leah's Response to Being the Unloved Wife

If the Bible were a modern novel or screenplay, we might expect that Jacob's marriage to Rachel one week after he married Leah would be followed by an in-depth narrative that would develop and deepen our understanding of these three characters. We would eagerly look forward to exploring how the characters perceive and emotionally respond to this extraordinary, dramatic love triangle. However, the Bible's literary style presents readers with a formidable challenge here. Typically, the Bible recites what its characters do, but not their emotions or motivations. It is left to us, with the help of midrash, to fill in their feelings by closely examining the slender textual clues.

The text has just described the two weddings and their consummation, expressing the fact—perhaps a direct consequence of those competing wedding nights—that Jacob loves Rachel more than Leah. The following sentence tells us how Leah responds. She does not withdraw in defeat, but instead will contend for Jacob's love through children.

The Lord saw that Leah was hated and he opened her womb;
but Rachel was barren. (Gen. 29:31)

The text thereby announces that this will be a rivalry involving the consequences of the sisters' sexual access to their shared husband. The number of children the wives provide will furnish at least the initial score of who is winning.

As noted earlier, many midrashic interpretations maintain that Jacob still loves Leah, but that he loves Rachel more. Now the text tells us that God, seeing that Leah is "hated" (*s'nuah*), intervenes. The Rabbis come up with a surprising number of finely nuanced explanations in their attempt to resolve this apparent textual contradiction.

One approach is to define away the problem by concluding that the term "hated" here doesn't mean detested or despised, but is a relative term—*less loved.*[12] Denying that Jacob hates Leah serves to defend the nobility of the Patriarch's character, which we have noted is very important for much of the classical midrash.[13]

Other commentaries accept the term "hated" in its ordinary sense, but add widely divergent interpretations of just how the word applies to Leah. According to some, the text does not say that Leah is hated, but rather that God sees Leah is hated. This could mean that Jacob always acts fully appropriately as a husband toward Leah, but God can see into Jacob's heart and knows his true feelings.[14] If only God, not Leah, sees Jacob's true feelings, then she would not necessarily be distressed, and can still hope that her husband will reverse his initial preference for Rachel after sufficient time has passed.[15]

Other commentaries conclude that the problem is not with Jacob at all. Jacob doesn't hate Leah, but she wrongly feels that he does, or at least she fears he will come to hate her. After Jacob's wedding to Rachel, Leah is even afraid that Jacob will divorce her so that he can enjoy an exclusive relationship with his new, beloved bride. Leah is distressed over her public humiliation in the event of such a divorce.[16] She may also fear that, if divorced, she would once again become a target for Esau's claims under their parents' betrothal pledges and therefore be subjected to Esau's wicked character, which would be hateful to her.[17] These commentaries conclude that Leah's fears result in new tearful prayers and entreaties by her, similar to those previously imagined by midrash to move God to have Jacob marry Leah first. Leah's new distress convinces God once again to act, by making her fertile, so that once Leah bears children for Jacob he will no longer want to divorce her.[18]

Even Rachel earns a role in contributing to Leah's distress. As mentioned earlier, midrash supposes that, during Leah's wedding week, as soon as Rachel learns that Laban and Jacob have agreed that Jacob can marry her at the end of that week, Rachel begins to wound her sister through proud and arrogant behavior.[19]

How should we choose among these various interpretations? A fair reading of the text indicates that Jacob's preference for Rachel continues or intensifies after his second wedding. It seems highly unlikely that Leah would be blind to this. After all, when we look at the Bible stories of the Matriarchs and Patriarchs, the Matriarchs seem to be the ones who receive prophetic insights, while the Patriarchs often suffer from blindness, both as to physical vision and factual or even ethical insight. Therefore, we can presume that for Leah the honeymoon is indeed over after her week of exclusivity with her new husband. She would have felt deeply disappointed and hurt. We are faced with a text that shows God intervening but fails to provide express clues as to exactly why God acts. Perhaps the simplest explanation is that God acts because Leah feels so hurt.

The verse that begins "The Lord saw that Leah was hated" goes on to describe what God did about Leah's situation: "he opened her womb." This could simply be the archaic language of delicacy sometimes used by the Bible to describe the process of conception. After all, in the classical view of the Bible and the early commentaries, human conception is a three-party transaction, requiring the successful involvement of the husband, the wife, and God's presence.[20] The early Aramaic translation of Genesis provides an example of interpreting the phrase "he opened her womb" here in this figurative sense: "he [God] gave her conception."[21]

But barrenness is a major theme for the biblical Matriarchs (Sarah, Rebekah, Leah, and Rachel), so it is natural for midrash to explore this bit of text in some depth. Is this wording telling us that there is some special reason that requires God to "open" Leah's womb? Some commentaries take the phrase literally to mean that Leah has some abnormal physical barrier interfering with conception, which requires miraculous intervention.[22] Other commentaries focus on the motivation for God granting Leah immediate fertility, concluding that God acts because God shares Leah's concerns that, if she remains barren, either she will suffer unjust public humiliation or Jacob will divorce her.

AND THE LORD SAW THAT LEAH WAS HATED (Gen. 29:31). Everyone hated [abused] her. . . . Even women behind the beams hated her: "This Leah is a hypocrite. She pretends to be a righteous woman, but is not. For if she were a righteous woman, would she have deceived her sister?" R. Judah bar Simon and R. Hanan said in the name of R. Samuel b. R. Isaac, "When our father Jacob saw that Leah had deceived him by passing herself off as her sister, he decided to divorce her. But when the Holy One, blessed be He, remembered her by giving her children, he [Jacob] said, 'Shall I divorce the mother of these children?'" (Midrash Rabbah, Genesis 71.2)

If Leah does not bear children, the townspeople will take her infertility as evidence that she is not a righteous person and not the proper wife of Jacob.[23] And Jacob might arrive at the same conclusion. So, to avoid a divorce, God makes it possible for Leah to give Jacob a son.[24] The text gives no indication of how much time elapses between Leah's wedding night and God's intervention to permit her pregnancy, but midrash finds a clue later in the text. At the end of Jacob's life, when he delivers a prophetic proclamation to each of his sons, he begins by characterizing Leah's first son, Reuben, as "my firstborn . . . first fruit of my vigor (*reishit oni*)" (Gen. 49:3). The Rabbis take this to mean that Reuben was not only Jacob's firstborn, but also the result of Jacob's first seminal emission.[25] If we assume that Jacob felt a righteous impatience to begin fathering the twelve children promised to him, and in light of all that the text and midrash say about what happened between him and Leah on their wedding night, it would be logical to infer that Reuben was conceived from Jacob's first marital intercourse with Leah.

Finally, this provocative verse concludes, "but Rachel was barren" (Gen. 29:31). Some commentaries presume that, since these were sisters or perhaps twins, Rachel would suffer from the same physical impediment to conception that afflicted Leah.[26] If this was the case, then the verse is telling us that God opens Leah's womb but, for the time being, does not similarly intervene for Rachel. But it is also possible that Rachel is initially fertile, and that God therefore has to actively render her infertile for some period of time in a divine attempt to bring more equality to Jacob's level of affection for his two wives.[27] The version of the text in the apocryphal book of Jubilees is clear about God's motivation, but grammatically ambiguous as to whether Rachel was already naturally barren or had to be actively rendered so by God: "And the Lord opened the womb of Leah, and she conceived. . . . But the womb of Rachel was closed, for the Lord saw that Leah was hated and Rachel loved."[28] Regardless of when Rachel became barren, the sisters' rivalry will henceforth be centered on this pivotal issue of bearing children for Jacob.

If there were any doubt about what it could mean for God to open Leah's womb, the Bible proceeds at once to make this clear.

Leah conceived and bore a son, and named him Reuben; for she declared, "The Lord has seen my affliction; for now my

husband will love me." She conceived again and bore a son,
and declared, "Because the Lord heard that I was unloved
and has given me this one also"; so she named him Simeon.
Again she conceived and bore a son and declared, "This
time my husband will become attached to me, for I have
borne him three sons." Therefore he was named Levi. She
conceived again and bore a son, and declared, "This time I
will praise the Lord." Therefore she named him Judah. Then
she stopped bearing. (Gen. 29:32–35)

In quick succession, four verses repeat the same basic details of the births of Leah's first children: Leah conceives, bears a son, names him, and explains what the name means. The explanations of the names provide a powerful insight into Leah's deeply felt hopes about these early stages of her struggle to win her husband's love and attachment. Such express statements of personal emotion are rare in biblical text, especially for a female character. The most important lines assigned to Leah in the Bible are actually the ones in these verses, where she is permitted to reveal her feelings indirectly, through the names she gives to her children.

When we read these words of Leah we feel some discomfort in learning of her desires because we know they will never be fulfilled. For despite Leah's eventual six sons, Jacob will continue his primary love for Rachel, even after Rachel's death.[29]

Even more surprising, Leah does not seem alone in her unrealistic hopes that producing children will change Jacob's affection. Midrash proposes that God gives these children to Leah because God thinks that the births will turn Jacob's hatred into love.[30] Do the Rabbis conclude that even God cannot predict the mysteries of love? More likely, the Rabbis would respond that all God wants is for Jacob to have sufficient feeling for Leah after her children's births that he will continue as her husband.[31] And he does.

The Rabbis notice that the names of Leah's first four sons

show a progression of expectations for her relationship with Jacob.[32] According to Leah, the name "Reuben" is from a form of "see" (r'u), and Leah explains it as God having seen her distress, so that with this firstborn son Jacob will come to love her. "Simeon" is from the word for "hear" (shamah), meaning God gives her a second son because God has heard that she is hated. "Levi" is derived from the root for "attached" or "joined," and Leah hopes that Jacob will finally become joined to her as a true husband.[33] Finally, "Judah" is from the word for "thanks" (hodu), and she gives thanks to God for him.[34]

In typical midrashic style, commentators add their own interpretations of the names, going beyond even what Leah herself expresses: The contemporary commentator Robert Alter finds thematic significance in Leah naming her first two sons for sight and sound. These are the two motifs that link the parallel deceptions by Jacob in the blessing tent and by Leah in the wedding tent. In the blessing episode, Isaac cannot use sight because of his blindness, and he disregards vocal sounds, instead relying on touch and smell (as well as taste). On Leah's wedding night, Jacob also lacks sight because of the darkness, and he ignores the differences in vocal sounds (or else he is fooled by Rachel speaking from under the bed). So he likewise must rely on his sense of touch (which may have been overwhelmed by Jacob's day of drinking or the sexually charged situation in the wedding tent).[35]

For some commentators, the fact that Leah provides this succession of names for her first three sons demonstrates her hopeful persistence. Although birth after birth fails to change her husband's feelings, Leah still clings to her dreams.[36] But other commentaries are even more nuanced when they point out how the text shows a gradual progression of Leah's state of mind, with hope diminishing as each birth fails to bring Jacob's love. With Reuben, she hopes that now, finally, her husband will love her. With Simeon, she realizes that Jacob hates her. This indicates that until her first child fails to make a difference, only

God, but not Leah, understands that this is not merely a situation where Jacob loves Rachel more. Jacob actually does hate Leah, so it is up to this second child to reverse his feelings. But Simeon's birth likewise fails to change Jacob's feelings. So with Levi, Leah's principal hopes have shattered. Her goal now is no more than having Jacob permanently attached to her. She wants to end her fear that Jacob will divorce her, thereby exposing her to the risk of becoming Esau's wife.

We wonder, however, whether Leah expects that the birth of Levi will finally join Jacob to her in affection, or does she now merely anticipate that three children will bind Jacob to her through obligation? Perhaps the name "Levi" shows the latter: Leah is finally resigned to settle for a permanent marriage with Jacob, even without his love.

To explain why Leah names her fourth son Judah (meaning, "praise") in thankful praise of God, midrash relies on the prophetic arithmetic, based on what the Rabbis presume was revealed to the Matriarchs: Jacob was destined to have four wives and twelve promised sons. This would call for three sons per wife.

AND SHE CONCEIVED AGAIN AND BORE A SON AND DECLARED, "THIS TIME I WILL PRAISE THE LORD" (Gen. 29:35). [S]ince the Matriarchs expected that each of [the four of] them would produce three sons, when Leah had given birth to a fourth son, she said, THIS TIME I WILL PRAISE THE LORD. (Midrash Rabbah, Genesis 71.4)

According to midrash, the first three sons are only Leah's fair share of Jacob's destined twelve sons. But Judah is beyond her entitlement, a true gift from God in recognition of her plight. Leah is appropriately thankful.[37] The Rabbis note that this is the first occasion in the Bible when a human blesses God.[38]

It is possible to agree with the rabbinic commentaries that interpret Leah's choice of the name "Judah" as proof that she has changed from an unhappy person focused only on what her sister possesses (Jacob's love), to a more contented person who can experience joy from the gifts she has been given (her children and her marital stability).[39] But at best this would only be one step in Leah's path to self-transformation. This development must be read in the context of Leah's entire story, and her story doesn't end here. We're about to see that Leah is not ready at this point to make the total change from competition to contentment. There remain important events (giving the handmaidens as wives to produce surrogate children and bargaining over the mandrakes) that will extend the period of harsh rivalry between the sisters. So although some commentaries don't recognize this, it is too soon at this point to conclude that Leah has totally changed her feelings about her husband, her sister, and her life.

A provocative commentary by Ibn Ezra, a major twelfth-century commentator, proposes an alternative view of the name "Judah." Leah's statement of "thanks" to God could have really been her declaration that she is satisfied with four sons and wants no more (perhaps because she is now resigned to the fact that Jacob's preference for Rachel cannot be swayed, no matter how many children Leah produces).[40] If her "thanks" actually means "enough," this could explain why, immediately after the naming of Judah, Leah "stopped bearing" (Gen. 29:35). God interrupts her childbearing until she later begins to pray for her fertility to resume. God wasn't punishing her by interrupting her fertility, but showing favor by granting her petition for at least a temporary respite.

The births and namings of these four children come one after another, with no pause to describe the sons or Leah's relationship and feelings toward them. It seems that the sons are only important to Leah for how they might affect her relationship with Jacob and Rachel. And perhaps this is not only Leah's focus. We can also imagine Rachel's feelings at this point, having to compete for her beloved Jacob's affections but consigned to barrenness while Leah becomes a childbearing machine.

The closing words of these four rapid-fire verses reciting the births of Leah's four sons—"stopped bearing"—may mark a new phase in Leah's rivalry with Rachel. A contemporary commentator observes that Leah's ceasing to bear children may not necessarily have been due to a sudden change in her fertility. Perhaps Leah stops having children simply because Jacob stops sleeping with her. Maybe he is the one who says "enough." We know that by the time of the later incident of the mandrakes (discussed below), Leah will have to bargain with Rachel to obtain the right to sleep with Jacob for a single night. That change in the physical arrangements may have begun when Leah gave birth to Jacob's fourth son. So perhaps it is not God's miraculous intervention, but Jacob's cessation of marital intercourse—a cessation that might even have been instigated by Leah herself—that causes Leah to stop bearing.[41]

Rachel Envies Leah and Demands Children

By now, our experience of reading Leah's story through the lens of midrash may have generated some misgivings about who is the real heroine of this family drama. Both the biblical text and the midrashic commentaries seem to focus on Rachel, not Leah.

But while Leah has said very little in the biblical text to this point, Rachel has said even less. Although the Bible has told us of Rachel's beauty and Jacob's great love for her, Rachel herself has yet said nothing.[42] That silence makes Rachel's first dialogue with her husband in the Bible rather surprising. She finally speaks, not with lovers' talk, but with angry, frantic, jealous demands. She is speaking to Jacob, but the text is all about her rivalry with Leah.

> When Rachel saw that she had borne Jacob no children, Rachel envied her sister; and Rachel said to Jacob, "Give me children, or I shall die." And Jacob's anger was kindled against Rachel, and he said, "Am I in God's place, who has denied you fruit of the womb?" (Gen. 30:1–2)

Rachel's first conversation in the Bible opens with the narrator's observation that she is envious. If we read this merely as a story of ordinary humans reacting to their situation in life, we would presume that Rachel is jealous of Leah's having sons or fearful that Jacob will be drawn closer to Leah because she has produced those sons. However, classical midrash rushes in to save the Matriarch Rachel's character from any accusation that she is acting out of jealousy. The Rabbis refuse to believe that Rachel is concerned about having sexual access to Jacob or losing his love.

WHEN RACHEL SAW THAT SHE HAD BORNE JACOB NO CHILDREN, RACHEL ENVIED HER SISTER (Gen. 30:1). Said R. Isaac, "[In Prov. 23:17 it is written:] LET NOT YOUR HEART ENVY SINNERS, and yet you say, SHE ENVIED HER SISTER? This shows that she envied her for her good deeds. She [Rachel] said, 'If she [Leah] were not righteous, would she have given birth?'" (Midrash Rabbah, Genesis 71.6)

Midrash converts Rachel's selfish jealousy into righteous envy. Rachel sees her sister's fecundity as evidence that God has intervened on Leah's behalf, which therefore must be a reward for Leah's good deeds. In contrast, Rachel sees her own barrenness as a sign that God has found her somehow lacking in merit.[43] So the Rabbis conclude that what Rachel envies is her sister's presumed piety and unspecified good deeds, not that Rachel is jealous of the births themselves.[44] The Bible can be read in many ways, but this may be an instance when a plain, natural reading of the family story does not support the moralistic praise-making of classical midrash. Rachel's envy suggests a rivalry with Leah over more than God's reward of children. Rachel also seems driven by competition for the affections of their shared husband and the stability of their respective marriages. It should not be necessary to deny that interpretation just to assuage rabbinic concerns for Rachel's piety.

But at least the Bible directly expresses something about Rachel's envy over Leah's four sons. At this point the text continues to be totally silent as to the feelings of those sons' parents, Leah and Jacob. Does Leah feel truly content with her marriage relationship once her sons are born, or does she act in an arrogant, hurtful manner toward her sister (as midrash accuses Rachel of acting when she was chosen to be Jacob's second wife)? Has Jacob shown some shift in his affection from Rachel to Leah because of the births of his sons, a change that might have triggered or perhaps justified Rachel's emotional response?

In any event, Rachel acts on her envy by sharply demanding that Jacob provide her with children, as he has done for Leah. Perhaps Rachel's outburst does not come without prelude, and we are meant to imagine some escalating domestic strife between Rachel and Jacob that has led to the first dialogue between them in the text. Since Rachel and Jacob don't say much in this interchange, the Rabbis jump in to elaborate.

A more literal translation of the Hebrew words of Rachel's outburst to Jacob would be: "Give me children; or if not, I am a dead person."[45] These few words launch a flotilla of commentaries. We are not certain of Rachel's tone of voice when she says this—the first statement to Jacob from any of his wives recorded in the Bible. It is possible that Rachel is not speaking in anger, but only in sorrow. The Rabbis take her statement as a proof text for the midrashic concept that there are four persons who are considered as if they were dead, and one of these is a childless person.[46]

But most commentators read Rachel's demand as one delivered in an angry, hysterical tone. What they don't agree on, however, is the target of her anger. Since Rachel is presumed to believe, as the Rabbis believe, that fertility requires divine cooperation, she could be angry with God. God appears to have forgiven Leah for her participation in the wedding-night deception, but continues to punish Rachel for giving to her sister the secret codes that allowed Leah's deception to proceed.[47] Other commentators see Rachel's anger directed at Jacob. And some commentators infer that Jacob responds in turn with anger toward Rachel because he still cannot forgive her for her role in the wedding deception.

We might find some insight into these complicated dynamics by considering how the Rabbis understand the process of forgiveness. In the talmudic tradition for the Jewish Day of Atonement (Yom Kippur), Jews cannot expect forgiveness from God for their sins against other persons until they first seek forgiveness from those persons.[48] Perhaps Rachel feels that until Jacob forgives her for her participation in the wedding-night switch, she cannot receive forgiveness from God, and her barrenness will continue.[49] Others propose a more specific basis for Rachel making her demand to Jacob for children. Since there is no suggestion in the text that Jacob is withholding marital relations from Rachel, it could be that she is demanding only that Jacob intercede for her with prayers to God.

However, some surprising midrashic commentaries conclude that Rachel is angry with Jacob precisely because her lack of childbearing is not due to physical infertility or divine punishment, but rather that Jacob is following an ancient practice of contraception.

> AND LAMECH TOOK TWO WIVES (Gen. 4:19). R. Azariah said in the name of R. Judah, "This is what the men of the generation of the Flood would do. Each of them would take two wives, one for procreation, the other for mere sexual pleasure. The one for procreation would sit like a widow in her own lifetime [once she had borne children]. The one for sexual pleasure would be given a cup of roots so that she would not become pregnant, and she would sit before her husband like a common harlot." (Midrash Rabbah, Genesis 23.2)

According to these explanations, Rachel has no children yet because Jacob is actively preventing her from pregnancy and motherhood (using herbs to render her temporarily sterile) in order to maintain his favorite wife's youthful figure and good looks.[50] This interpretation serves to further elaborate an earlier midrashic discussion about whether it is somehow improper or beneath Jacob's righteous dignity to fall in love with Rachel because she is more attractive than Leah. Now we can see the terrible price that Rachel might be paying for her beauty.

A contemporary commentator reminds us that this is the second time that Jacob has been confronted with a demand from someone who asserts urgency because of facing death: Rachel's demand echoes Esau's earlier demand for the stew that led to the transfer of the birthright to Jacob.[51] But while Esau will continue on to a long life of strength and power after his demand to Jacob for food, Rachel's demand to Jacob for children hides a dark irony. She will likewise eventually receive what she asks for—two sons (her demand is for *banim*, "sons" in the plural)—but it will be her struggle in giving birth to her second son, Benjamin, that will indeed make her a "dead person."[52]

Avivah Zornberg finds much poignancy in what she sees as a classic love triangle, because we observe each of these parties unhappily pursuing an unattainable goal while failing to experience gratification from what she or he has already been granted. Leah, the spinster, at last has a husband and children (something that was not certain before Jacob's arrival), but she desires greater closeness with Jacob and an end to his preference for her sister. Leah wants to be Rachel. On the other hand, Rachel, who now has the loving husband of her desires, finds that without children, her marriage and her husband's love are not enough. Rachel wants to be Leah.

Jacob came to Haran in part to find an appropriate wife and to have the children who were promised to him at Bethel. Now he has clearly begun to achieve all those goals with his two wives and four children, but he still desires a closer, perhaps exclusive, relationship with his beloved Rachel. As Zornberg points out, a broad gulf between their gender-typical attitudes now separates Rachel and Jacob. Rachel feels driven to achieve both aspects of a woman's traditional role in life—to be a mother as well as a wife—while a baffled Jacob (depicted up to this point as a romantic lover but an uninvolved father) can't understand why his abiding love alone is not enough to bring happiness to Rachel.[53]

Jacob's response to Rachel's outburst is to react to her words instead of hearing her hurt. "And Jacob's anger was kindled against Rachel, and he said, Am I in God's place, who has denied you the fruit of the womb?" (Gen. 30:2). She spoke in the heat of desperation; he responds with cold indignity. But just as the target of Rachel's anger was not obvious (Leah? Jacob? Herself? God?), the source of Jacob's responding anger is also unclear. The Rabbis propose alternatives. Jacob's anger might be understandable if he thinks Rachel is demanding that he provide her with the child she seeks, rather than asking him to pray to God, the source of her infertility. Or he might be taking her dramatic demand literally, as threatening him with her death if he cannot remedy the situation. Perhaps the simplest explanation here is the best one: Jacob is stung by the realization that, without providing children, his love isn't enough to satisfy Rachel.[54]

Another possibility sees Jacob as disturbed that Rachel is asking him to pray to God on her behalf rather than praying herself. Midrash expands this point by imagining important additional dialogue between Jacob and Rachel as they argue over his praying for her to be blessed with children.

> [Jacob said to Rachel:] "AM I IN GOD'S PLACE, WHO HAS DENIED YOU FRUIT OF THE WOMB (Gen. 30:2)? From you he has withheld children; he has not withheld them from me." She said to him, "Is this what your father [Isaac] did for your mother? Did he not gird his loins [entreat God] for her?" He answered her, "But he had no children, while I do have children." So she said to him, "But your grandfather [Abraham] had no children, and he likewise girded his loins for Sarah." He said to her, "Can you do as my grandmother did?" She said to him, "And what did she

do?" He said to her, "She brought her rival [Hagar] into her own household." She [Rachel] said to him, "If that's the impediment, then HERE IS MY MAID BILHAH. GO IN TO HER, THAT SHE MAY BEAR ON MY KNEES AND THAT THROUGH HER I TOO MAY HAVE CHILDREN (Gen. 30:3). Just as she [Sarah] was given descendants through her rival, so I shall be given descendants through my rival." (Midrash Rabbah, Genesis 71.7)

Jacob understands that Rachel is not asking him for a child, but only that he pray for God's intervention. What angers him is that, in the midrashic imagination, Rachel went further and complained that by not praying for her, Jacob was failing to do for her what his father did for his mother (Isaac had prayed for the barren Rebekah to conceive a child, Gen. 25:21). Jacob responds coldly, making lawyerlike arguments to distinguish his situation from his father's.

According to some commentators, Jacob thinks that, unlike Rebekah, Rachel is physically incapable of conceiving a child—it would take a miracle, and the righteous do not pray for miracles for others. Only Rachel can pray for such a miracle.[55] But other commentaries condemn Jacob for this view, pointing out that it is an essential function of the righteous to pray for miracles for others, at least to comfort them by the process.[56]

Also, when Rebekah was barren, Isaac had no descendants, while Jacob already has four sons by Leah. Jacob therefore sees Rachel's barrenness as not his problem, not even as a problem that he shares with her, but strictly as an issue between Rachel and God.[57] When Rachel counters that Abraham had prayed for Sarah to conceive even after he had a son (Ishmael), Jacob responds that Abraham's prayers did not cause the birth of Isaac. Isaac was God's reward to Sarah for her prior act of selflessness in giving her handmaiden, Hagar, to Abraham as a second wife. According to midrash, that interpolated conversation explains the leap in the biblical text from Jacob's final retort in Gen.

30:2 ("Am I in God's place, who has denied you the fruit of the womb?") to the next lines of Gen. 30:3–4 (where Rachel gives her handmaiden, Bilhah, to be Jacob's third wife).[58]

And the Rabbis go further, envisioning God's strong disapproval of that sharp, sarcastic retort by Jacob ("Am I in God's place?").

AND JACOB'S ANGER WAS KINDLED AGAINST RACHEL, [AND HE SAID, "AM I IN GOD'S PLACE?" (Gen. 30:2)] Said the Holy One, blessed be He, to him, "Is this the proper way to answer women in distress? By your life, your children are destined to stand before her son [Joseph, who will similarly respond to them, 'AM I IN GOD'S PLACE?' (Gen. 50:19)]." (Midrash Rabbah, Genesis 71.7)

The Rabbis imagine that God rebukes Jacob for his cold insensitivity to Rachel's anguish. God promises Jacob that one day there will be a shift in the balance of power in this rivalry over children. One day, Leah's children will bow down in subservience to Rachel's son. This midrash is based on the passage at the conclusion of Genesis where Rachel's son Joseph, then viceroy of Egypt, will use that same phrase ("Am I in God's place?") to reassure the sons of Leah as they bow before him, trembling in their fear that he will exact his revenge after Jacob has died (Gen. 50:19).[59] It is noteworthy that this early strand of midrash expresses a well-deserved feminist critique of Jacob's attitude toward Rachel as expressed in the biblical text. Still, once again it is difficult for us to feel comfortable with a biblical concept of justice that proposes using the fear and terror of Jacob's ten sons as an instrument of Jacob's posthumous correction.

Rachel Gives Bilhah to Jacob

It took the Bible only four lines to report that, when God saw that Leah was unloved, she conceived four sons. Leah's names for her first four sons make clear that she didn't view her children as compensation for her unhappiness, but rather as tools to repair her relationship with Jacob. Now the Bible's next four lines describe Rachel's response to this challenge by her rival. But Rachel ends up with a very different strategy—not conceiving children with the help of God, but giving to Jacob her handmaiden, Bilhah (her half sister, according to midrash), to become a surrogate mother for her.[60] Rachel's escalation of her competition with Leah appears to be a desperate move, since it creates yet another potential rival for Jacob's time, affection, and sexual access.

> She said, "Here is my maid Bilhah. Go in to her, that she may bear on my knees and that through her I too may have children." So she gave him her handmaiden Bilhah as a wife, and Jacob went in to her. (Gen. 30:3-4)

In the biblical text, Rachel expresses her purpose in providing her handmaiden to Jacob: "that she may bear upon my knees and that through her I too may have children" (Gen. 30:3). That is, Bilhah's children will be counted as if they are Rachel's. As noted above, this act of a barren wife giving her handmaiden to her husband in order to produce children is a reenactment of Sarah giving her handmaiden, Hagar, to Abraham to produce a child (Ishmael, Isaac's older half brother) (Gen. 16:2). In that earlier instance, Sarah expressed the same purpose that Rachel indicates: "perhaps I will be built up through her" (Gen. 16:2), which the Rabbis read as meaning that since Sarah could live on beyond her death only through her children, she needed Hagar's child to serve this function because it appeared that Sarah was barren.[61]

Midrash also offers an alternative reading of Sarah's statement. Perhaps she will be "built up" in merit for her selfless act of providing Hagar to bear Abraham's child.[62] Midrash goes on to credit Sarah's meritorious act with earning her the miracle of ultimately conceiving Isaac. (And it certainly was a miracle. The Bible tells us that at the time of Isaac's birth Abraham was one hundred years old, and Sarah was ninety and had already gone through menopause, Gen. 17:17 and 18:11).

In Rachel's case, Midrash asserts that she too provides her handmaiden not just for the children who could ensue, but also as an act of merit that she hopes will be rewarded by conceiving a child of her own. So under this interpretation, Rachel's immediate strategy to obtain surrogate children does not preclude her ultimate desire to bear her own children.[63]

The Rabbis may have been aware of some unexpressed irony of their own when they emphasized these parallels between Rachel and Sarah, since the question of Sarah's "merit" regarding Hagar receives some harsh commentary in midrash about that earlier episode.

AND HE [Abram] WENT IN TO HAGAR, AND SHE CONCEIVED (Gen. 16:4). R. Levi b. Hiyyata said, "She became pregnant from the first intercourse. . . . Hagar would tell [women visitors], "My mistress Sarai is not inwardly what she is outwardly: she appears to be a righteous woman, but she is not righteous. For had she been a righteous woman, look how many years she has not become pregnant, whereas I became pregnant in one night." (Midrash Rabbah, Genesis 45.4)

The Bible tells us that after Hagar sees that she has conceived in her initial act of intercourse with Abraham, Sarah is wounded by what she sees as Hagar's "lighter" attitude (*va-tekal b'eineha*) toward her mistress (Gen. 16:4). Hagar apparently becomes insubordinate because she concludes that Sarah cannot be truly righteous if she has been barren for many years while Hagar conceives immediately.[64] The commentators note that this only happened when Hagar "saw" that she had conceived—when Hagar's pregnancy became evident. Perhaps it isn't Hagar's attitude that vexes Sarah, but rather what Sarah fears will be the community's judgment on her character: that God rewarded Hagar with fertility and punished Sarah with infertility. Being compared with the visibly pregnant Hagar will indeed make Sarah appear "lighter" (*kal*, the Hebrew root used twice in the text) in the community's eyes, in the physical as well as moral sense (Gen. 16:4–5).

Midrash has Sarah reacting to Hagar's pregnancy just as Rachel later reacts to the births of Leah's first four children. Sarah angrily rebukes Abraham for her continued barrenness. She does not accuse him of failing to pray to God, as Rachel later accuses Jacob. Rather, Sarah complains that Abraham has been praying only for children for himself and not also praying for Sarah to be the woman to bear those children. The Rabbis conclude that Sarah went further, putting the "evil eye" on Hagar's pregnancy and causing her to miscarry.

> Since it was earlier written: AND HE [Abram] WENT IN UNTO HAGAR, AND SHE CONCEIVED (Gen.16:4), why is it later stated [to Hagar]: BEHOLD, YOU WILL CONCEIVE (Gen. 16:11)? This teaches that an evil eye [from Sarai] possessed her and she aborted [and so Hagar had to conceive again to give birth to Ishmael]. (Midrash Rabbah, Genesis 45.5)

Under this midrashic analysis, Ishmael is born only later, as a result of Hagar's second pregnancy.[65] And of course, when the biblical text continues after Sarah's "merit" has been rewarded with the birth of Isaac, it raises further questions as to the ethics of her dealings with Hagar when Sarah escalates the rivalry by causing Abraham to exile Hagar and Ishmael (who becomes the ancestor of Islam) into the wilderness (Gen. 21:9–21). In a sense, Leah and Rachel will also follow this pattern, expanding their rivalry to engulf all their family interactions and the interactions of their children and descendants.

Since modern readers lack personal experience with the biblical convention of multiple wives and concubines, it is difficult for us to understand the full implications of Rachel's (and later, Leah's) act in giving her handmaiden to Jacob in order to produce children. In particular, what family status did Bilhah and Zilpah attain after being given for childbearing to Jacob? Did they continue to be servants but with new sexual duties, did they become concubines (a long-term sexual partner but without the status of a wife), or did they receive full status among Jacob's multiple wives? It is difficult to answer these questions because the biblical text itself uses different terms at different points. Rachel gives Bilhah "her handmaiden" or "maidservant" (*shivhatah*) to Jacob "as [or for] a wife" (*l'ishah*) (Gen. 30:4). The same language is used a few lines later when Leah likewise gives her maidservant, Zilpah, to Jacob "as a wife" (Gen. 30:9). This phrasing could indicate an elevation in status from maidservant to wife. Or the phrase "as a wife" might just be a delicate way of expressing what the servants' new duties will include—"wifely duties."

Subsequent descriptions of Bilhah and Zilpah in the text are inconsistent. Sometimes they are referred to as maidservant/handmaiden (Gen. 30:10, 12; 31:33; 32:23; 33:1–2, 6; 35:25–26). Sometimes they seem to be included together with Leah and Rachel in references to Jacob's wives (Gen. 30:26; 31:17, 50). Sometimes Bilhah and Zilpah appear to be included as wives, but with a status inferior to Leah and Rachel (Gen. 37:2). And we will see that ultimately, even after Rachel's death, Bilhah is still referred to as Jacob's "concubine" (*pilegesh*) in describing Reuben's actions with her, although this may be a shorthand description of how Reuben regarded her (Gen. 35:22).

As is often the case when the biblical text is unclear, the commentators have more opportunity to read their own interpretations into the text. Here, they are faced with the status of Bilhah and Zilpah, two of the mothers of the tribes of Israel. One modern translation renders "as a wife" to read "as a concubine" because that is what Bilhah is later called. However, the contemporary commentary accompanying this text minimizes the historical distinction between wife and concubine, which reflected no more than whether the husband had to pay a formal bride-price to initiate the relationship.[66]

Earlier commentators were greatly concerned that reducing Bilhah and Zilpah to the status of concubines could seriously diminish the status of one-third of the tribes of Israel, and so they conclude that Bilhah and Zilpah were indeed Jacob's wives. They point out that the term "concubine" (*pilegesh*) is outweighed by the multiple references to the women as *shivhah* (generally translated as "handmaiden," "maidservant," "bondswoman," or "female slave belonging to a mistress") and that these terms describe only the previous status of Bilhah and Zilpah. This analysis presumes that, by giving their handmaidens to Jacob "as a wife," Leah and Rachel granted freedom to their handmaidens and ensured that their children would thereby be fully legitimate.[67]

In contrast, other commentators contend that even if Bilhah and Zilpah and their children were granted freedom and legitimacy, they never achieved full equality with Leah, Rachel, and their children (Gen. 31:4, 33:2, 37:2).[68] And modern readers may feel disappointed that both the Bible and midrash completely ignore Bilhah and Zilpah at this point, as if these women would have had no emotional response to their own marriages and children.[69]

Rachel's and Leah's Surrogate Children

Just as when Sarah provided Hagar to Abraham, Rachel's gift of Bilhah to Jacob quickly leads to Bilhah's pregnancy. But unlike Sarah's reaction in both the text and midrash, the sharp contrast between Bilhah's ready fertility and Rachel's own barrenness does not trigger second thoughts or complaints from Rachel. She is happy for both of Bilhah's sons, whom she counts as her own and credits with a divine judgment that her worth is now equal to Leah's.

> *Bilhah conceived and bore Jacob a son. And Rachel said, "God has judged me; He has heeded my plea and given a son to me." Therefore she named him Dan. Rachel's handmaiden, Bilhah, conceived again and bore Jacob a second son. And Rachel said, "With mighty wrestlings have I wres-*

tled with my sister, and I have prevailed." So she named him
Naphtali. (Gen. 30:5–8)

Just as with Leah's first four sons, we learn about Rachel's feelings
through the names she chooses for Bilhah's sons and the explanations she gives for those names. Rachel names the first son
Dan, because God "has judged me" (*danani*). She also rejoices
that God has given that son "to me" (Gen. 30:6). For purposes
of Rachel's rivalry with Leah as well as her standing in the eyes
of the community, Rachel counts Dan as her own son, not Bilhah's. Again, as with the births of Leah's sons, there is no discussion about the child as an individual and no mention of how
Rachel, Bilhah, or Jacob feels about Dan.

The next line of the text simply repeats that Bilhah again
conceives and gives birth to a son. Rachel names him Naphtali, from the word for wrestling or twisting, stating that she
has wrestled with her sister with great "wrestlings" (or "twistings"; in Hebrew, *naftulei*) and prevailed (Gen. 30:8). The Rabbis explore these words, "wrestling with great twistings," and
reach various interpretations.[70] But the contemporary commentator Robert Alter expands on the classical midrash by noting
how the name "Naphtali" (or, "wrestlings") repeats a theme that
points the reader to consider additional literary counterparts
within the story: Rachel has been wrestling with her sister just as
Jacob wrestled in the womb with his brother.[71] And later, Jacob
will literally become "the wrestler" when he wrestles with the
stranger and God changes his name to Israel, "one who wrestles
with God" (Gen. 32:25–29; 35:10).

But Rachel's claims of triumph, expressed through the names
she gives to Bilhah's children, prove to be premature. Immediately after Bilhah's two sons are born, the now-barren (or, at least
for a time, nonbearing) Leah accepts the implicit challenge and
gives her handmaiden, Zilpah, to Jacob as a wife.

When Leah saw that she had stopped bearing, she took her
maid Zilpah and gave her to Jacob as a wife. And Leah's

maid, Zilpah, bore Jacob a son. Leah said, "Fortune has come!" So she named him Gad. And Leah's maid, Zilpah, bore Jacob a second son. Leah declared, "Happy am I, because daughters will call me happy." So she named him Asher. (Gen. 30:9–13)

Although the text says nothing about Leah's motives for this action, midrash doesn't hesitate to weigh in. As expected, some commentaries suggest lofty motives: Leah knows that Jacob wants (or is destined) to have more children, and since at this point neither she nor her sister are pregnant, Leah's giving Zilpah to produce children could have been another selfless act.[72]

Other commentators presume that Leah's action is far from selfless. Even if she isn't trying to compete with Rachel, perhaps Leah is concerned that Jacob's drive to beget children might push him to seek outside wives who would be even further beyond Leah's control than her own handmaiden. Alternatively, since these stories demonstrate such close similarities between Leah and Rachel, some attribute to Leah the same motivation that the Bible text expressly reveals for Rachel—competition born from envy. The version of the story related in the book of Jubilees makes this clear: "And when Leah saw that she had become sterile and did not bear, she envied Rachel, and she also gave her handmaiden, Zilpah, to Jacob to wife."[73]

One interpretation praises Leah on the assumption that she is acting out of empathy for Zilpah. Further elaborating on the midrashic story that Zilpah and Bilhah are sisters (Laban's daughters from a concubine), it presumes that Zilpah is older than Bilhah, since Laban gave her to Leah, the elder sister. This midrash therefore concludes that Leah gives Zilpah as a wife to Jacob because Leah would certainly identify with the plight of an older sister faced with seeing her younger sister (Bilhah) marry first. Another midrash counters this, however, by asserting that Laban was so crafty at Leah's wedding that he gave the younger of the handmaidens (Zilpah) to Leah (then posing as

Rachel) to maintain the semblance that Jacob was marrying the younger Rachel.[74]

In any event, it is surprising to us that Rachel, who at times is attributed by some commentators with prophetic powers, seems not to have foreseen that providing Bilhah to Jacob would trigger Leah's response of providing Zilpah. Even novice Bible readers would expect such a development if they have paid attention to the handmaidens' almost identical roles in the family saga so far. The first clue is Laban giving Zilpah and Bilhah to Leah and Rachel in identical situations as wedding gifts (Gen. 29:24, 29). And even the handmaidens' rhyming names, "Zilpah" and "Bilhah," telegraph a certain interchangeability of these stock characters, alerting readers to expect further similarities in their roles.

Just as Rachel named Bilhah's two sons, Leah now names Zilpah's two sons. The first, Gad, is generally translated as being derived from Leah's declaration that he is a sign of *b'gad* ("luck," "fortune"), indicating that good fortune has come to her. But since biblical Hebrew is written without vowel sounds and sometimes exhibits variations in spelling, the Rabbis argue over the meaning of "Gad" here. Some connect it to *bagad*, referring to "betrayal."[75] But then the Rabbis can't agree on which betrayal she means. One commentary concludes that for Leah this surrogate birth shows that she had been betrayed (that she might lose the rivalry with Rachel) by her own barrenness. Another finds that Leah is complaining that it is Jacob who betrayed her by accepting Zilpah without protest and by promptly proceeding to have marital relations with the handmaiden.[76] We are left to ponder whether the Rabbis are saying that even a prophetic Patriarch becomes no more insightful than any ordinary husband when it comes to marital relationships. It apparently doesn't occur to Jacob that Leah's offer of Zilpah's sexual services could have been an offer that Leah desperately wants Jacob to refuse.

Still another interpretation of "Gad" poses a different root for his name and concludes that Leah perpetrates a new variation of her original wedding-night deception. This presumes that Gad's name is derived from *beged*, "garment," suggesting that Leah gives Zilpah to Jacob surreptitiously, placing her own garment on her maidservant to fool Jacob into having marital intercourse with her handmaiden.[77] Leah reenacts her own wedding-night switch.

Leah's bestowing the name "Asher" on Zilpah's second son is also open to a variety of interpretations. In the text, Leah says that she chooses the name because she is *asher*—"happy" (or "blessed," "fortunate")—because daughters will call her so. But who are these daughters who will deem Leah fortunate? She could be referring triumphantly to Rachel, but the plural form would make sense only if she is referring to both Rachel and Bilhah, and there is no suggestion that Bilhah is voluntarily involved in any sibling rivalry. Leah might be referring to the women of the community, whose opinion is so important to her. But she could also be referring to future generations, which might explain her use of the word for "daughters" (*banot*) instead of "women" (*nashim*). This could prefigure the later episode in the book of Ruth when the townspeople wish fertility to the newlywed Ruth and her husband, Boaz, by invoking the names of both Rachel and Leah (Ruth 4:11).

So we see that the Bible and midrash go into some detail about how Leah responds when Rachel uses Bilhah to produce two sons for Jacob. But it may nevertheless remain difficult for modern readers to fully comprehend why Leah reacts by providing her own handmaiden, Zilpah, in order to produce two more sons. Perhaps the answer lies in the precise equivalence between Rachel's and Leah's actions here: two sisters who aren't pregnant providing two handmaidens to Jacob, each resulting in two more sons for Jacob, regarded as the sisters' own and named by them.

If we were to ignore this strong correspondence, we might conclude that when Leah arranges for Zilpah to be yet another wife, she is taking a desperate, extreme act that must be driven by her extraordinarily fierce rivalry with Rachel. After all, Leah herself has recognized that she has already been rewarded with a sufficient number of Jacob's sons—or (if we accept the view in some midrashim that Leah had prophetic knowledge of the twelve-sons prophesy at Bethel) even more than her share of Jacob's sons. If the Bible were telling a "nice" family story, shouldn't Leah be content with her already-achieved victory?

But if we view Leah's response to Bilhah/Rachel's two sons in the most favorable light, perhaps the story's clear and measured parallelism is not accusing Leah of escalating the rivalry, but rather telling us that Leah goes out of her way to do no more than counter Rachel's actions by exactly matching them. This could show Leah exercising a laudable measure of restraint. Presuming that Leah retains some control over her handmaiden's marital relationships with their now shared husband, Leah does not try to exacerbate the sibling rivalry by having Zilpah—arguably the youngest and thus most likely to conceive of Jacob's four wives—bear more sons than Bilhah.

Perhaps the most enigmatic figure at this point in the story is not either of the sisters, but Jacob. Although he accepts the handmaidens as his wives by promptly having sexual relations with them, Jacob does not otherwise respond to these events. Since we are already familiar with the rest of the story, we know that Jacob will ultimately grow into a man of action, strength, and initiative. Even his name will be changed to reflect this. But his role in these handmaiden marriages and the four births presents an embarrassing picture of inexplicable passivity for this man who is to become a hero.

Both Bible and midrash agree that Jacob's deception of his father, Isaac, was instigated and orchestrated by his mother, Rebekah. Now it seems that the women in Jacob's life continue to control him. In silent obedience to his first two wives, he takes two more wives, in apparent insensibility to the strong rivalry between his first wives. Jacob's lack of awareness reminds us of his father. If you read this portion of Genesis through the traditional lens of the Rabbis, it seems that the divine plan for history is being enacted here though the vision and action of the Matriarchs, not the Patriarchs.

The principal emotion Jacob has expressed so far is love—his instant, intense, and abiding romantic love for Rachel. Perhaps his lack of response to the situation of his new wives and children is meant to suggest that Jacob still remains totally love struck. And his obsession with Rachel, even after he has conceived four sons with Leah and four more with the handmaidens, must have hurt Leah deeply. We are drawn to acknowledge and respect her ability to somehow get beyond that hurt and keep functioning within this complex family.

Leah's Lessons from Early Married Life

By closely examining Leah's early married life, we can already see how she becomes a great Matriarch. At this point, the breakneck pace of the biblical narrative doesn't allow time to describe Leah's insights and reactions to her predicament. But it discloses much. We know that the speedy march of events after her bizarre wedding must have forced Leah to reach equally speedy judgments and take prompt actions to deal with her awkward situation. Despite being thrust into the wedding tent with a man so deeply in love with her sister, Leah controls her responses to maintain the dignity of her own person and that of her rival. So far, at least, she has not permitted even her severe trials to diminish her noble character. She has embarked on a life of moral heroism.

Leah provides us with a model of how to meet adversity. Indeed, she gives us two great lessons: With the naming of her first three sons, Leah shows us that when life's circumstances are beyond our control, we might have to respond by adjusting to more realistic goals. Leah shows wisdom in making realistic changes to her expectations, rather than getting trapped in the fullness of her initial hopes. This permits her to control the ethical quality of her further competition with her sister. And with the naming of her fourth son ("thanks," perhaps signaling "enough"), and then apparently limiting her own handmaiden's children to no more than the two, Leah teaches us that even in the midst of desperate rivalry, a person of high moral character can still impose limits on herself, in consideration for the dignity and humanity of the other.

But for all her nobility of character, Leah has still not won the prize she really seeks—Jacob's love. So at this point we're left wondering whether her hunger for love will cause her to change strategies and escalate the conflict, in a final attempt to achieve what she wants most: to become Leah the Loved.

4

LEAH CONTINUES THE CONFLICT

Leah and Rachel Bargain for the Mandrakes

Surely the involvement of Bilhah and Zilpah must have produced a further intensification of the rivalry between the sisters, or perhaps new vectors of dissention among the four wives. We might even anticipate conflicts or varying alliances among the eight young sons of Jacob from three different mothers. But biblical style often does not detail events, dialogue, or descriptions that directly describe developments of character or plot background. Instead, the Bible may use some seemingly interpolated stand-alone episode to serve as a gloss on what is obscured or skipped in the main narrative. Familiar examples of such interpolated episodes in Genesis include Abraham and King Abimelech in Gerar, when Abraham claims that Sarah is his sister (Gen. 20:1–18), and Judah's encounter with Tamar, his daughter-in-law (Gen. 38:1–30). It is left to the reader to find the implications in such episodes that can illuminate the main story line. Such an episode appears in our story immediately after Zilpah gives birth to her two sons, when Leah and Rachel bargain over the *dudaim* plants that Leah's first son, Reuben, gathers from the fields.

Once, at the time of the wheat harvest, Reuben found some mandrakes [dudaim] in the field and brought them to his mother, Leah. Rachel said to Leah, "Give me, please, some of your son's mandrakes." But she said to her, "Was it not enough for you to take away my husband, that you would also take my son's mandrakes?" Rachel replied, "Therefore he shall lie with you tonight, in return for your son's mandrakes." (Gen. 30:14–15)

The episode opens with Reuben retrieving the *dudaim* from the fields and bringing them to his mother, Leah. The Rabbis begin their analysis with a dispute over what the Hebrew word *dudaim* means. The context suggests that it is some kind of wild plant or herb, perhaps the mandrake plant. *Dudaim* ends in *-im*, a Hebrew suffix that typically signifies a plural noun, and the mandrake plant may have had this plural form of name because its root is forked, resembling the legs of a human body. And perhaps because of this shape, the plant was deemed in folklore to possess magical aphrodisiac or fertility powers.[1] (Robert Alter notes a further suggestive relationship between the word *dudaim* and the word for lovemaking, *dodim*.)[2]

But the Rabbis recoil at the idea that the Matriarchs would quarrel over possession of a magical plant.[3] Jews are not supposed to believe in magic; the miraculous is God's realm. Some commentators argue that Reuben does not bring his mother the anthropomorphic mandrake root for its power to aid fertility. He brings her only its fragrant fruit for its pleasant aroma.[4] Or perhaps the plant was not a mandrake at all, but some other fragrant plant or herb such as a jasmine or violet,[5] because, while Leah and Rachel might have desired a source of floral aroma for their own pleasure (or, more likely, for increasing their attractiveness to Jacob), they would not have stooped to sorcery. Other commentators acknowledge that the mandrake plant had the power to assist in fostering pregnancy, but reject any suggestion of magic, noting that such powers are no more than the ordinary medicinal qualities naturally found in many herbs and plants.[6]

Despite the valiant rabbinic efforts to deny that Rachel wanted the *dudaim* to become fertile, it seems most likely that this was indeed her motive. This would explain why this apparent interpolation was placed in the midst of the story of the sisters' rivalry over bearing Jacob's children. And this conclusion might be reinforced by its consistency with Rachel's later actions (Gen. 31:19) when she steals Laban's teraphim (icons of household gods), perhaps also for magically inducing conception.

There follows in this mandrakes story what becomes (ironically, from our point of view) a high point for Leah's presence in the text—the first of Leah's only two lines of direct dialogue in the entire Bible. This first line is her only dialogue with Rachel, and the language makes Leah seem like an unpleasant, mean sister. Rachel has carefully used words of politeness ("Give me, please" or "Give me, I beg you"—*t'ni-na li*) to ask for the mandrakes that Reuben brought to Leah. Leah responds in a biting, sarcastic tone: "Was it not enough for you to take away my husband, that you would also take my son's mandrakes?" Perhaps Leah answers in this way because both women see the mandrakes as a love or fertility potion. If so, Leah may be treating Rachel's request as an escalation of their rivalry for Jacob's affection through seeking to have children.[7]

The coldness of Leah's reply indicates that this rivalry is far from over. What could be crueler for Rachel than to hear Leah refer to Jacob not by name but as "*my* husband"? In attacking Rachel for taking Jacob from her, Leah certainly seems to have forgotten the dramatic circumstances of how Jacob became her husband in the first place, especially if we credit the midrashic account of Rachel's role in enabling that marriage by giving Leah the secret signs of identification.

But perhaps Leah's manifest anger is really about something else. Rachel answers her, "Therefore he shall lie with you tonight, in return for your son's mandrakes." This certainly indicates that Jacob was scheduled to sleep with Rachel that night, and further suggests that Rachel may have exclusive sexual access to

Jacob at this point. At the least it appears that Rachel is acting as his chief wife, with the power to determine Jacob's sleeping arrangements among his four wives.[8] So Leah may be complaining about more than Rachel taking Jacob's affections. Leah's real complaint may be that Rachel had been diverting Jacob from his spousal obligations of intercourse with Leah. This interpretation is supported by a modern commentary noting that Rachel's word for Jacob sleeping with Leah this night (*yishkav*) is used in Genesis to describe sex not accompanied by normal marital love.[9] Thus, the mandrakes incident can be read to show these sisters competing for sexual gratification from Jacob.

Perhaps surprisingly, the Rabbis are not generally critical of Leah for her sharp response to her sister. Instead, most commentaries strongly condemn Rachel for her offer to have Jacob sleep with Leah.

> R. Simeon b. Yohai taught, "Because she [Rachel] treated that righteous man with contempt [by giving up marital cohabitation in exchange for mandrakes], therefore she was not buried with him, THEREFORE HE SHALL LIE WITH YOU TONIGHT (Gen 30:14), indicating, "He will lie with you [for eternity]; he will not lie with me." R. Berekhiah said R. Eleazar and R. Samuel bar Nahman [discussed this as follows]: R. Eleazar said, "Both lost and both gained. Leah lost the mandrakes but gained the tribes [the two that were born to her after the exchange]. Rachel gained the mandrakes, but lost the tribes [the two that would have been Rachel's in addition to the ones she ultimately produced]." R. Samuel bar Nahman said, "Leah lost the mandrakes but gained the tribes and burial with Jacob. Rachel gained the mandrakes but lost the tribes and burial with Jacob." (Midrash Rabbah, Genesis 72.3)

According to the Rabbis, not only is it unseemly for Rachel to be bargaining away her right to sleep with Jacob in exchange for a handful of plants, but she is also voluntarily giving up an opportunity to produce a child for Jacob. They conclude that for relinquishing her role in the holy task of producing the remaining children promised to Jacob, Rachel will receive two severe punishments: In light of the close parallelism between Leah and Rachel, midrash presumes that, until the mandrakes event, Rachel has been destined to bear the remaining four sons prophesied for Jacob in midrash. But because she bargains away even one night of cohabitation with Jacob, two of those sons will be taken away from her and given to Leah to bear.[10] Second, Jacob and Leah will be buried in the Cave of Machpelah, joining the other Matriarchs and Patriarchs (Abraham, Sarah, Isaac, and Rebekah). Rachel will be the only Matriarch not buried there.[11]

When Jacob came home from the field in the evening, Leah went out to meet him and said, "You must come in to me, for I have hired you with my son's mandrakes." And he lay with her that night. (Gen. 30:16)

For Leah's second and final line of dialogue in the Bible, she goes out (*va-tetze*) to meet Jacob that evening as he returns from the fields and tells him, "You must come in to me; for I have hired you with my son's mandrakes" (Gen. 30:16). Once again Jacob makes no reply; the text reports only that he indeed lay with her that night.

As we have previously seen, the Rabbis often put great effort into finding a morally acceptable interpretation of such situations. When the Matriarchs or Patriarchs display seemingly coarse language or actions that would be inconsistent with their character, midrash strives to make sense of the incongruity. Some commentators closely examine the text to find an interpretation that can exonerate the biblical hero or heroine from criticism. Others are content to read the text as merely reporting natural, understandable human urges. Still others will search later in the text to find some appropriate divine punishment for what they deem an inexcusable lapse. All these approaches appear in the extensive midrash on Leah's second and final line of dialogue.

First, midrash engages in a broad discussion over the propriety of Leah's unusual aggressiveness in going out and demanding that Jacob come to her that night. Some commentators infer that Leah is acting from pure and saintly motives. Without her intervention, Jacob would have gone to Rachel's tent, which is by then Jacob's regular sleeping place, or at least where Jacob is scheduled to sleep that night. So by demanding that her husband change his arrangements, Leah saves her sister from the embarrassment of having to explain the bargain to Jacob and send him from Rachel's tent to Leah's.[12] Another justification for what the Rabbis see as Leah's sexual aggressiveness is familiar by now: she is acting purely out of the motivation to bear more children for Jacob.

Midrash points to the fact that Leah will conceive a son that night as evidence that God has rewarded her for one or more of these righteous acts.[13] Thus, even though the Rabbis see Leah's "going out" as an act of forwardness, most conclude that her conduct here is acceptable behavior. Indeed, the Talmud states that where the purpose is procreation, it is appropriate for a wife to tastefully solicit her husband for sex (and the reward is said to be a wise child).[14]

But as we have repeatedly seen, the judgments of midrash are seldom uniform. One reading takes a very pragmatic view of Leah's motivation: Leah goes out to intercept Jacob because she is worried that if he ever gets to Rachel's tent, he will be spending the night there, regardless of the sisters' bargain.[15]

For this night's marital relations, the sisters together make the arrangements for their unaware husband, echoing the sisters' earlier collaboration (according to midrash) in substituting Leah as Jacob's bride on his first wedding night. Contemporary commentator Rabbi Bradley Artson points out that because the Bible was written and compiled in a gender-biased culture, it often labors under a presumption that nothing much important happens unless a man is involved.[16] The bargaining over the mandrakes is one of the rare instances where the Bible records a dialogue between two women, but even here classical midrash manages to criticize both of them: Rachel, because she passes up the opportunity of that night's cohabitation with her husband, and Leah, because her sexual forwardness in going out (*va-tetze*) to Jacob will become the model for her daughter, Dinah, later going out (*va-tetze*) to meet Prince Shechem (Gen. 34:1).

The Bible confirms the formal terms of the bargain when Rachel states that Jacob will lie with Leah "this night," and the text goes on to echo that phrase when it reports that Jacob lay with Leah "that night." But Rachel's bargain turns out to be quite an ironic one for her. The magical mandrakes fail to relieve Rachel's barrenness, while "that night" immediately leads to the end of Leah's barrenness and the birth of her final children.

Leah's Final Children

If midrash stopped at this point, the commentary would be overwhelmingly favorable in its assessment of Leah's bargaining with Rachel for access to Jacob. And the Bible seems to validate such a favorable assessment by immediately reporting the births of Leah's final children, her fifth and sixth sons, Issachar and Zebulun (followed, we shall soon see, by the birth of her daughter, Dinah). But the Rabbis prove themselves just as wary of uncritically accepting seemingly good narrative developments as they are of accepting apparently bad ones. Whether the text shows good things or bad things happening to the good people of the Bible, midrash persists in excavating meanings hiding beneath the surface.

> God listened to Leah, and she conceived and bore him a fifth son. And Leah said, "God has given me my reward for having given my handmaid to my husband." So she named him

Issachar. And Leah conceived again and bore Jacob a sixth son. Leah said, "God has endowed me with a good dowry; this time my husband will dwell with me, for I have borne him six sons." So she named him Zebulun. (Gen. 30:17–20)

The first puzzle is the text's introduction to Leah's reward: "God listened (*va-yishma*) to Leah, and she conceived" (Gen. 30:17). God listened to Leah, but what was it she said? Did she pray? Complain? Cry? Did we miss a third line of dialogue from her, or was God responding to her silent inner thoughts? One clue is that the Hebrew word root, *sh-m-ʿ*, often translated as "listen," contains the same ambiguity inherent in its English counterpart. "Listen" can have the sense of "hear," the physical-neurological phenomenon of the body receiving and processing sound waves, or it can have the sense of "harken" (originally "*hear*ken"): paying attention to, responding to, or heeding something that, in poetic usage, need not even be an auditory phenomenon (as when we listen to the dictates of our conscience).

For example, when Jews use this word to introduce the core prayer of their liturgy, *Sh'ma Yisra'el* ("Hear, O Israel: the Lord our God, the Lord is One"), they aren't being told merely to hear the following four Hebrew words that declare God's unity. They are being told to harken—to pay attention to the content of the words and to obey the moral commands implicit in Judaism's majestic concept of monotheism.

As midrash notices, the Bible tells us that God listens now to Leah but does not tell us what, if anything, she has said. So the Rabbis conclude that, since the text does not relate any prayer that Leah may have spoken, God must be responding to her unspoken desire to produce more sons for Jacob.

LEAH WENT OUT TO MEET HIM (Gen. 30:16). This teaches that she did not even give him time to wash his feet. AND SAID, "YOU MUST COME IN TO ME" (Gen. 30:16). R. Abbahu said, "The Holy One, blessed be He, saw that her only intent was to produce tribes. Therefore it was necessary

for Scripture to use language [that under other circumstances would be deemed coarse]: YOU MUST COME IN
TO ME." Said R. Levi, "Come and see how appropriate the
mandrakes exchange was, for because of the mandrakes,
two great tribes arose in Israel, Issachar and Zebulun."
(Midrash Rabbah, Genesis 72.5)

According to this midrash, God "listens" when God rewards
Leah (giving her two more tribes in Israel) for relinquishing the
mandrakes in order to have marital intercourse with Jacob for
the purpose of further procreation.[17]

But perhaps we should read any divine grant of fertility here
as not being a reward for Leah's righteousness, but rather as a
further divine accommodation for her marital despair. The text
previously told us that Leah ceased giving birth after her first
four sons (Gen. 29:35, 30:9). We have considered how this could
mean that she became temporarily infertile, but it could also
mean that she stopped having children because she stopped
having intercourse with Jacob. (The text doesn't say that Leah
became barren; it says only that she stopped bearing.)[18] Jacob's
affections may have become exclusively focused on Rachel. If
this is the situation, then Leah has once again become unloved,
just as she was immediately after her wedding. At that earlier
time, God caused her to bear sons so that Jacob would cleave
to her. Perhaps this time, when Jacob resumes having relations
with her as a result of the mandrakes exchange, God responds
to Leah's similar distress at being unloved, and again causes her
to conceive and bear further sons.

Some modern readers might react to a different aspect of the
question of what God listens to that leads to the birth of Leah's
fifth son. The absence from the text of Leah's express prayer or
petition could simply be another example of gender bias in the
Bible. We don't get to read Leah's prayer, not because it would not
have proven illuminating and instructive, but because the Bible
seldom gives women direct voices in communication with God.

Just as with her first four sons, Leah's expression of thoughts and emotions at the time of giving birth to these next two sons is limited to her choice of names, together with her one-line explanations of those names. But something is different this time: the Rabbis decide that Leah gets it wrong. She is quite specific in naming her fifth son Issachar, saying, "God has given me my reward [in the sense of "wages" or "hire"] for having given my handmaid to my husband" (Gen. 30:18). In the text, Leah chooses the name Issachar as a play on the word *s'khari*, my reward, seemingly unconscious of the fact that she has just used a word from that same root, *sakhor*, to tell Jacob that she has "hired" him for the night with the mandrakes. So while Leah expressly identifies her reward of bearing another child as relating to her having previously provided her handmaiden, Zilpah, to Jacob as a fourth wife, midrash connects the name with the bargain over the mandrakes that brought Jacob to her for the night when Issachar was conceived.[19]

Following the now-familiar pattern for announcing the births of Jacob's children, the Bible does not relate anything about Issachar or how his parents or aunts feel about him. Instead, the next line of the text immediately reports that Leah conceived and bore a sixth son to Jacob. This absence of further mention of Issachar signals that the sisters' rivalry persists unabated and that Leah's children are still primarily only tokens to use in her competition with Rachel for Jacob's affection.

For Leah, her sixth son is evidence that God has endowed her (*z'vadani*) with a good endowment (*zeved*), and she names him Zebulun. Midrash translates the word for "endowment" in the sense of "portion," which could refer to this sixth son being the assurance that Leah will have borne at least as many of the promised twelve sons as all of Jacob's other wives combined— surely a goodly portion.[20] Leah confirms this when she continues her explanation for the name by expressing her hope: "Now will my husband live with me, because I have borne him six sons" (Gen. 30:20).

With her first three sons, Leah's names and explanations showed her longing for the affection that Jacob lavished on Rachel. Now Leah seems to have recalibrated her hopes to better conform to her unfortunate reality. She may finally be resigned to never being able to supplant Rachel in their husband's primary affections. So perhaps Leah now hopes that by sheer number of children, she may at least overcome her sister's control or exclusivity regarding Jacob's sleeping arrangements. Leah may hope that, since she has been granted fully half of Jacob's destined sons, her tent will finally become his main residence, and she will become Jacob's chief wife, even if Rachel might forever remain his beloved.[21]

The Birth of Dinah

A fascinating coda to this episode of Leah giving birth to her final two sons is expressed in a single, curiously abrupt line (curiously abrupt even for the often spartan text of the Bible).

> *And afterward she bore a daughter, and named her Dinah (Gen. 30:21).*

The line is even more succinct in Hebrew (just six words). Midrash often regards what is missing from the text as equally significant with what is expressly stated. Therefore, the Rabbis fill in the textual gaps here by inventing another elaborate midrashic supplement to the biblical story.

"Afterward She Bore"

As previously noted, some midrashic commentaries find that Leah's handmaiden, Zilpah, was the younger of the two handmaidens (and therefore presumably the most fertile of Jacob's four wives). The source text for that analysis is the Bible's statement that Zilpah bore two sons to Jacob, but without the text first reciting the standard formula that she had conceived (Gen. 30:10, 12). This verbal omission, the Rabbis conclude, signifies that no one had noticed that Zilpah was pregnant. They took this to imply that she was a young, pubescent girl whose menstrual periods had not yet achieved regularity.[22]

But, just as for Zilpah, the text we're reviewing here likewise fails to state that Leah conceived before giving birth to Dinah (Gen. 30:21). What can the Rabbis say about the omission of the conception language in this context? A mature mother of six would surely know if she was pregnant, as would those around her. Midrash therefore deduces a simple reason why the Bible states that Leah gives birth to Dinah, but without the text first reporting that she had again conceived: Dinah must already have been conceived—she must have been Zebulun's twin. So "afterward" in the text must mean that Dinah emerges immediately after Zebulun (as Jacob did immediately after Esau).[23]

Since Jacob and Esau are twins, and some commentators speculate that Leah and Rachel are also twins, we should not be too surprised to see midrash raise this theme of twins to explain the verse about Dinah's birth. What may be surprising, however, is that the Rabbis fit this specific explanation into a far broader midrashic tradition that each of Jacob's twelve sons (perhaps with the exception of Joseph) is born with an unnamed twin sister. Each of these female twins later marry another son of Jacob (again, except for Joseph). The point of this midrashic legend apparently is to raise the level of purity of the twelve tribes by having Jacob's sons follow the tradition of Isaac and Jacob (avoiding marriage to local Canaanite women) after they return to the Promised Land.[24]

"A Daughter"

We have already explored several instances where midrash seizes on a single word or phrase ("Leah had weak eyes," "Behold, it was Leah," "Leah was hated," "[Leah] ceased bearing," "Leah went out," etc.) and builds upon that slender textual clue a rich and often unexpected commentary. There is no more dramatic example of finding Leah in midrash than reading how the Rabbis expand on the single word that the Bible uses to describe

Dinah: *daughter*. Midrash recognizes the anomaly of the Bible reporting that Leah gives birth to a daughter after her six sons (born in addition to Jacob's other four sons so far, from Bilhah and Zilpah). Even if we credit the midrashic legend, absent from the text, that each of the sons of Jacob is born with a twin sister who later marries another of Jacob's sons, Dinah's birth is obviously quite different. Her birth is recorded in the Bible, and she receives a name.

There has to be a story hiding behind this unique event, so midrash creates a fascinating one.

IF A MAN'S WIFE IS PREGNANT AND HE SAYS, "MAY IT BE PLEASING [to God] THAT SHE BEAR [a male child]," . . . THIS IS A VAIN PRAYER. And such prayer will not make a difference. R. Joseph objected, "AND AFTERWARD SHE BORE A DAUGHTER, AND NAMED HER DINAH (Gen. 30:21). What is the meaning of AND AFTERWARD?" Said Rab, "After Leah had judged [*din*] herself, saying, 'Twelve tribes are destined to come forth from Jacob, six from me, four from the handmaidens, so there are now ten. If this one should be a male, then my sister, Rachel, will not even be equivalent to one of the handmaidens.' Forthwith the baby was turned into a girl. For it is said, AND SHE NAMED HER DINAH (Gen. 30:21)."

[A potential objection could be raised:] We cannot argue from a miraculous event. [But in response to that objection:] If you like, I shall say that the matter involving Leah took place within forty days of conception. This is according to that which has been taught: For the first three days [after sexual relations] a man should pray that the semen not putrefy. From the third day to the fortieth he should pray for mercy that the child be male. From the fortieth day to the end of the third month he should pray for mercy that it not be a sandal [a flattened, aborted fetus]. From the end of the third month through the sixth, he should pray for mercy that there not be a miscarriage. From the sixth to the ninth he should pray for mercy that the baby should be delivered safely. (Talmud, *Berakhot* 60a)

According to this midrash, Dinah was not originally intended to vary from the history of exclusively male children already recorded for Jacob. She began in the womb as a son (Jacob's eleventh son), and was originally destined to be Zebulun's twin brother.[25] But Leah intervened to change the gender of her unborn child.

Those Rabbis who reach this miraculous explanation rely on their understanding that Leah, like other Matriarchs and Patriarchs, sometimes had prophetic foreknowledge of future events. Leah knew that Jacob was destined to have twelve sons (of which her son Zebulun would be the tenth). Leah also knew that Zebulun's twin, whom she was carrying, was likewise a male. She recognizes that this would account for eleven of Jacob's sons, leaving no more than the final one who could yet be born to her sister Rachel. This would mean that Rachel would not be permitted to produce even as many sons as either of the two handmaiden-wives. To spare Rachel this humiliation, Leah prays during her pregnancy that her seventh child will be born a female. God grants her prayer and transforms the fetus into a female.[26]

It is not necessary for us to reject the entirety of this midrashic miracle story because it presumes Leah's prophetic awareness of Jacob's destiny to produce twelve sons and establish twelve tribes. The Rabbis may simply be conveniently transposing the later biblical story of twelve sons/tribes to create an earlier story of divine prophecy and destiny. Likewise, it is not necessary to accept that a single grammatical difficulty (the text referring to the stones around Jacob's sleeping place at Bethel in the plural form at night but using the singular form the next morning, Gen. 28:11, 18) is sufficient to imply a divine promise of twelve sons/tribes to Jacob.[27] Instead, Leah's actions here could be read to demonstrate merely her desire to limit competition in producing sons for Jacob out of concern for her sister and co-wife, Rachel (who at this point in the story continues to be barren).

Previously, midrash explained what happened on Leah's wedding night by presuming that Rachel had cooperated with the bridal switch to save Leah from humiliation. Now this midrash on the birth of Dinah explains Dinah's gender by asserting that Leah changed her unborn son into a female to save Rachel from humiliation. But the story about Leah's extraordinary kindness regarding Dinah's birth seems even more startling since it comes in the midst of the intense rivalry that the sisters have been waging primarily though competing to produce sons. At this point, Rachel remains Jacob's chief and beloved wife, while Leah's names for her sons show her continuing unanswered yearnings for Jacob's love and connection. But Leah now ends these baby wars by entreating God to permit Rachel to give birth to the remaining two sons. Leah thereby risks establishing Rachel forever as Jacob's clear favorite. This is a remarkable act of righteous selflessness by Leah.

The situation is all the more extraordinary because the midrash indicates that Leah prayed for this outcome after she became pregnant, and the majority of commentators presume that this must have happened after the gender of the child had initially been determined (at forty days, according to the Rabbis' understanding). To change gender once it has been determined would require a miracle, and the Rabbis strongly oppose the idea of praying for miraculous alteration of natural laws and processes already set in motion.[28] The Rabbis generally honor the principle that "the world pursues its natural course"—the natural order is mechanistically amoral, not governed by ethics. And the Rabbis generally prohibit a vain prayer. We are forbidden to pray for alteration of an existing fact, as opposed to a permissible prayer for something that hasn't yet happened.[29] So when midrash tells how Leah changes Dinah's gender, this is a notable recognition of an extraordinary miracle attributable to Leah's righteousness.[30]

We can note some variations to the basic midrashic legend that Leah changes Dinah's gender through prayer. One story says that it is Rachel's prayer, not Leah's, that makes the miracle.[31] In another version, Bilhah and Zilpah come to Leah and say that they all have enough sons already, so that the next son should be for Rachel. Then all four wives unite in prayer asking that Rachel should bear a son.[32]

A further variant of the story proposes that an even more spectacular miracle occurs at Dinah's birth. Since the biblical verse about Dinah's birth to Leah will be followed immediately by the verse reciting Joseph's birth to Rachel, some speculate that these were concurrent pregnancies, with Leah originally having conceived Joseph, and Rachel originally having conceived Dinah. Through the force of the women's prayers, it isn't that Dinah's gender is changed, but that the two children are miraculously exchanged in utero.[33] According to this telling, the story of Jacob's married life in Haran, which began with the switch of Leah and Rachel in the wedding tent, now closes with the switch of the sisters' children, Dinah and Joseph, in their wombs.

"And Named Her Dinah"

The Bible reports Dinah's birth in an extremely minimal fashion (although we will see how the text later devotes a separate chapter, Genesis 34, to telling the troubling story of Dinah and Shechem). The text here says nothing about the significance of the only daughter of Jacob recorded in the Bible, or whether Leah's producing that daughter affects the rivalry with Rachel. Leah has lost even the indirect voice that she exercised with her other six children when she expressed, in speech or thought, her hopes and emotions by explaining her choice of names. Leah names Dinah, but no explanation is given in the text. Midrash presumes that the name is derived from the root for "judgment" (*din*), just like Dan's name. Apparently, Leah made a judgment upon herself when she prayed to change Dinah's gender in order to spare Rachel from humiliation.[34]

The midrashic tale of Leah praying to change Dinah's gender parallels the opening scene in their marriages when the midrash relates how Rachel gives Leah the secret codes and hides in the wedding tent. And just as Rachel's initial act of graciousness enabled her sister's married life to begin, now Leah's reciprocal act of graciousness will permit Rachel's married life to be fulfilled. Rachel's barrenness ends, and she will finally give birth to her first son.

Leah's Lessons from Her Continuing Rivalry for Children

We have just examined two of the most dramatic episodes in Leah's life: the exchange of the mandrakes and the birth of Dinah. Both these events express the full development of Leah's ethical heroism. The mandrakes episode begins with Leah's harsh retort to Rachel as quoted in the text. This is reminiscent of Leah's previous harsh retort to Jacob on the morning after their wedding, as imagined in midrash. But just as with that earlier dialogue, Leah does not follow up her sharp words over the mandrakes with sharp actions. Instead, Leah magnanimously gives up the mandrakes even though the sisters presumably share the belief that the plant could help Rachel to bear children for Jacob. Leah does not allow the intense sibling rivalry to obliterate family ties. At the beginning of her story, Leah's tears convinced God that it would be unfair if she were forced to marry her unworthy cousin, Esau. And now, when the same principle of fairness calls for some assistance to Rachel, Leah stays true to her values. She acts to mitigate the injustice of Rachel's barrenness, even though changing that condition could end forever any hope that Leah's sons will ultimately draw Jacob's love to her.

The second incident, the birth of Dinah, triggers a midrashic tale that serves as the pinnacle of Leah's moral heroism. Leah gave birth to six of Jacob's sons. With her unborn seventh son, Leah may have finally held complete victory in her hand (or more precisely, in her womb). But out of concern for her sister's humiliation, Leah makes the momentous decision to give up what could be her sole advantage in the fierce rivalry with Rachel. Leah recognizes that her total victory can only be achieved at the cost of total disaster for her sister. So Leah restructures her competitive efforts. Instead of trying to match Rachel's continuing allure for Jacob, Leah now attempts to emulate Rachel's previous sacrifice for Leah's dignity at the wedding.

In the midrashic story of Leah's wedding night, the Rabbis weave a tale of incredible self-sacrifice by Rachel when she gives Leah the secret signs, and even hides under the bed to answer for Leah throughout the intimate conversations of the wedding night. Now Leah chooses to reciprocate. By her prayers to change the gender of her seventh child, Leah turns her back on her own goals, and instead acts in a way that will almost certainly further her sister's competing goals.

In both these key episodes of the mandrakes and Dinah's birth, Leah subverts self-interest to the principle of fairness. Leah elects to limit her central rivalry with Rachel in order to act in an ethical manner consistent with the finest points of her own character. In these two instances, Leah offers us a model of consistency of character in the face of the natural, almost irresistible temptation to win at all costs. The episodes of the mandrakes and, even more, the birth of Dinah constitute high points in the midrashic depiction of Leah's moral heroism.

5

LEAH AND THE FAMILY
LEAVE HARAN

Rachel's Ascendancy

The birth of Dinah does not mark the end of Leah's story, but it does inaugurate a significantly different role for Leah in the balance of the story. It is true that up to this point in the family saga, Leah has been frustrated in her efforts to become the focus of Jacob's love, or even his attention. Nevertheless, Leah's position as his first and most fertile wife has at least kept her at center stage. In the eyes of some traditional commentators, Leah possesses a unique claim to being Jacob's only legal wife (since later-revealed Jewish law will prohibit a man from marrying his wife's sister during the first wife's lifetime). And there is no question about who is ahead at this point in Leah's competition with Rachel to have Jacob's children. Leah has given birth to six of Jacob's sons (as well as his only daughter, Dinah), and the handmaidens have produced another four sons, while Rachel is still barren.

But finally it is Rachel's turn to become the star of this family drama. Seven years have elapsed since Jacob married the sisters. He has now labored for Laban a total of fourteen years. More significantly, Rachel is about to bear Jacob a son, his eleventh. This event will set in motion the events leading to the end of Jacob's sojourn in Haran. Unfortunately for Leah, the end of her sister's barrenness seems to remove the sole remaining impediment standing in the way of Rachel's total dominance in the household. From now on, it clearly will be Rachel, not Leah, who will assume the role of Jacob's primary wife during the family's remaining six years in Haran.

Rachel Gives Birth to Joseph

Rachel's momentous pregnancy is announced in a single, terse sentence.

> *And God remembered Rachel, and God listened to her, and opened her womb. (Gen. 30:22)*

As we have seen before, midrash searches for the deeper significance by closely examining the biblical verse.

"And God Remembered Rachel"

A God of perfection obviously can't forget, so midrash reads this word "remembered" as indicating that God intervenes for Rachel because God "remembered" (took into account) a particular act by her that merited reward.[1] Some commentators specify that Rachel's merit here is having given the secret identification signs to Leah on the wedding night.[2] But if this is true, then why is the reward for Rachel's act of compassion so delayed? Perhaps God withholds the reward to Rachel until Leah first expresses her gratitude by her reciprocal act of compassion (changing Dinah's gender). One commentary concludes that the righteousness of Leah praying for her sister at the birth of Dinah is so great that God is moved to respond. God recognizes that if Leah, a mere human being and thus by nature a harshly competitive creature, can be so moved by pity for Rachel, then surely an infinitely merciful God should exhibit comparable pity.[3] Other commentators attribute Rachel's reward to other factors.

AND GOD REMEMBERED RACHEL (Gen. 30:22). What did He remember? It was the silence that she [Rachel] kept for her sister's sake when they gave Leah to Jacob. She [Rachel] knew about it but she remained silent. AND GOD REMEM-BERED RACHEL. That was only just, for she brought her rival [Bilhah] into her home. (Midrash Rabbah, Genesis 73.4)

God doesn't remember Rachel for what she said (telling Leah the codes or answering from under the wedding bed) but for her dutiful silence in the face of her father's injustice toward her when he switched the brides. Alternatively, God rewards Rachel for giving her handmaiden, Bilhah, to be Jacob's wife and produce children. Still other commentators conclude that God is answering Rachel's desperate desire to produce children for Jacob, which she had demonstrated by bargaining for the magical mandrakes.[4] On this point, however, one commentator asserts that the mandrakes episode had the opposite effect, actually restraining God from sooner granting Rachel's wish for children. God delays helping Rachel until now to make it clear that her pregnancy is God's miracle, and not the result of some magical plant.[5]

Classical midrash also makes the case that God is responding to Rachel's or Jacob's fear that Esau might claim Rachel as his wife so long as she has not borne children. We will see later that when Jacob eventually presents his family to Esau upon their return to the Promised Land, the commentators note various family actions taken regarding the women: Jacob hides Dinah from Esau (Gen. 32:23); Jacob places Leah and Rachel behind the handmaidens for protection (Gen. 33:2); and Joseph shields Rachel from Esau's view (Gen. 33:7). According to midrash, all these maneuvers are attempts to deter Esau from seizing these attractive women by force.[6]

"And God Listened to Her"

In addition, the Rabbis find that God is moved to end Rachel's barrenness by more than her past deeds. God also listens to the prayers that midrash imagines Rachel is continually offering for fertility.[7] One commenter suggests that Rachel has learned she must pray for herself as a result of Jacob's earlier angry response when she demanded that he give her children and pray to God on her behalf. Now God listens to her because she is offering her own prayers.[8] Another commentator concludes that Rachel's prayers are finally answered because they have been reinforced by the prayers of Leah, Bilhah, and Zilpah.[9]

"And [God] Opened Her Womb"

We previously noted how modern readers might assume that when the Bible speaks in terms of God opening a mother's womb, this may be nothing more than quaint, old-fashioned language. But just as when this phrase was previously used for Leah (Gen. 29:31), midrash assumes here that such language may hide a deeper layer of significance. The Rabbis speculate that Rachel, like her sister (and perhaps twin), is sterile due to some anatomical blockage or abnormality, and therefore a similar divine miracle is necessary to permit Rachel to conceive.[10]

☙

And she conceived and bore a son, and said, "God has taken away my disgrace." So she named him Joseph, saying, "May the Lord add another son for me." (Gen. 30:23–24)

Rachel bases her son's name (Joseph—*Yosef*) on two different wordplays, both of which she expresses in the text. First, she declares, "God has taken away [*asaf*] my reproach." Joseph is the instrument taking away her disgrace—her barrenness, which had been a public sign of her unworthiness.[11] But midrash notes that the word she uses, *asaf*, does not technically mean "to remove," but rather "to gather in," in the sense of hiding or bringing under cover.[12] This is a telling psychological observation. Giving birth to Joseph may have made Rachel's former barrenness no longer a topic of public comment. But past humiliation is often internalized as a permanent wound. Perhaps nothing can ever expunge the feelings of shame and bitterness produced by those seven years of barrenness at the height of her harsh rivalry with the fertile Leah.

Others speculate that Rachel's disgrace, which God has "taken away" through Joseph's birth, comes not just from public gossip over her childlessness. It might also refer to humiliation she suffered from Leah's cruelty toward her during that period, or to Rachel's shame for not having been able to accept Bilhah's children as her own.[13] And as previously mentioned, midrash even speculates that Rachel is distressed because the community might be viewing her childlessness as indicating that Jacob had followed the early pagan practice of marrying one wife (Leah) to have children, but rendering a second wife (Rachel) sterile so that childbearing would not diminish her beauty or make her less available for sexual pleasure.[14]

The second basis in the text for Joseph's name is found in Rachel's next statement, "May the Lord add [*yosef*] another son for me." It expresses her desire to be the one to bear Jacob's next—and final—son.

The Family Prepares to Leave

Once Rachel gives birth to Joseph, we might expect that Jacob will be ready to end his fourteen-year exile in Haran and take his family back to the Promised Land. Jacob has now had children with each of his four wives, so all those relationships appear to be permanent. Most importantly, Jacob has paid his brideprices for Leah and Rachel. But while the completion of his contract to labor for Laban may have legally freed Jacob to take his family and leave, he is as penniless as he had been the day he first arrived in Haran fourteen years earlier. All his work to this point had been solely for Laban's benefit; he was not able to build up any flocks or other wealth for himself.

Now, however, Laban has come to recognize that Jacob's righteousness and skills have blessed Laban with ample pure water and great increase in his flocks. In a scene strikingly reminiscent of their initial bargaining over the terms of Jacob's service, negotiated a month after he had arrived at Haran, Laban now once again asks Jacob to name his wages for managing the flocks. Jacob responds by agreeing to continue to oversee Laban's animals, but this time with an opportunity to build up his own personal wealth. As his wages, Jacob asks only to keep all the animals that are born with spotted or streaked color markings. Laban readily agrees, and Jacob proceeds to use his herdsman's skills to selectively breed the flocks so that his portion would consist of the stronger animals. After six years of this, Laban and Laban's sons become jealous of Jacob's new prosperity. Finally, for the first time since Jacob's ladder dream at Bethel, God reappears to Jacob, telling him to return with his family to the Promised Land (Gen. 31:3).[15]

Jacob has now received two strong indications that he should leave Haran immediately. He has perceived danger from the jealousy shown by Laban and his sons, and he has heard God's command to return to his homeland. We might expect that his response would be simply to flee, repeating in reverse his initial hasty flight from his homeland to Haran twenty years earlier. However, the story of Jacob's return is a very different tale, focusing not on the similarities between the two journeys, but on their differences.

> *And Jacob sent and called Rachel and Leah to the field to his flock. . . . And Rachel and Leah answered him, saying, "Have we still a share in the inheritance of our father's house? Surely, he regards us as strangers, now that he has sold us and has used up our purchase price. Truly, all the wealth that God has taken away from our father belongs to us and to our children. Now then, do just as God has told you." (Gen. 31:4, 14–16)*

The earlier story told how Jacob fled from his parents' home immediately after he had obtained the firstborn's blessing by tricking Isaac. That account showed a husband-wife dynamic between Jacob's parents, Isaac and Rebekah, marked by secretiveness, dissembling, manipulating, and almost total lack of real communication between the spouses. Jacob appears to have learned from that, and now, even after God has commanded him to leave Haran, Jacob first consults with Rachel and Leah, in a field where they won't be overheard. (Perhaps the location of this meeting is also meant to signal that Jacob has finally become a man of action, strength, and cunning—a man of the fields, like Esau, Gen. 25:27.) Jacob tells Rachel and Leah how, with God's help, he has manipulated the animal breeding to acquire wealth from Laban, and how God has now told him to return. Jacob is apparently seeking his wives' assent, and they quickly agree to leave with him.

At the start of Leah's story, when Jacob arrived in Haran, we saw how both Leah and Rachel cooperated with Laban's deception. The Rabbis partly justify the sisters' complicity on the grounds of filial duty or parental force. But the biblical text has not yet told us how either sister feels about Laban's scheme. Now, when Jacob tells his wives about his plans to take the family and flee from Haran, Leah and Rachel finally have the opportunity to express their feelings about their father. They complain that Laban has appropriated their bride-price (the economic fruits of Jacob's service during his two seven-year terms of labor) rather than setting it aside for them and their children as he was obligated to do.[16] Even though they say no more, both have ample basis for more complaints about Laban.

Although the Rabbis conclude that Rachel participated in the wedding hoax to spare Leah humiliation, or perhaps in acceptance of what Rachel saw as God's will, that analysis does not preclude the likelihood that Rachel deeply resented her father's engineering the bridal switch. We might expect that the natural target of Rachel's resentment would be Leah, and midrash does tell us that Rachel distressed her sister with hateful words during Leah's wedding week.[17] But many commentaries see Laban as having forced an unwilling Leah to participate in the wedding-night deception. And so it is possible that Rachel's resentment for the hoax is focused on her father.

Midrash even proposes that Laban's deception of Jacob did not begin with the wedding. The Rabbis invent a tale of how Laban intercepted all of Jacob's loving notes to Rachel during the initial seven years when he first tended the flocks. Laban even seized the gifts Jacob sent to Rachel and redirected them to Leah.[18] Midrash credits Rachel with additional merit for her silence throughout all these acts. However, it remains likely that even a dutiful daughter such as Rachel must have harbored some bitterness toward her father for this.

There is much less discussion in the commentaries about Leah's feelings toward Laban. Even if we accept that Laban dragged Leah into the wedding tent against her will, it is not as easy to presume that she necessarily resents Laban for this. Leah may have been an otherwise unmarriageable, weak-eyed woman who faced life as an old maid. If so, it was only due to Laban's audacious scheme that Leah married at all.

Even in the morning-after argument between the bride and groom as imagined by the Rabbis, Leah never expresses blame or criticism of her father. Instead, she defends herself by attacking Jacob for his comparable deception of his own father.[19] However, the classical commentaries also imply that, even if the wedding hoax was beneficial for Leah, Laban was not acting from any concern for her. Laban planned the wedding hoax to keep Jacob in Haran for another seven years, in order to retain his valuable herdsman's services and to extend the miraculous replenishment of the community's water wells.[20] This suggests another possible reason for Leah's resentment—that her father was only using her as a pawn in his struggle to obtain economic advantage from Jacob. But Leah certainly didn't express any distaste for becoming Jacob's first wife. So perhaps Leah's real resentment is for Laban's unjust appropriation of her bride-price, exactly the complaint the sisters express in the field. But this injustice seems to have been remedied by the great wealth Jacob has built up in his final six years in Haran. And so we can see why, after the discussion in the field, Leah ceases to have any remaining issues with her father. From this point on in the narrative, it is Rachel who deals with Laban.

Jacob summons "Rachel and Leah" to the field. He disregards Leah's status as older sister and first-married wife by calling Rachel first. The wives' response is even more significant: "And Rachel and Leah answered." The Rabbis note that the word used for "answered" (*va-ta'an*) appears in the singular form; they interpret this to mean that Rachel speaks for both the sisters, or at least that she answers first. Of course, it is possible to "correct" the biblical grammar and translate this as "they answered," as some modern interpreters do.[21] But consider what a world of commentary would be lost by such a modification.

According to Rashi, Rachel is mentioned before her older sister in this conversation for two reasons. First, Rachel is Jacob's principal wife, having the chief duties of managing his complicated households, and he apparently spends the most time with her. Second, Jacob's love for Rachel is the whole reason that he had stayed with Laban, and that led to all four marriages.[22] Thus, regardless of the wives' respective statuses at this point, Rachel deserves most of the credit for all that has happened in Jacob's family, and so is entitled to respond first. Other commentators conclude that Rachel answers first because she loves Jacob more than Leah does, or else that, while Rachel is the only one who expresses the reply, we must presume that she would have first properly consulted with her older sister.[23]

In the book of Ruth, the townspeople bless the marriage of Ruth to Boaz (who is Leah's descendant) by praying that God will make Ruth "like Rachel and Leah," thus repeating Rachel's priority by mentioning her name first (Ruth 4:11).[24] Rachel also comes before Leah today in the traditional *Mi She Berakh* prayer for healing the sick, and in the blessing recited for daughters on

Shabbat. And the order of names in the contemporary version of the *Amidah* prayer is typically "Sarah, Rebekah, Rachel, and Leah" (although Leah is named before Rachel in some Reform prayer services).[25]

Contemporary Judaism's practice of naming Leah last may seem like quite a rebuff for Jacob's first (and perhaps only legal) wife. But from Leah's point of view, the current practice is actually an improvement. In previous centuries, the Matriarchs were referred to only in women's prayers, and most of those totally omitted Leah's name and mentioned only "Sarah, Rebekah, and Rachel."[26] Thus, as reflected in contemporary liturgy, Judaism has largely accepted Rachel's precedence over her older sister, Leah, a precedence foreshadowed in their conversation with Jacob in the field. Rachel seems to have become our third Matriarch, while Leah, the older sister and Jacob's first wife, has been somehow relegated to the fourth position. Leah has become our Lost Matriarch.

Rachel Steals the Teraphim

Once his wives have consented to leave, Jacob immediately begins preparations for the journey back to his homeland. He lifts his sons and wives onto the camels and then leads away his livestock and all the possessions and property he acquired in Haran. (Gen. 31:17–18) The only other preparation mentioned in the Bible is performed by Rachel.

> *Meanwhile Laban had gone to shear his sheep, and Rachel stole her father's teraphim. (Gen. 31:19)*

Teraphim are physical icons of pagan household gods. But the commentaries disagree on how these icons were made, what role they played in pagan households, and most importantly, why Rachel stole them from her father's house. As is typical in classical midrash, some of the Rabbis impute virtuous motives to Rachel for taking these objects, such as saving her father from worshiping these false gods or removing unclean objects from his house.[27] These explanations are not really satisfying, however, because Rachel does not destroy the icons, as did young Abraham (recounted in Midrash Rabbah, Gen. 38.13). Instead, Rachel carefully hides the idols from both her father and from Jacob (Gen. 31:32, 34–35).

Another midrashic attempt to justify Rachel's theft of the teraphim presumes that pagans such as Laban used them as tools for divination.[28] By taking them, she prevents her father from getting early news of their flight and destination. But this explanation is problematic, because if she takes the teraphim to stop Laban from learning where the family has gone, it would mean that Rachel herself believes in their magical powers. This would not be an implausible state of mind for Rachel. She was raised in a pagan household, and she had previously demonstrated an apparent belief in the magical fertility powers of the mandrakes. Biblical Judaism tries to restrict the miraculous solely to God's agency, so Rachel's desire to interfere with Laban's powers of divination would not be a redemptive motivation for this Matriarch.

Perhaps the most likely reason for Rachel's theft is that it is simply another attempt to achieve her primary and continuing goal—to bear children for Jacob. Since Rachel's deeply felt need to have children had already driven her to desperate measures, it seems likely that she steals the teraphim because they are idols of the pagan goddess of fertility and childbirth.[29]

Rachel's stealing the teraphim marks the beginning of Leah's marginalization in the family drama—to the point of near-total exclusion. Leah, who has had only two lines of direct dialogue in the text, now becomes entirely silent. Rachel becomes the central female character in the remainder of Genesis, even after her death. So she not only steals the teraphim, she also steals the spotlight. We're about to see this in the closing scenes of the flight from Haran, when Laban appears for his last confrontations with Jacob and with Rachel—confrontations from which Leah is noticeably absent.

When Laban finally learns that Jacob has fled with his wives, children, and flocks, Laban gathers an armed force and hurries off in pursuit. But before he can catch up with the family, God appears in a dream and warns him not to harm or impede Jacob. Therefore, when Laban does overtake the group, he professes to have come after them only to say a proper farewell to his daughters and grandchildren (Gen. 31:26–28). The complaint actually raised by Laban, however, is not really about his missed opportunity for family kisses and celebration. Laban charges that Jacob or someone in his party stole Laban's household gods—his teraphim.

> [Laban complains to Jacob:] "Why have you stolen my gods?" And Jacob answered Laban, saying, . . . "Anyone with whom you find your gods shall not live." For Jacob did not know that Rachel had stolen them. (Gen. 31:30–32)

Jacob denies any theft, and goes on to issue a fearsome curse: "Anyone with whom you find your gods shall not live." The text goes on to make certain that the reader does not miss the terrible irony—that Jacob may be unwittingly cursing his beloved Rachel with death. The Rabbis make much of Jacob's curse, since they are confident that blessings and curses by the righteous have significant consequences. One midrash compares such a blessing or curse to the decree of a king, which once made cannot be revoked.[30] Jacob fled from his homeland because he had received a blessing intended for Esau, which his father was powerless to cancel once it had been given. Now Jacob is returning to his homeland, and he answers his father-in-law by declaring a curse that unintentionally falls upon Rachel, a curse that will likewise be unalterable. On this basis, some Rabbis conclude that Jacob's curse will cause Rachel's early death (they know that later in the story Rachel will die giving birth to Benjamin). But the commentaries are divided on whether Jacob's curse is responsible for Rachel's death. As we can expect by now, some come up with various ingenious arguments to shield Jacob from guilt here.[31] And perhaps this is not a curse. Jacob could be saying "If you can find someone who stole your *gods*"—that is, "gods" (Laban's clay idols) that were not gods, making this an ironic declaration of monotheistic faith.

Now Rachel had taken the teraphim and placed them in the camel saddle and sat on them. And Laban rummaged through the tent without finding them. And she said to her father, "Let not my lord be angry that I cannot rise before you, for the manner of women is upon me." Thus he searched, but could not find the teraphim. (Gen. 31:34–35)

At Jacob's invitation, Laban searches the family's tents for the teraphim. Laban searches Leah's tent in precisely the same perfunctory manner that he searches the handmaidens' tents (Gen. 31:33); he does not speak with any of them. Instead, it is Rachel who plays the leading role in the search scene. The casting is dramatically appropriate, since we know (but Jacob and Laban do not) that Rachel indeed has the teraphim. She evades detection by a most audacious stratagem.

Rachel hides the teraphim in her camel saddlebag and sits on it. When her father enters her tent, she coolly informs him that she cannot get up because she is menstruating, considered in that culture to be a highly contaminating state that men must avoid.[32] (According to one contemporary commentator, Rachel is pregnant with Benjamin by that time and therefore would not be menstruating.)[33] Regardless of whether or not Rachel is lying, her stratagem works. Laban searches the rest of her tent but does not find the idols.[34]

And Laban answered and said to Jacob, "The daughters are my daughters, and the children are my children, . . . and what can I do this day for these my daughters, or for their children whom they have borne?" . . . [And Laban said,] "If you shall afflict my daughters,

or if you shall take other wives besides my daughters, although no man is with us, remember, God is witness between me and you.". . . And early in the morning Laban rose up, and kissed his sons and his daughters, and blessed them; and Laban departed, and returned to his place. (Gen. 31:43, 50; 32:1)

After some angry posturing and threatening, Laban finally parts from Jacob with a covenant of peace, which they mark by erecting a pile of stones. Laban warns Jacob not to ill-treat his daughters or take any other wives, and then Laban kisses and blesses his daughters and grandsons and returns home. The Rabbis calculate that Jacob served Laban for twenty years (a period that is about to be followed by two years of journeying home). The Rabbis proceed to painstakingly examine the precise wording of Laban's final charge to Jacob regarding Laban's daughters.

AND LABAN ANSWERED AND SAID TO JACOB, "THE DAUGH-TERS ARE MY DAUGHTERS [. . . AND WHAT CAN I DO THIS DAY FOR THESE MY DAUGHTERS" (Gen. 31:43)?] R. Reuben said, "All [including the concubines] were his daughters, for THE DAUGHTERS ARE MY DAUGHTERS refers to two, and WHAT CAN I DO THIS DAY FOR THESE MY DAUGHTERS refers to another two, making four in all." [Other] Rabbis reach the same conclusion from the following verse: IF YOU SHALL AFFLICT MY DAUGHTERS refers to two; and . . . IF YOU TAKE OTHER WIVES BESIDES MY DAUGHTERS (Gen. 31:50) refers to another two, making four. (Midrash Rabbah, Genesis 74.13)

Because in the text Laban refers twice in the same sentence to his "daughters" rather than using the expected pronoun "them" the second time, midrash infers that Laban is talking about two different pairs of daughters—if the first reference is to Leah and Rachel, then the second must be to Bilhah and Zilpah. According to midrash, this indicates that the handmaidens are also Laban's daughters, although by a concubine rather than a legal wife.[35]

By this point in the narrative, Jacob's four wives have already collectively given birth to eleven of the twelve promised sons, and Rachel is pregnant with the twelfth. It therefore may seem a little late for Jacob to receive advice from his father-in-law about potential complications of his marital relations. But we know that those complications are far from resolved. They will continue to plague this family throughout Jacob's lifetime and beyond.

In the text the scene ends when Laban finally departs in peace. However, midrash adds two significant additions to the story. First, the Hebrew text doesn't say that Laban returned "to his home" or "to Haran." The word in Gen. 32:1 (*li-m'komo*) says that Laban returned "to his place." Midrash takes that to mean that Laban returned to his original place in life: his status at Jacob's arrival in Haran, when Laban had only meager flocks barely surviving the drought. Midrash imagines that while Laban was away pursuing Jacob, robbers broke into his home and stole all his wealth.[36]

Second, midrash strongly doubts the sincerity of Laban's peaceful words. The Rabbis presume that, as soon as his fear and awe from being visited by God while pursuing Jacob dissipate, Laban will start to feel bolder. He will regret not having attacked Jacob and seizing his wealth by force when he had the chance. So, according to the midrashic tale, in a final act of treachery toward his son-in-law and family, Laban sends a message to Esau warning him of Jacob's approach. Laban discloses the great wealth in Jacob's caravan and urges Esau to commit the attack on Jacob that Laban is too fearful to attempt himself.[37]

Leah's Lessons from Her Flight from Haran

As the family's stay in Haran ends, we are aware that both sisters' roles in the family's story will soon be over. We can see that Leah no longer plays a central part in the story, and while Rachel has some important dramatic scenes remaining, we know that she will soon die. But from their lives to this point in both the text and the midrash, it has already become clear that, twins or not, these sisters display some close similarities and some distinct differences. The pattern for comparing the sisters was set by the previous descriptions of Jacob and Esau, who appear as major archetypical opposites in the overall story: smooth versus hairy, herder versus hunter, Momma's favorite versus Papa's favorite, man of thought versus man of action. And the Rabbis go further, reading the brothers as symbols for good versus evil—the people Israel versus their oppressor, Rome.

But the sisters present a more complex picture; they are not simply opposites. So how similar or different are Leah and Rachel? As to physical attributes, some commentators emphasize their differences, imagining a beautiful, young Rachel and an unattractive, older Leah. However other commentators conclude that these sisters are twins, or at least are essentially equal in beauty. As a purely literary matter, this latter interpretation has much to offer. Thinking of Leah and Rachel as similar in appearance and age intensifies the level of dramatic conflict between them.

For narrative purposes, making the assumption that the sisters are similar in age and appearance also fits well with the story as it has developed so far—even offering a natural explanation for how Jacob could have failed to recognize the bridal substitution on the wedding night. Similarity in appearance would also heighten the significance of differences in the sisters' conduct.

In terms of their respective characters, this portion of the biblical text does not demonstrate consistent moral superiority of Rachel over Leah. For example, we read the sharp contrast between Rachel's name for her new son, Joseph (asking for "another" son), and the name Leah previously chose for her fourth son, Judah (meaning, "giving thanks"). Rachel ignores the miraculous birth granted to her after so many years of barrenness and immediately makes more demands on God. On the other hand, Leah not only expressed gratitude for her fourth son, but may have been graciously signaling her contentment with already having been favored by God and her willingness to allow Jacob's eventual other three wives to bear the rest of Jacob's sons.

In the story so far, it seems that Rachel has not yet achieved Leah's ethical excellence. Indeed, much of the midrash on this portion of the text appears driven by an effort to raise Rachel's character to at least equal Leah's. But we don't have to accept the common midrashic bias for making pious justifications to elevate the characters of the Matriarchs and Patriarchs.[38] We don't have to justify Rachel's bold actions in pursuit of what has become her obsession to have children—providing Bilhah to produce surrogate children for Rachel, bargaining for the mandrakes to overcome her barrenness, pushing herself in front of her older sister in the conversation in the field, stealing Laban's teraphim, and finally claiming her impure status of menstruation to stop her father from finding his household gods.

Such assertiveness contrasts with the moral heroism that Leah displays in silence. Unlike their cousin Esau's example, Leah doesn't complain when Rachel ignores the prerogatives of the firstborn by answering in the field. Unlike Rachel's insistence on obtaining the magical mandrakes and teraphim, Leah is willing to give up the mandrakes for marital access to Jacob, and she plays no role in stealing the teraphim. And unlike Rachel's lie to her father to escape detection of her theft of the teraphim, Leah appears to have been a passive, even reluctant participant in the original wedding hoax, perhaps acting out of filial obligation.

Rachel began the family story with her magnificent self-sacrifice of giving the secret signs to Leah (and perhaps answering for her in the wedding tent). Now Rachel displays her more assertive, selfish side; she seems consumed with having a second son. This is in contrast to Leah's silence about leaving Haran.

And perhaps we can find more than just a relative measure of Leah's character here. The very fact that the text does not describe any actions by Leah during the family's departure may imply that there is nothing to report. If we are entitled to conclude that Leah's character remains constant, then Leah is showing us that heroic moral character is more than an individual instance of good behavior; it requires consistent responses to life.

6

LEAH COMES TO THE
PROMISED LAND

Confronting Esau

Although Leah's already limited presence in the text becomes even further diminished with the family's journey from Haran, the Bible is not finished with her just yet. We can still learn more about her life and her character from several indirect references to her in the remaining narrative. To view those references, however, we must try to catch a glimpse of Leah through the screen of a story that now primarily focuses on Jacob and Rachel.

The family's journey back from Haran is more than a simple return to Jacob's homeland in Canaan. Jacob is returning to face the situation from which he fled two decades ago: confronting his brother Esau. The Bible doesn't indicate that Jacob or anyone else in Haran had any contact with Jacob's parents or brother during all this time. Jacob returns after twenty-two years—a period that his mother had assured him (with manipulative understatement? a mother's unrealistic hope? narrative irony?) would be only "a few days," until Esau's anger over the stolen blessing had cooled (Gen. 27:44).

Without having heard anything in the interim, Jacob still doesn't know what reaction to expect from Esau. Esau had likewise thought that he was postponing his revenge against Jacob only for some "days"—until the conclusion of the days of mourning for Isaac's anticipated death. (Due to his blindness, even Isaac seems to have thought that he was about to die, which explains why he was so anxious to bless his firstborn son.) But even assuming that Esau would stand by his resolve not to take revenge until Isaac's death, Jacob does not yet know whether Isaac still lives. (Later in Jacob's life, his son Joseph will also be exiled. Midrash notes that for twenty-two years Joseph makes no attempt to contact a grieving Jacob, despite Joseph's rise to a position of immense power in Egypt. Midrash sees this as a measure-for-measure punishment for Jacob having subjected his parents to the same period of anguish when he was alive and well in Haran.)[1]

From the time of their first struggles in Rebekah's womb through their development as children competing to win their parents' favoritism, Jacob and Esau exemplify two opposing characters. Perhaps these twins are meant to depict two different sides of a single personality.[2] If so, Jacob might really be returning to confront himself, attempting to vanquish the darker aspects of his own soul.

What has changed is that now Jacob has himself been subjected to connivance and deception by Laban and has seen the sufferings that flow from sibling rivalry. Chastened and reformed by the harsh lessons of his life in Haran, he is finally ready to come to terms with his older brother. The metaphor for this self-struggle will be the famous scene just before he meets his brother, when Jacob wrestles through the night with a mysterious stranger (Gen. 32:25–33). Variously interpreted as wrestling with God, with God's angel, with Esau's protecting angel, or with Esau, Jacob really may be wrestling with himself—with the side of himself that he must overcome before he can meet his brother.

For Leah's story, however, perhaps the most telling aspect of Jacob's meeting with Esau is what Jacob's management of that meeting reveals about his relationships with his wives and children.

And Jacob went on his way, and the angels of God met him.
And when he saw them, Jacob said, "This is God's camp"; and
he called the name of that place Mahanaim. (Gen. 32:2–3)

Jacob's flight from Canaan began at Bethel with his dream of
the angels on the ladder as he reached the border when leaving his homeland (Gen. 28:12). Now his reentry into Canaan is
marked by another vision of angels.[3] This time Jacob names the
location Mahanaim—"two camps"—apparently because there
is now a camp of angels beside his family's camp. But from his
family's point of view, "two camps" describes how Jacob treats
his several wives and children at this critical and dangerous
juncture.[4] Jacob's harsh actions in dividing his family will make
brutally clear how he feels toward each of his family groups.
The text describes how Jacob makes two successive divisions
of his family.

Then Jacob was greatly frightened and distressed; and he
divided the people with him, and the flocks and herds and
camels, into two camps. And he said, "If Esau comes to the
one camp and attacks it, the other camp may yet escape."
(Gen. 32:8–9)

His first division is a coldly calculated combat strategy. Jacob
explains, "If Esau comes to the one camp and attacks it, the
other camp may yet escape." With Jacob's family in two camps,
if Esau's approaching army attacks the first camp, the ensuing
battle will cause a delay, allowing at least the second camp to
flee. The Rabbis speculate on a whole range of possibilities about
how Jacob makes this first division. The advance camp could
consist only of Jacob's fighting men, who would delay Esau with
armed opposition in order to protect the wives and children in
the second camp. Or it could be unarmed, to avoid the appearance of hostility and thereby encourage Esau to accept Jacob's
peaceful overtures, while Jacob's armed forces would hide in
the second camp. Or the first group could hold all the flocks

and property, to see if that is all that Esau wants. Or, despite God's promise of protection (which could have been directed exclusively to Jacob and his future issue, and not necessarily include his present children), Jacob might have divided his family between the two camps to make sure that at least some of his present descendants would survive.[5]

Perhaps the text doesn't tell us more because the details of Jacob's division into two camps are not important. The lesson is simply that Jacob's life (as is true to some extent for everyone) is marked by division: Jacob and Esau, Jacob and Laban, Leah and Rachel, internal piety and external trickery. When Jacob prays for God's help immediately after he has divided his people into two camps, he describes his pitiful plight in these same personal terms: "and now I have become two camps" (Gen. 32:11). So the name that Jacob gives to the place—Mahanaim, Two Camps—may be intended to show Jacob's recognition of his lifelong issues of internal division and inconsistent actions.[6]

Jacob then makes his second division. As Esau approaches with his army, Jacob divides his family, arranging them for formal presentation to his brother.

> Looking up, Jacob saw Esau coming, accompanied by four hundred men. He divided the children among Leah, Rachel, and the two handmaids. And he put the handmaids and their children first, and Leah and her children next, and Rachel and Joseph last. (Gen. 33:1–2)

This time the text makes it painfully clear just how Jacob makes the division. He places "the handmaids and their children first, and Leah and her children next, and Rachel and Joseph last." Midrash is equally clear as to Jacob's unstated rationale: Jacob presumably makes this second division for the same reason he previously divided his camp—as a defensive strategy that would allow at least the rear group a chance to escape if Esau (with his menacing 400-man army) attacks the forward group. This, in turn, implies that Jacob loves and values his formal wives (Leah and Rachel) and their children more than the maidservants (Bilhah and Zilpah) and their children, and moreover that he still prefers Rachel to Leah.[7] Since midrash paints Esau as a man of unbridled sexual appetites, there is some speculation that the specific attack Jacob fears is that Esau will attempt to seize and violate the women. Jacob thus regards the handmaidens as expendable in his attempt to protect his favorite wives. As Rashi succinctly points out, "The further back, the more dear."[8]

It is troubling to us that Jacob is willing to express his preferential love so openly and apparently without regard to how his wives will feel about this. And Jacob likewise ignores the feelings of his sons, who lose their individuality in their father's eyes when they are treated as mere extensions of their mothers. Contemporary commentator Burton L. Visotzky expresses this latter aspect when he notes that by placing the maidservants in front with their sons, Jacob is telling those sons that they are simple cannon fodder, unlike his valued, cherished sons from Rachel and Leah, who are sheltered in the back.[9]

It is easy to see how the jealousies engendered by Jacob's arrangement of his family in this episode may later contribute to the terrible treatment of Joseph, Jacob's favorite, at the hands of the brothers Jacob here deems more expendable. Visotzky also asks whether Jacob's callous expression of parental favoritism might more immediately be the cause of the next episode of outraged violence in Genesis—when Dinah's brothers, Simeon and Levi, exact their bloody revenge on the Shechemites as their expression of the precious family unity and protection they have never received (Gen. 34:25–31).[10]

Visotzky notes that Jacob's original exile to Haran was the direct result of being an object of his parents' clashing preferential treatment of their sons. Now Jacob returns from two decades of laboring in exile, and almost the first action he takes is to repeat the corrosive display of parental preference from which he and Esau have suffered.[11] The power of parental modeling triumphs over what should have been the lessons of painful personal experience.

⌖

Then the maidservants, with their children, came forward and bowed low; next Leah, with her children, came forward and bowed low; and after, Joseph and Rachel came forward and bowed low. (Gen. 33:6–7)

Midrash also observes that when Jacob initially divides his family, the text ends with "Rachel and Joseph" (Gen. 33:2), but when the family members are then presented to Esau, the order is reversed: "and after, Joseph and Rachel came forward" (Gen. 33:7). This change suggests a significance that is not expressed in the text, so the Rabbis proceed to speculate on the meaning.

THEN THE MAIDSERVANTS CAME NEAR (Gen. 33:6). In the case of all [the others in the family], it says, THEN THE MAIDSERVANTS CAME NEAR, THEY AND THEIR CHILDREN, AND THEY BOWED DOWN. AND LEAH ALSO WITH HER CHILDREN CAME NEAR, AND BOWED THEMSELVES (Gen. 33:6–7). But in the case of Joseph it is written AND AFTER CAME JOSEPH NEAR AND RACHEL, AND THEY BOWED DOWN [naming the child before the mother] (Gen. 33:7). Joseph said, "That wicked man [Esau] has desiring eyes; this [how I am walking] is so he shall not look upon my mother." So he drew up to his full height and covered her. (Midrash Rabbah, Genesis 78.10)

The commentators generally conclude that Joseph comes before his mother to shield her from Esau's view. She is still outstandingly beautiful and has to be protected from Esau, who might claim her as the bride he was promised (according to the midrashic tale of the family marriage contracts between Rebekah and Laban), or perhaps seize her in lust (consistent with the Rabbis' insistence on portraying Esau as the embodiment of lust and violence).[12]

In contrast, the Rabbis consider it a mark of Leah's superior confidence in God that she does not likewise seem to fear being presented to Esau. Midrash on early parts of the story has her disfiguring her eyes by copious weeping in her distress that Esau will claim her under their parents' agreement. Now Leah seems to have come to trust that God's justice will protect her. Perhaps she is simply confident that since she has provided six sons to Jacob, it is impossible for Esau to still claim her. In any event, she apparently doesn't feel the need to have any of her six sons (all older than Joseph) shield her.[13]

If this is a fair measure of Leah's attitude, then the contrast with Rachel here might suggest some of what Leah has learned from her life struggles, which may now have become a source of strength and confidence for her. She has continued to reinvent herself, creating for herself an identity beyond that of being only a victim of unfair circumstances.

Of course, Leah's attitude at this juncture is only speculation. It may be that Leah's sons do not try to protect her because they feel alienated from her. They could be resentful of having been used—indeed, of having been born at all—as mere tactical maneuvers in Leah's conflict with Rachel. They could feel abandoned because Leah has failed to protect them against Jacob's obvious preference for Rachel and Joseph. But the Rabbis are content to presume that the biblical word-order cue that triggers speculation about Joseph protecting his mother implies by contrast that Leah has grown in self-confidence.

As for the actual meeting of the brothers (Gen. 33:3–15), the Rabbis create extensive midrash in an attempt to resolve the ambiguities in the Bible's description. Many of the commentaries conclude that Esau's apparently affectionate greeting of Jacob is insincere, just as Laban's was when Jacob first arrived in Haran. Midrash sees Jacob as the hero who, without resorting to armed battle, manages to deflect (at least temporarily, and with God's help) Esau's continuing thirst for vengeance.[14]

That same night he arose, and taking his two wives, his two maid-servants, and his eleven sons, he crossed the ford of the Jabbok. (Gen. 32:23)

In the verses just discussed, the Bible has unfolded the vivid story of Jacob returning to Canaan to meet Esau. But just prior to that meeting, the text appears to go out of its way to specify that he brought with him his two wives, his two maidservants, "and his eleven sons [or 'eleven children']." So where was Leah's daughter, Dinah?

Modern readers might see the text's failure to mention Dinah as merely another example of the Bible's gender bias. But rather than ignoring Dinah's absence, the Rabbis play with it. They speculate why she may not have been mentioned in the description of the family members Jacob brought into Canaan. The midrashic response is woven from two strands of biblical and midrashic material.

The first story line is found in the next chapter of the Bible, which will be devoted entirely to Dinah. It tells the dramatic story of her unexpected relationship with the prince of Shechem and how her brothers forcefully react to that situation. Since Dinah suffers greatly there, the Rabbis are challenged to find some reason why God would so afflict her. Perhaps Dinah's omission from the family list might signal some basis for a measure-for-measure divine punishment about to be inflicted on the family in the incident involving Dinah and Shechem that follows.

A second story line comes from the repeated midrashic portrayal of Esau as a man who acts impulsively out of lust. Many midrashic tales recount how his evil nature—at this point even more threatening because Esau now has military power and proximity—keeps Leah, Rachel, Jacob, and Joseph fearful that he will claim Leah or Rachel. Most commentators don't miss a chance to highlight any new facet of Esau's villainous character in order to contrast him with his virtuous twin. So the Rabbis create a midrash blaming fear of Esau for why Dinah is omitted from the list of family members entering the land.

> AND HE ROSE THAT NIGHT, AND TOOK HIS TWO WIVES, AND HIS TWO MAIDSERVANTS, AND HIS ELEVEN SONS, AND PASSED OVER THE FORD OF THE JABBOK (Gen. 32:23). Where was Dinah? He [Jacob] put her in a chest and locked it. He thought, "That wicked man has desiring eyes. This is so that he will not take her from me." R. Huna, in the name of R. Abba the Priest, said, "The Holy One, blessed be He, said to him, 'You did not have her married in an acceptable way [married to Esau], so she will be taken in a forbidden way [by Shechem, without marriage].' So it is written: AND DINAH WENT OUT (Gen. 34:1)." (Midrash Rabbah, Genesis 76.9)

The midrashic tale that results from combining all these elements proposes that Dinah is omitted from the list of entering family members because Jacob was fearful that Esau would seize her. To avoid this, Jacob brings Dinah into the Promised Land hidden in a wooden chest.[15] Midrash goes on to connect this to the grief suffered by Dinah and her family in the next chapter where some commentaries conclude that Jacob is wrong to have withheld Dinah from Esau, ignoring his obligations to his older brother.[16]

One chauvinistic commentary even speculates that if Esau had married Dinah she could have reformed his character, since he was, after all, the son of Isaac and Rebekah and so must have inherited some genetic disposition toward goodness.[17] Thus, Jacob is faulted for taking matters into his own hands when he conceals Dinah.[18] He should have followed the earlier example of Leah, who prayed for God's protection against the threat of being claimed by Esau. In the midrashic imagination, we hear God telling Jacob that since he withheld Dinah from Esau, a Jew whom she could have reformed for the benefit of the Jewish community, God will give her to Shechem, a non-Jew whom she will not have an opportunity to reform, and this will be a great loss to both the Shechemites and the Israelites.

Although most modern readers may be uncomfortable with a divine justice that can punish Dinah for her father's actions, we know that biblical justice often affects innocent parties or future generations. Perhaps the term "justice" is misleading; "consequences" may be more accurate. It is a fact of life that our bad actions often impose negative consequences on innocent third parties. The Rabbis understand that view, just as we today understand that actions taken by some, such as polluting the environment or starting a war, can bring suffering for many future generations of innocent parties.

The Dinah Episode

Although Leah is not actually a character in the story of her daughter, Dinah, and Prince Shechem in Genesis 34, she is referred to once in the text, and even blamed by the Rabbis for her daughter's misfortunes. When midrash examines the moral implications of what happens to Dinah, the Rabbis' casting of blame becomes relevant to our understanding of Leah's character. The episode of Dinah and Shechem is often referred to as the "rape of Dinah," but it is unclear what actually happens. The biblical text leaves so much unsaid that the Rabbis feel compelled to provide their own detail.

We will explore these rabbinic elaborations, but first, a summary of the Bible text: After Jacob and Esau finally meet without incident, they separate, and Jacob and his family settle in the land of Shechem. Dinah goes out to see the daughters of the land, whereupon Prince Shechem, son of King Hamor, takes her and has sexual intercourse with her. Shechem then falls in love with her and implores his father to arrange for their marriage. When Shechem and Hamor come to negotiate with Jacob and his sons for the marriage, Jacob's sons trick them. The sons agree to the marriage and the joining of the two nations, on the condition that all the men of Shechem are first circumcised. Prince Shechem is eager to accept, and he and the king convince all the males of Shechem to undergo the procedure. But on the third day after the circumcisions, when the men are still in pain from the procedure, two of Dinah's brothers, Simeon and Levi, slay Prince Shechem, King Hamor, and all the men of the city, taking Dinah back to the family home. The other brothers then plunder the city, seizing livestock, wealth, and the women and children. Surprisingly, the Rabbis begin their interpretations by focusing on the one significant character who is absent except for a seemingly incidental reference—Leah.

And Dinah the daughter of Leah, whom she bore to Jacob, went out to see the daughters of the land. (Gen. 34:1)

This initial verse makes it clear that the story's main character will indeed be Dinah. But the verse goes beyond simply naming Dinah when it identifies her as "the daughter of Leah, whom she bore to Jacob." This detail seems excessive, since there is only one Dinah mentioned in the Bible. Surely the reader will not have forgotten the birth and naming of Dinah, which appeared just four chapters earlier. But the Rabbis' belief that the Bible is a divinely written or divinely inspired document requires presuming that every word of the text has separate meaning and purpose. Therefore the mention of Dinah's parentage signals that some special significance is hidden in these apparently superfluous words.

Rashi examines the words of the text closely and asks why Dinah is referred to as the daughter of Leah (who does not appear further in the chapter) rather than as the daughter of Jacob, or of Jacob and Leah. His answer relies on the next word of the verse (which has even more prominence as the first word in the Hebrew text): "[Dinah] went out" (*va-tetze*). Rashi notes that this is the same word that described Leah's actions in the episode of the mandrakes, when Leah "went out" (*va-tetze*) to tell Jacob that he was to sleep with her that night because of her bargain with Rachel (Gen. 30:16).[19] Although in that earlier story Leah seemed to be rewarded by God for relinquishing the mandrakes to her sister—Leah's barrenness ended immediately—some commentaries nevertheless criticize her for initiating sexual activity, a role presumably appropriate only for husbands. The Rabbis see her behavior as suggesting some measure of immoral wantonness. Now, in the story of Dinah and Shechem, the Rabbis see Leah's punishment finally emerging, delayed but still measure for measure, in what they believe is the manner of divine justice. Having the text use the same word to describe their respective goings out signals that Leah's daughter is repeating her mother's offense. Dinah is "going out" just as Leah did, which suggests that Dinah is acting from the same motivation attributed to Leah—to initiate sexual activity.[20] So this rabbinic analysis of what some read as a story of rape manages to fix blame on both the women mentioned in the story, Leah as well as Dinah.

It seems odd that the majority of the midrashim here blame Leah for Dinah's actions in "going out"—enticing Prince Shechem. In the earlier mandrakes episode, midrash only mildly condemned Leah herself for going out to claim her night of marital relations with Jacob.[21] And God appeared to approve of Leah's role in the mandrakes exchange, since she immediately conceived (Gen. 30:17). So this is not a situation that would seem to support a "measure for measure" explanation, even on the part of commentators who believe that God's justice generally works on that basis.

And while Dinah is not dealing with a husband, she receives rabbinic blame for wrongful enticement based on what seem to us to be relatively benign actions, even in connection with strangers: Some commentaries criticize her for merely exposing herself to the gaze of a male without family protection, while others presume that Prince Shechem's extreme response must have been caused by some culpable actions by Dinah, perhaps dressing alluringly (by wearing jewels) or immodestly (by bar-ing an arm).[22] Dinah is presumed to be the enticer, and therefore receives censure when she becomes the victim. These justifications for blaming Dinah tell us more about the worldview of the Rabbis than anything about Dinah's character.

Midrash does include some significant minority views that attempt to defend Leah and Dinah from blame. Unfortunately, some of these defenses seem tepid when contrasted with the majority view of the classical commentators that Dinah was wrong in intentionally provoking attention by going out and that Leah was somehow at fault for this.[23]

Modern readers may be disturbed that this neat pairing of the Rabbis' condemnations of Leah and of her daughter does not reflect any inherent rule of morality, but rather reveals the restricted gender roles in sexual matters that male writers in patriarchal societies imposed during biblical and classical midrashic times. For the authors of early midrash, however, the conclusion is clear. They find that Dinah going out, as Leah previously had gone out, is the proof text for the biblical adage "Like mother, like daughter" (Ezek. 16:44).[24]

One of the most intriguing questions in the "rape of Dinah" story is whether it was indeed a case of rape in the standard sense of that term.

> Shechem the son of Hamor the Hivite, prince of the country, saw her, and he took her, and lay with her, and defiled her. (Gen. 34:2)

Once again, the biblical text seems to tantalize readers not so much by what is stated, but by what is omitted. Out of delicacy and reverence, the Bible often uses certain standard euphemisms to describe subtle variations in sexual acts. For example, when Leah was brought to the wedding tent, the text reads that Jacob "[went] in to her" (Gen. 29:23), a term that may indicate sexual intercourse in the absence of romantic marital love.[25] When the Bible describes rape by force, however, the text typically says that the man "grabbed her" or "took hold of her" (hazik-bah) (see Deut. 22:25 and 2 Sam. 13:11, 14).[26] That key term is missing here, inviting a whole range of interpretive speculation by the commentators.

The Bible's description of Shechem's initial act certainly doesn't sound like an act of love: Shechem "saw her, and he took her, and lay with her, and defiled her" (Gen. 34:2). Some commentators therefore conclude that this unadorned series of harsh physical acts clearly depicts a physical, even brutal, rape in which Dinah was an unwilling victim. A modern commentator also points out that the Hebrew phrase used for "lay with her" (*va-yishkav otah*) omits the preposition "with," indicating that Dinah was an object, presumably an unwilling object, of Shechem's act, reinforcing the interpretation that this was rape.[27]

In considering such conclusions, we should be aware of the extreme discomfort that many of the classical commentators may have experienced with their need to justify the widespread slaughter and pillage about to be executed by Jacob's sons upon the entire country of Shechem in revenge for this act. Under the cultural mores of the time, Dinah's brothers may have been expected to seek bloody revenge for the insult to their family honor, even if this were only an act of seduction or mutually consensual sex.[28] Nevertheless, the Rabbis may have found it more comfortable to excuse the brothers' retaliatory treachery and violence by concluding that this was a case of rape by physical force.

Even acknowledging the possible bias of the Rabbis, the majority interpretation seems correct. The close analysis, above, of the text is sufficient to support the conclusion that the Dinah-Shechem incident at least begins with an act of rape. But whatever the nature of Shechem's initial act with Dinah, the text paints a very convincing picture of his love for her immediately after their initial interaction.

And his soul was drawn to Dinah the daughter of Jacob, and he loved the maiden, and spoke tenderly to her. And

Shechem spoke to his father Hamor, saying, "Get me this girl as a wife." (Gen. 34:3–4)

Midrash is more divided when analyzing this development. Some commentators accept the explicitly romantic text on its face—"his soul was drawn to Dinah . . . and he loved the maiden." Regardless of what happened before, love strikes Prince Shechem in the aftermath of intercourse with Dinah. Others stop short of fully endorsing Shechem's sincerity. They acknowledge that perhaps Shechem's love does develop, but they focus on the fact that he "spoke tenderly to her." They suspect that these kind words may not be the spontaneous outpourings of his loving heart. Perhaps they are only an attempt to placate Dinah's anger and hostility, which she naturally feels because he forced himself on her.[29]

We can also consider the contrast between how Dinah was identified in the first verse ("Dinah the daughter of Leah, whom she bore to Jacob") and how she is identified two verses later, describing the object of Shechem's sudden love: "Dinah the daughter of Jacob." Why at this point would the text call her anything more than simply Dinah? This new identification of Dinah as Jacob's daughter suggests that Prince Shechem may be motivated by political considerations rather than just personal love. He is Shechem, prince of (and bearing the name of) his father's kingdom. She is Dinah, not Dinah the beautiful, but Dinah the daughter of Jacob, the new foreign tribe now in the midst of the Shechemite kingdom. Perhaps after sexual relations with Dinah, Shechem's lust for Dinah cools sufficiently for him to realize the serious political and military threat his rash act has engendered. He might then see how this threat might be evaded if he can convert the sexual incident into a marriage of state joining the two powers.

It is even possible that not only did Shechem's after-the-fact words of kindness and love lack sincerity but even his initial act of seduction or rape itself is not motivated by love or even lust. Perhaps that initial act merely marks the opening gambit in a coldly manipulative game of statecraft. If so, then Dinah is repeatedly violated in this story: she suffers the physical act of Shechem's taking her; she is used as an object of Shechem's political maneuverings to obtain a protective pact with a potentially threatening neighbor; and later in the story she is used once again as a pawn in the political game, this time by her own family when they in turn exploit the incident to secure their position in the land and plunder the wealth of the Shechemites.[30] The real challenge in understanding chapter 34, however, is not the difficulty of interpreting Shechem's words of love, but dealing with the silence of Jacob and Leah.

> *Jacob heard that he had defiled his daughter Dinah; but since his sons were in the field with his cattle, Jacob kept silent until they came home. (Gen. 34:5)*

To place Jacob's silence in context, we should not imagine him as a weak old man who has been supplanted by his vigorous young sons. Dinah's story occurs no more than a year or two after Jacob performed as a man of action, wrestling all night with the stranger and then strategically preparing to battle Esau's army. Moreover, midrash reports that Jacob will participate militarily in his sons' coming battle against Shechem and in subsequent wars. And in the story of Joseph in Egypt, the Bible itself will show that Jacob continues to be very much in charge of his family even after his sons mature.

We should also remember that, according to midrash, Jacob had recently protected Dinah by hiding her in a box when they encountered Esau. If Jacob went to such measures to safeguard his daughter from his brother, Esau, we now should certainly expect Jacob to make a vigorous response to Shechem's actually taking Dinah, regardless of whether Shechem's act was seduction or rape. That's why the text is so baffling when it says that, upon hearing of the incident, "Jacob kept silent" until his sons returned from the fields.

One commentator suggests that the answer might be found in the opening verse of this chapter, which identifies Dinah as Leah's daughter. Perhaps Jacob is still reenacting the parental favoritism that he suffered as a child. If he still resents Leah for the wedding deception or for her subsequent actions in the marriage, this may have cooled his reaction to her daughter's plight. Another commentator proposes that Jacob is silent because the Patriarch apparently holds the chauvinistic view, expressed in the classical midrash, that it is in a woman's nature to be a gadabout, and that she is therefore to blame if bad consequences result.[31]

The puzzle of Jacob's silence only deepens when his sons return. In contrast to the absence of any indication of emotional response by Jacob, his sons are grieved and very angry (Gen. 34:7). So we see that the Bible can describe emotions when it wants to. And although Hamor and Shechem address both Jacob and his sons in negotiating the marriage, only the sons answer (Gen. 34:11–13). Jacob's silence continues.

Jacob will finally speak only after the murder and pillage of the Shechemites, and then it is only to chastise Simeon and Levi for the attack. Even in that exchange, Jacob makes no mention of Dinah, but frames his rebuke strictly in terms of the resulting political and military danger to himself (and by implication to his family) from Shechem's surrounding allies. The last word in the chapter goes to his sons, who defend their treacherous aggression on the basis of what Shechem did to their sister— explicitly referring to Dinah as "our sister," as if to contrast the sons' actions with Jacob's silent, passive disregard for his daughter (Gen. 34:30–31).[32]

Thus, the Bible depicts Jacob as a mere observer of the family's vengeance in this incident. Perhaps this is simply a bit of the old Jacob showing through the new Israel. Jacob began by being directed by his mother, Rebekah, in the blessing episode. He was also led by Rachel and Leah to take their handmaidens as wives and have children with them. Now, even after his new assertiveness in wrestling at the Jabbok and confronting

Esau, it appears that Jacob has relapsed into his old passivity. He is content to let his sons take the active role in dealing with Dinah's misfortune.

In contrast with Jacob's role, Dinah's mother, Leah, is not only silent, but totally absent from the story. This omission is likewise difficult to understand. While the time of Leah's death is not stated in the Bible, the commentators calculate that Leah is still alive at the time of Dinah's involvement with Shechem.[33] Leah's early tears and prayers over her fear of being claimed by an evil Esau had been sufficient to move God. As a result, Leah was able to become Jacob's first wife, and God promptly intervened to end her barrenness so that she could give her husband the sons who would secure her marriage. It seems inexplicable that Leah now would not likewise cry or pray or speak out at her daughter's predicament. It also seems unjust that the Rabbis create midrashic tales to support Jacob's character but say nothing in defense of Leah. And if we find it puzzling that Dinah's parents remain silent, where at least is the voice of Dinah herself in all this? With excruciating ambiguity, the text tells us only what happens when Dinah's brothers, Simeon and Levi (Leah's second and third sons, and thus Dinah's full brothers), take action.

> *And it came to pass on the third day, when they were in pain, Simeon and Levi, two of Jacob's sons, brothers of Dinah, took each man his sword, came upon the city unmolested, and slew all the males. They put Hamor and his son Shechem to the sword, took Dinah out of Shechem's house, and went out. (Gen. 34:25–26)*

Once again the Rabbis read a clue in the apparently superfluous identification of already-named characters: "Simeon and Levi, Dinah's brothers."

TWO OF THE SONS OF JACOB, SIMEON AND LEVI, DINAH'S BROTHERS, TOOK EACH MAN HIS SWORD (Gen. 34:25)....

DINAH'S BROTHERS: Now was she sister of only those two? Was she not sister of all the tribal founders? But because they risked themselves for her, she is called by their name [in this verse]. (Midrash Rabbah, Genesis 80.10)

The midrashic inference from the description of Simeon and Levi as "Dinah's brothers" is that they were acting as true brothers should act, defending their sister at the risk of their lives. This is an implicit criticism of Jacob's silence and passivity, and perhaps also a criticism of Leah's other sons, who fail to act similarly for their sister.[34]

Simeon and Levi take advantage of the Shechemite men's indisposition after their circumcision and kill Hamor, Shechem, and all the males of the kingdom. Then the two brothers "took Dinah out of Shechem's house, and went out." Should we understand from this that Shechem was forcibly keeping Dinah a prisoner in the palace as a hostage to the political negotiations between the two nations? Or did Dinah perhaps remain there voluntarily because, like a Juliet, she has now fallen in love with an outsider, her forbidden prince?[35] One midrashic tale rejects both these views and instead envisions a Dinah who acts more like an Esther than a Juliet.

Haddakum, the grandfather of Shechem, and his six brothers would not be circumcised, and they were greatly incensed against the people of the city for submitting to the wishes of the sons of Jacob. . . . They chided Shechem and his father for doing a thing that their fathers had never done, which would raise the ire of the inhabitants of the land of Canaan against them, as well as the ire of all the children of Ham, and that on account of a Hebrew woman. Haddakum and his brothers finished by saying: "Behold, tomorrow we will go and assemble our Canaanitish brethren, and we will come and smite you and all in whom you trust, that there shall not be a remnant left of you or them." When Hamor and his son Shechem and all the people of the city heard this, they were sore afraid, and they repented what they had done, and Shechem and his father answered Haddakum and his brothers: "Because we saw that the Hebrews would not accede to our wishes concerning their daughter, we did this thing, but when we shall have obtained our request from them, we will then do unto them that which is in your hearts and in ours, as soon as we shall become strong."

Dinah, who heard their words, hastened and dispatched one of her maidens whom her father had sent to take care of her in Shechem's house, and informed Jacob and his sons of the conspiracy plotted against them. When the sons of Jacob heard this, they were filled with wrath, and Simon and Levi swore, and said, "As the Lord liveth, by to-morrow there shall not be a remnant left in the whole city." (Ginzberg, *Legends of the Jews*, 308–9)

According to this tale, the brothers' attack is in response to Dinah's disclosure of a treacherous plot threatening annihilation of the Israelites.[36] Such a twist on the story would, of course, absolve the brothers of moral culpability for their slaughter of the Shechemites. Midrash converts the operation into a preemptive military strike justified by the necessity of self-defense. Nevertheless, even in this midrashic tale we still don't know with certainty if Dinah initially remained in the palace as willing lover or reluctant prisoner.

[Simeon and Levi] TOOK DINAH OUT OF SHECHEM'S HOUSE, AND WENT OUT (Gen. 34:26). R. Yudan said, "They dragged her out." . . . R. Huna said, "She said, 'And I, where shall I carry my shame?' (2 Sam. 13:13), [refusing to leave] until Simeon swore that he would marry her." (Midrash Rabbah, Genesis 80.11)

Some commentaries go even further and presume that the brothers don't go to rescue Dinah from being held against her will. Instead, even after they have slain Shechem, they have to drag her away from the castle, or at least convince her to leave because of her deep shame at what has happened to her.[37]

Although the Bible doesn't deal with Dinah's reaction to this episode or what happens after the brothers retrieve her, midrash imagines that Dinah at first refuses to return to her family after the incident because she fears that her life has been ruined and she will never be married. She finally agrees to return only when Simeon promises that he will marry her.[38] This would have been in accordance with the general midrashic concept that each of Jacob's sons except for Joseph is born with a twin sister, and each son marries a twin sister of his brother. Dinah is Zebulun's twin (or perhaps his triplet, in addition to his regular, unnamed, twin sister), and so could be an appropriate wife for Simeon.[39]

To support their tale of Simeon marrying Dinah, the Rabbis cite the later genealogy identifying one of Simeon's sons, Shaul, as the "son of the Canaanite woman" (Gen. 46:10)—presumably referring to Dinah, who acted like a Canaanite woman when she was intimate with a Canaanite.[40] Other commentators go further still, to conclude that the Shaul included in the list of Simeon's issue is actually Dinah's son fathered by Shechem.[41]

But surely the most imaginative midrashic legend about this incident, which also has Shechem fathering Dinah's child, goes further. In this tale the child is a daughter who, in an elaborately plotted narrative, ends up becoming the wife of Joseph in Egypt. This creative midrashic tale and its variants explain that Dinah's daughter is born after Dinah returns to Jacob's household. Because she is born as a result of Shechem's rape, the brothers want to do away with the baby. Jacob saves her life by abandoning the child in the wilderness after giving her a necklace with a Hebrew inscription that identifies her as his granddaughter. She is found (by an angel, or perhaps just a passing trade caravan, as Joseph was) and taken to Egypt, where Potiphar and his wife adopt and raise her as their own and name her Asenath. Joseph reads the necklace (as viceroy, or earlier as a slave in Potiphar's household) and realizes who she is. Later, when Pharaoh seeks to reward Joseph for saving Egypt from famine, Joseph asks to marry Asenath (see Gen. 41:45).[42]

This midrashic legend of Dinah's daughter becoming Joseph's wife does more than merely create a pure Jewish heritage (through matrilineal descent) for the tribes of Joseph's sons, Ephraim and Manasseh. The story also serves to finally reunite the rival sisters, Leah and Rachel, by merging their bloodlines in joint descendants.

Regardless of how we read Dinah's story, it is difficult not to be dismayed at the nature and extent of the vengeance exacted by Jacob's sons against the entire population of Shechem. The Rabbis too are uncomfortable with what the brothers do. The commentaries therefore struggle to evaluate the ethical niceties of the Israelites' murder and plunder, as well as their deceptive negotiations that lead up to it. This is, of course, a special challenge for the classical commentary, which often insists on somehow coming up with a story consistent with the Rabbis' presumption of the essential righteousness of Jacob and his sons.

And the sons of Jacob answered Shechem and Hamor his father deceitfully, and said, because he had defiled Dinah their sister. (Gen. 34:13)

The initial moral issue is presented when the brothers negotiate "deceitfully" by agreeing to Dinah's marriage on condition that all male Shechemites become circumcised. They appropriate what should have been an honorable negotiation between nations and convert it into a dishonest ploy to render the Shechemites vulnerable. It may be true that their father likewise began as a deceiver, but Jacob is subsequently portrayed as learning from his experiences and developing into a man of total righteousness. Even his name is changed from Jacob ("deceiver," "supplanter") to Israel ("one who has wrestled with God and himself and prevailed"). But now we are confronted with his sons reverting to their father's old style of winning through deceit.

Even worse, it seems especially distasteful to observe the Israelites using their sacred ritual of circumcision as an instrument of retribution. It is even possible that the writers of the biblical text or commentaries saw circumcision as a step in a non-Jew's conversion to Judaism. If so, the morality of the brothers' negotiations, transforming a rite of conversion into a pretext for annihilation, is even more troubling. (However, a contemporary commentator defends the use of circumcision as the mechanism for the brothers' revenge as measure-for-measure justice—the body organ subject to circumcision was used by Shechem to perpetrate the rape of Dinah.)[43]

Midrash defends Jacob's sons in various ways. The word used in the Hebrew text describing the brothers' negotiations (*b'mirmah*), which is commonly translated as "deceitfully" or "with treachery," can also mean "with subtlety," "cleverly," or "craftily." Some commentators even translate the problem away by reading the word in a totally positive light as meaning "with wisdom."[44]

The contemporary commentator Robert Alter notes that the word here (*b'mirmah*) was previously used by Isaac (*b'mirmah*) to describe how Jacob took the blessing (Gen. 27:35), and comes from the same word root used by Jacob (*rimmitani*) when he complained about Laban's deceiving him by substituting Leah for Rachel in the wedding tent (Gen. 29:25).[45] This suggests that the sons are, indeed, reenacting the family theme of deception rather than learning from it. Jacob gained the blessing by deception, Laban got Jacob to marry Leah by deception, and now the sons exact revenge on Shechem by deception.

But the verse itself provides some rationale for elevating the morality of the sons' actions: they speak as they do "because he had defiled Dinah their sister." Rashi concludes that the sons' negotiating statements should not be condemned as deceit, because they are made in order to be able to impose the appropriate punishment for Shechem's act of violating Dinah.[46]

But even if the brothers' deceptive plot against Prince Shechem were warranted by his inexcusable acts with Dinah, midrash must still grapple with how to justify their killing all the males of the kingdom and seizing the women, children, and property. The Rabbis come up with a broad range of justifications, but many seem unconvincing.

A more recent commentary embraces this episode as an example of necessary violence in defense of the people Israel. Samson Raphael Hirsch, the great nineteenth-century European rabbi, comments on this issue in the then-contemporary light of his fellow Jews' desperate need for self-preservation in the increasingly hostile and threatening modern world of the Diaspora. Hirsch determines that the brothers were right to use ultimate violence when needed to deter future violations. As Hirsch stirringly proclaims, potential bullies must be shown that although Jews are committed to the peaceable voice of Jacob they will also raise the sword of Esau when needed for self-preservation.[47]

We can see that midrash, whether in the form of classical commentary or modern analysis, struggles with the story of Dinah. Although contemporary readers may be tempted to read Dinah's story as a cautionary example of the perils of Jewish intermarriage, the classical commentaries do not express that view. The Rabbis even create a "happy ending" story in which Dinah becomes the second wife of Job, another gentile of the Bible.[48]

Even if the Dinah story does not provide a lesson about individual intermarriage, it could still be read as a geopolitical commentary on the Israelite acquisition of the Promised Land: perhaps the story is speaking about the need for the ancient Israelites to avoid assimilation and intermarriage with those Canaanite tribes already occupying the land that God promised to Abraham, Isaac, and Jacob—the very Canaanite tribes who will have to be ousted through purchase or conquest so that the Hebrews can acquire the land.

But the classical commentators take a simpler view of guilt and culpability in this story. They line up to apportion blame among the various actors for the moral shortcomings that may have brought on such a tragedy. And there's plenty of condemnation to go around—shared by Dinah, Shechem, Jacob, the sons of Jacob, and the townspeople of Shechem.[49] And we have seen how midrash even assigns a significant measure of blame to poor Leah, who is totally absent from the story.

Contemporary readers, however, may conclude that patriarchal views and national chauvinism have distorted both the biblical text and the traditional midrash. How else could it be that Dinah is granted no voice in her own story? It seems that the classical commentaries here don't elucidate the biblical text as much as they reflect the contemporary world conditions and the religious-philosophical orientations and biases of the respective commentators.

Leah's Lessons from Arrival in the Promised Land

As we have seen, Leah's major influence—indeed, essentially her very presence—in the family saga seems to have ended with the birth of Dinah and the family's exodus from Haran. Nevertheless, the story of their arrival in the Promised Land still reveals some noteworthy things about Leah.

First, the details of the family's meeting with Esau clarify Leah's position in Jacob's concerns and affections. In presenting the family to Esau, Jacob places Leah and her sons after the maidservants and their families in the procession, but before Rachel and Joseph. The order of the family procession appears to precisely calibrate Jacob's relationship to his wives and sons at this point.

Looking back over all that we have gleaned from the midrashic commentaries on Leah's life, we can see how the Rabbis expend much energetic inventiveness in trying to put the best face on Leah's actions. Nevertheless, the classical interpretations are not entirely satisfying to us in their analysis of our heroine's questionable early behavior as it progressed from participating in the wedding hoax to bearing children. Perhaps the point of the present text is to show us that Leah has finally changed.

She has grown to control and overcome her earlier unrealistic responses to her marriage. When Jacob places her and her sons behind the handmaidens but in front of Rachel and Joseph, the meaning of this demonstration of preference must have been painfully obvious to Leah. Unlike her previous behavior, however, now she does not offer tears, prayers, or protests. Leah participates in the family procession for presentation to Esau without complaint; she registers no fear or insecurity. It is presumed that she walks alone, as the head of her family. In contrast, Rachel is shielded by Joseph.

Why does Leah exhibit such self-confidence? Since God previously intervened several times in response to her cries and prayers, perhaps she has come to trust in God's continuing protection and no longer feels the need to plead for divine assistance at each turn. Leah has changed. Her character has developed as a consequence of the pain that she has already suffered. And since she has learned how to master hardships by adjusting to circumstances, she is not paralyzed by fear. In biblical terms, she has learned to trust in God. Perhaps she has also learned to trust in herself.

And what can Leah teach us in the Dinah-Shechem episode? After all, Leah is almost totally absent from the story. But if we read Genesis 34, the chapter about Dinah and Shechem, from a Leah-centric aspect, we can glimpse some hidden lessons there. First of all, it is significant that Leah does not play any active role in this story. While the actions of all the other Israelites (her daughter, her husband, her sons) raise major questions about each actor's morality, Leah's lack of participation in the drama can be read as another indication of her superior moral character.

Secondly, what can we learn from reading how classical midrash is quick to condemn Leah for the acts of her daughter? After all, that is not the long-term judgment expressed in the Bible, for Leah becomes the ancestress of Israel's priesthood, monarchy, and the Messiah to come. And she alone of all Jacob's wives will be buried next to him with his parents and grandparents at Machpelah. In the Dinah-Shechem episode, the Rabbis seem to blame Leah for a variety of reasons. Some appear to presume that this mother has transmitted some genetic, gender-linked taint of female wantonness. Others believe that Leah merely set a bad example. In accordance with their worldview, still others conclude that Leah's brazen behavior in the earlier mandrakes incident in Haran has now triggered divine punishment in Shechem measure for measure. It is not necessary for us to defend Leah against these attacks. If we conclude that many of the midrashic commentaries are unfair, perhaps it is sufficient for us simply to learn from Leah's story how the speedy moral judgments of a particular culture may not stand up to inspection when ultimately examined through the long lens of history.

7

THE DEATHS OF RACHEL,
LEAH, AND JACOB

The Death of Rachel

Soon after devoting an entire chapter (the thirty-one verses of
Gen. 34) to the dramatic story of Dinah and Shechem, the Bible
turns to a new tragedy: the death of Rachel.

> And they set out from Bethel; but when they were still some
> distance short of Ephrath, Rachel was in childbirth, and she
> had hard labor. When her labor was at its hardest, the mid-
> wife said to her, "Fear not; for it is another son for you." But
> as she breathed her last, for she was dying, she named him
> Ben-oni; but his father called him Benjamin. So Rachel died,
> and was buried on the road to Ephrath, which is now Bethle-
> hem. And Jacob set up a pillar on her grave; that is the pillar
> at Rachel's grave to this day. (Gen. 35:16–20)

In contrast to the chapter about Dinah, Rachel's story is told
in only five verses, even though the events covered include the
birth of Jacob's twelfth son (Benjamin), the names given him
by Rachel and by Jacob, Rachel's death in childbirth, her burial,
and the monument Jacob sets up at her grave site. As we might
expect by now, midrash compensates for the brevity of the text
by extensively exploring many important questions surrounding Rachel's death.[1]

For our story of Leah, however, we're more directly concerned with the consequences that Rachel's death has for Jacob and Leah, and especially their relationship together. Up to the point of Rachel's death, Leah has lived her entire married life as Jacob's first wife, but always in the shadow of his abiding preference for Rachel and with the additional complication of the handmaiden wives. Jacob's complex household of four wives and multiple children precariously endures in a delicate balance that must be significantly upset by the death of Jacob's favorite, Rachel.

Avivah Zornberg notes how Rachel's death results in a simpler, more ordinary marital structure.[2] Rachel was never satisfied with Jacob's spousal devotion. After her wedding to Jacob, Rachel may have felt more like a mistress than a wife because Jacob expected her to be available to him sexually and emotionally, but until the last few years she was not able to participate in fulfilling Jacob's destiny of a great legacy. She almost seems to have been playing the role of "the other woman" in this complicated family.[3] So Rachel craved children. And although her wish was eventually fulfilled, it cost her dearly. Rachel won only by forfeiting her life and with it the special relationship that had never been enough for her—unity with her loving husband.

On the other hand, Rachel's death is clearly a deep loss for Jacob. He loved Rachel for herself. Unlike Rachel, Jacob was not primarily focused on whether she would be the one to produce sons and tribes for him. And regarding that issue, there is some irony in the fact that before her death Rachel had already given birth to Joseph, who will go on to become the great hero of the final third of Genesis—the savior of the Jews and the entire ancient Middle East. But despite already having been granted a son favored with such a magnificent destiny, Rachel dies as a consequence of her yearning to produce another son.

According to one midrashic interpretation, at the moment Jacob first meets Rachel at the well, he weeps because of his prophetic foreknowledge of her early death. We will see that he continues to mourn her after she dies, even up to his last statements on his deathbed. Yet Jacob's grand, romantic devotion to Rachel was never enough to satisfy her.

The Rabbis repeatedly assert that both sisters are driven to compete in giving birth to Jacob's sons by their prophetic knowledge of God's promise about Jacob's descendants on the night of the ladder dream at Bethel. For midrash that divine promise is expressed in the text when the twelve stones surrounding Jacob's makeshift bed miraculously fuse into a single pillow stone. Even if we are to accept this as a symbol of fusion rather than a scribe's error, however, the concept of fusion seems more appropriate to describe national solidarity rather than family harmony. So any miracle of the pillow stone should foretell twelve tribes unifying to becoming a nation, not just twelve sons becoming a family.[4] It follows that if Leah and Rachel have to compete, they should be competing over establishing tribes, not bearing sons.

And this is a source of deep irony for both Leah and Rachel. We have already heard the rabbinic tale of how Leah intervenes to change the gender of her last child, Dinah, so that Rachel can bear Jacob's last two sons. Midrash explains that Leah takes this extraordinary step to save Rachel from humiliation by allowing her to produce at least as many sons as each of the maidservants. But later, on his deathbed, Jacob will give separate inheritance portions in the Promised Land directly to Joseph's two sons and the tribes they will establish (Gen. 48:5). This in effect will elevate Manasseh and Ephraim to the status of sons of Jacob. Thus, Jacob's ultimate bequests to Joseph's two sons will transform both Leah's magnificent sacrifice at Dinah's birth and Rachel's ultimate sacrifice of her own life in bearing Benjamin into unnecessary acts. With Jacob's adoption of Joseph's sons, Rachel would have been the ancestress of two tribes of Israel (Manasseh and Ephraim), the same as the maidservants, even if she had given birth only to Joseph, and even if Leah's seventh child had been a son.

The text says nothing explicit about Leah's reaction to the death of Rachel—her rival, her sister, and perhaps her twin. But it would seem that, on the surface at least, Leah has finally won the grand conflict. As the survivor, Leah might naturally expect that she has finally achieved exclusivity and unity with Jacob. With Rachel gone, she can now presume that Jacob will surely love her above all others. (Midrash calculates that Rachel died at age thirty-six and that Leah survives for another eight years.)[5]

We will soon explore midrashic legends showing that upon Leah's death, Jacob and his entire family gather in respect and sorrow to mourn her. There is even a version of the legend where Jacob eventually comes to truly love Leah.[6] However, the Bible itself is silent as to whether even Rachel's death is sufficient to give Leah any gratification from finally attaining the position she always craved—becoming Jacob's chief wife. Immediately after the death of Rachel we find one of the most problematic sentences in the entire biblical story.

> And it came to pass, while Israel lived in that land, that Reu-
> ben went and lay with Bilhah, his father's concubine; and
> Israel heard of it. Now the sons of Jacob were twelve. The
> sons of Leah: Reuben, Jacob's firstborn, and Simeon, and
> Levi, and Judah, and Issachar, and Zebulun. (Gen. 35:22–23)

Reuben, Jacob's firstborn, "went and lay with Bilhah." Jacob (now called Israel) hears of it, but doesn't respond. At the simplest level of *peshat* (interpreting the text according to its plain meaning), it would appear that Reuben has intercourse with Bilhah. Perhaps he does this to make the point that Bilhah and Zilpah are only concubines (*pilagshim*, plural of *pilegesh*, the word used in this verse), and that his mother, Leah, is now Jacob's only remaining legitimate wife.[7] Midrash proposes several alternative interpretations.

The book of Jubilees offers a romantic version of this episode, detailing how, during Jacob's absence from the camp, Reuben sees Bilhah bathing and is smitten with love for her. (This start of the Jubilees story seems conspicuously similar to the beginning of the David and Bathsheba story in 2 Sam. 11:2.) Reuben sneaks into Bilhah's bed and has intercourse with her when she is asleep. When Bilhah awakens, she drives him off and later tells Jacob. Reuben is not punished, since the law prohibiting sexual relations with a father's wife has not yet been given at Sinai; however Jacob stops having marital relations with her.[8]

Later, in the story of King David, the Bible tells how David's son Absalom asserts political victory in his rebellion against his exiled father by making a public show of sleeping with David's concubines (*pilagshai*, from the same word used in the Bilhah story) on the roof of the palace (2 Sam. 16:22). A modern commentator concludes that Reuben has sexual relations with Bilhah as a means of asserting his own political claim to leadership as the firstborn son, in order to supplant his father.[9] As enticing as these textual similarities appear to be, however, there is no suggestion in the text that Reuben is leading a political rebellion against Jacob. Indeed, it is difficult to learn anything from this single cryptic verse because Jacob keeps silent, as he does so often.

One clue indicating that Reuben's act cannot have been as grave as either civil rebellion or actually having intercourse with Bilhah appears in the genealogy stated in the very next verse (Gen. 35:22–23; later confirmed in Gen. 46:8, 49:3). The Bible recites that Jacob has twelve sons and that Reuben continues in the status of being Jacob's firstborn son even after the Bilhah affair. Under midrashic logic, if Reuben does not do anything that results in the immediate loss of his firstborn status, then he cannot have committed a grave offense against Jacob. Therefore the Rabbis conclude that if Reuben's offense cannot have been something so serious as having sexual relations with Bilhah, then his sin must have been something related only very generally to intercourse—in this case, moving or disturbing her (or Jacob's) bed.[10]

Midrash comes up with a very wide range of inventive scenarios for why Reuben would have moved Bilhah's bed. But despite the difficulties that the Rabbis have in agreeing on what happened, they all seem to accept one overall implication of this episode: that even after Rachel's death, Jacob still takes a passive role in making marital sleeping arrangements. It seems that for all the crucial issues regarding Jacob's marriage bed—his wedding night, the births of his first children, his marriages to the handmaidens, and his resumption of sleeping with Leah as a result of the sisters' bargain over the mandrakes—Jacob's arrangements are decided for him by Laban, Leah, Rachel, or even by God's intervention.

Now it seems that Reuben has taken his turn (perhaps as proxy for his mother, Leah) to determine where and with whom Jacob will sleep. And once again, Jacob utters no response. But Reuben's manipulations may have had some significant effect. Jacob has no further children, and we never again hear of his having marital relations with any of his surviving wives. Indeed, except for being identified in genealogical reports, Leah, Bilhah, and Zilpah do not appear again after Rachel's death and Reuben's incident with Bilhah. We know that they do not later accompany Jacob and the family into Egypt, because they are not included in the Bible's detailed list of the family members who make that journey (Gen. 46:8–27). However, the text does not report their deaths or (except for Leah) their burials. From the aspect of literary narrative, it is as if Leah and the handmaidens simply died with Rachel—and perhaps for Jacob, they did.

The Death of Leah

The only time that the Bible mentions anything further about Leah is when Jacob, on his death bed, incidentally refers to Leah's burial. While the Bible can thus permit Leah to make her final exit from the stage silently, without adding anything further to her story, midrash cannot resist the need to fill in such a major gap in the family narrative. But even the Rabbis stop short of attempting to create a death scene for Leah that might compete with Rachel's dramatic death during childbirth. Instead, they use this occasion to further develop their vision of the relationship between Jacob and Leah after Rachel's death. The resulting midrashic tale also brings a measure of closure to the story of Jacob's lifelong struggles with Esau.

In the midrash, when Leah dies some eight years after Rachel's death, Jacob and all his sons gather at a fortress to mourn her.[11] This development alone would confirm the view that after Rachel's death, Jacob comes to love Leah, and she is finally elevated to the status of his chief wife. Jacob's grief upon the death of Leah is touchingly (if perhaps excessively) detailed in the book of Jubilees.

> [Jacob] was lamenting her [Leah]. For he loved her exceedingly after Rachel, her sister, died; for she was perfect and upright in all her ways and honored Jacob, and all the days that she lived with him he did not hear from her mouth a harsh word, for she was gentle and peaceable and upright and honorable. And he remembered all her deeds that she had done during her life, and he lamented her exceedingly; for he loved her with all his heart and with all his soul. (Jubilees 36:22–24)

Midrash goes on to describe an elaborate battle story. While Jacob and all his sons are mourning Leah's death, Esau and his sons and army secretly surround the Israelite fortress and suddenly attack. Jacob tries to argue for peace, but Esau won't listen. Jacob shoots two arrows from the fortress, the first killing Esau's general (perhaps one of Esau's sons) and the second wounding Esau in the thigh. Esau's sons carry him away, and their army continues the attack. Jacob's sons, led by Judah, run out the fortress gates to confront the enemy, thereby saving Jacob and the family. In answer to the prayers of Jacob's sons as they emerge from the fortress, God causes a great sandstorm that blinds Esau's army and allows Jacob's sons to slaughter them.

Jacob's sons perform heroic feats of great courage and fantastic strength, enabling them to overcome Esau's large army.[12]

Jacob's sons then pursue Esau's sons. Esau dies from the wound in his thigh (in contrast to the midrashic tale of how the sun miraculously heals the wound in Jacob's thigh after his night of wrestling with the stranger just before previously meeting Esau).[13] Esau's sons, fearful of having to confront their cousins in direct battle, abandon their father's body and flee back to their castle at Mount Seir. Jacob's sons, showing proper reverence, pause in their pursuit to bury their uncle Esau. The next day they continue to the castle at Mount Seir and besiege it until Esau's sons enter into a peace treaty and agree to serve and pay tribute to the sons of Jacob.[14] This servitude and tribute fulfill exactly Isaac's earlier prophesy when he blessed Jacob (Gen. 27:29).

After Abraham, Sarah, Isaac, and Rebekah have been buried in Machpelah, there are only two grave sites remaining, which should have been allocated to Esau and Jacob, as Isaac's sons. According to one midrashic tale, when Isaac dies, he leaves all his property to his two sons equally. (This story conveniently ignores what seems to have been the central conflict between the twins: determining which of them was entitled to the firstborn's right of double inheritance.) However, after the brothers bury Isaac, Esau insists that the inheritance be divided into two shares so that the brothers can have separate ownerships. As the firstborn, Esau demands that Jacob make the division into two portions, but then Esau should have the first right to choose one of the shares. Jacob allocates all the material wealth (Isaac's flocks, goods, money, and personal property) to one share, and to the other share he allocates the only three things of value to him: the rights to the land promised to Abraham and Isaac, the burial places in Machpelah, and the portion in the world to come earned by the merit of the twins' parents and grandparents.[15]

This legend has Esau's choice echo the brothers' very first negotiation when Esau traded his birthright for a bowl of stew. While Jacob shows that he understands what is truly valuable, Esau has not changed. He is still driven by his appetite for immediate gratification. Esau does not want the rights to the land, since it would have to be wrested from the Canaanites who already live there. And he is unconcerned with a future burial place, much less a position in the next world. So Esau chooses the portion containing immediate material wealth. He settles his family in Seir (outside the borders of the Promised Land), and executes a deed to Jacob for the other portion of the inheritance, including his grave site in Machpelah. This is what permits Jacob to bury Leah in Machpelah.[16] This might even explain why Esau and his sons choose the occasion of Leah's death to attack Jacob and his family—perhaps they finally realize that Leah is about to be buried in Esau's place in Machpelah, after which they may never be able to contest the inheritance agreement between Esau and Jacob.

The Death of Jacob

Although the biblical text is silent about Leah's death, Jacob's thoughts turn to both her and Rachel as he lies on his deathbed. And here again the sisters are presented in terms that suggest contrast and rivalry.

As we might expect from Jacob's lifelong love affair with Rachel, his first deathbed reference to his wives is about Rachel. Previously Jacob summoned Joseph (now the powerful viceroy of Egypt) and made him swear not to bury him in Egypt, but to place his remains in the family burial place (Machpelah) in the Promised Land (Gen. 47:29–31). Jacob's health then worsens, and Joseph brings his two sons to visit their ill grandfather (Gen. 48:1).

From his deathbed, Jacob recounts to Joseph the promise by God to give the land to Jacob's descendants, and declares that for this inheritance Jacob will treat Joseph's two sons, Manasseh and Ephraim, as direct sons of Jacob, each receiving a full share with Jacob's other sons (Gen. 48:3–6). Jacob follows this adoption of Joseph's sons by blessing them. The fact that the Bible details this scene in which Jacob blesses his grandsons immediately signals the reader to be alert for similarities and contrasts with Jacob's own blessing scene in Isaac's tent. The new episode does not disappoint. The text reveals Jacob repeating the troubling family pattern that began his adult life—a blessing that promotes the younger over the older. The text even points out that Jacob's eyesight has failed with age, just as had Isaac's at the blessing of Jacob (Gen. 48:10). But midrash points out that, perhaps unlike Isaac, Jacob fully understands what he is doing. His blessings intentionally prefer the younger because of Jacob's prophetic knowledge that Ephraim will become the more prominent. (He will be the ancestor of Joshua and the founder of the tribe of Ephraim, whose name will be used to signify the entire Northern Kingdom of the ten tribes of Israel).[17] So Jacob crosses his hands to place his right (preferred) hand on the head of the younger grandchild, Ephraim, and he mentions Ephraim's name before that of his older brother, Manasseh (Gen. 48:14–20).

Jacob's grant of the separate inheritance shares to Joseph's two sons in effect awards to Joseph the firstborn's traditional birthright of a double-inheritance portion. What Jacob previously had to cleverly bargain away from Esau, he now voluntarily gives to Joseph. In the earlier episode, some of the Rabbis justify Jacob's obtaining the birthright by arguing that he was actually the true and intended firstborn, before Esau's manipulations in the womb reversed the natural birth order.[18] Now midrash similarly suggests that Joseph, the eleventh son, was always Jacob's intended firstborn. Jacob intended to marry Rachel, so her Joseph was supposed to be the product of Jacob's first wedding night (rather than Leah's son Reuben). Because Rachel sacrificed her happiness by cooperating in the wedding switch in order to spare Leah humiliation, Rachel is now rewarded by Joseph regaining the firstborn's birthright of the double-inheritance share originally destined for him.[19] Just before Jacob blesses Joseph's sons, however, the biblical text describes a strange interruption. Jacob seems to break his chain of thought by describing Rachel's death and burial.

> *And as for me, when I came from Padan, Rachel died on me in the land of Canaan on the way, when still some distance short of Ephrath; and I buried her there on the road to Ephrath—now Bethlehem. (Gen. 48:7)*

A standard midrashic explanation for this is that it is not related to the grandsons' inheritance, but is a sudden return to Jacob's previous discussion with Joseph. In that earlier conversation Jacob had Joseph pledge to bury Jacob in Machpelah. Now Jacob feels he must return to the topic of burial to acknowledge that he appreciates the difference between what he has asked from Joseph and how deficiently Jacob himself provided for the burial of Joseph's mother, Rachel—not even taking her body to nearby Bethlehem, much less to Machpelah.[20]

Midrash imagines an additional conversation where Jacob goes on to offer Joseph some justifications for burying Rachel on the road: Jacob had to do so in order to implement Rachel's destiny, as related in Jer. 31:14–16, that her cries for the passing exiles would move God to promise their return.[21] An alternative interpretation proposes that Jacob explains how he had no choice, because of being burdened with responsibility for his flocks, family, and property, all requiring a slow pace of travel. But due to the bloody circumstances of Rachel's death in childbirth (which would have been deemed especially contaminating), her burial had to be immediate and could not be postponed until the family's eventual arrival in Bethlehem.[22]

Still other commentaries examine Jacob's particular language: "as for me . . . Rachel died on me." It seems that Jacob interrupts the inheritance discussion because he is thinking about Rachel's death, not her burial. His words suggest that he is either referring to how that death affected him, or perhaps acknowledging that he feels responsible for it. His declaration seems to be the heartfelt romantic expression of a still-grieving husband. Indeed, midrash uses Jacob's statement as the basis for a general proposition that the quality of grief borne by husbands over the death of their wives is unique.[23]

> It has been taught: A MAN DIES ONLY FOR HIS WIFE, AND A WOMAN DIES ONLY FOR HER HUSBAND. A man dies only for his wife [she is the one who primarily feels his death], as it is said, AND ELIMELECH, NAOMI'S HUSBAND, DIED (Ruth 1:3). And a woman dies only for her husband, as it is said, AND AS FOR ME, WHEN I CAME FROM PADAN, RACHEL DIED ON ME (Gen. 48:7). (Talmud, *Sanhedrin* 22b)

Some read Jacob's statement as saying that a large part of him has already died with Rachel. As the contemporary commentator Robert Alter notes, Jacob's comment is inserted as an apparently spontaneous non sequitur to show that his feelings go beyond ordinary recollection or grief. This literary structure confirms that Jacob remains obsessed with Rachel throughout his lifetime, even after her death. The text is telling us that, even while Jacob is on his deathbed, he continues to regard the loss of Rachel as the greatest misfortune of his life.[24]

Some commentators say that Jacob's deathbed reference to Rachel may be expressing guilt over her death. Others see Jacob as feeling more than just personal loss or general guilt for Rachel's death and burial—that the source of his distress is his concern that his actions have also diminished Rachel's role as a Matriarch. Jacob feels guilty that Rachel will not be remembered in future generations as much as she deserves, either because he caused her death before she was able to bear more tribes, or because he couldn't bury her in a place of prominence in Machpelah with Israel's other Matriarchs and Patriarchs.[25] It seems that even after all his wives have died, Jacob continues struggling to balance the outcome of their rivalry.

But Jacob's statements about Rachel's death and burial may not be an unrelated retrospective interruption after all. Perhaps they are intended to explain why he has just doubled Joseph's inheritance portion by adopting Manasseh and Ephraim as separate tribes. Jacob fears that his beloved will be forgotten, so he increases the number of tribes descending from Rachel from two (Benjamin and Joseph—a number that would have been no more than the number of tribes from Bilhah or Zilpah) to three (Benjamin, Manasseh, and Ephraim), trying to make up for the future children she didn't survive long enough to bear.[26] Since Rachel thus would be credited with three of the twelve tribes who inherit, she thereby attains her full one-quarter share of the twelve and will have more than either of the handmaidens.

We might note a historical irony in this picture of Jacob's concerns for how Rachel will be remembered because of where he has buried her. The burial site at Machpelah is to this day a venerated location.[27] However, it is difficult to say today that it is more prominent than Rachel's tomb—a tomb revered not just for marking her grave, but also for the miracle that occurred there when Rachel's cries for the exiles moved God to mercy.[28] And as for descendants of these rival sisters, it is true that Joseph's reign in Egypt will be short when compared to the Davidic royal line descended from Judah, Leah's son (a line that God promises will continue until the coming of the Messiah). Nevertheless, it was Rachel's Joseph who saved Israel, Egypt, and the surrounding world from famine. So it is far from obvious that Jacob needs to be concerned over whether he has diminished Rachel's prominence for the Jewish people.

If Jacob's deathbed recollections of his wives are supposed to provide a sort of summary of the complex relationships among Jacob, Leah, and Rachel, then the contrast between what he says about each of his wives tells us much about who won and who lost in the Leah-Rachel rivalry. We have just examined Jacob's obsessively romantic, guilty recollection of Rachel's death and burial. Now his mention of Leah comes at the end of blessing his sons, as he is about to die, when he instructs his sons to bury him at Machpelah.

> *There they buried Abraham and Sarah his wife; there they buried Isaac and Rebekah his wife; and there I buried Leah.* (Gen. 49:31)

He identifies Machpelah with great specificity and detail, stating its location and reciting the history of Abraham's purchase of the property. As a literary matter, this language seems more like the formal provision in a legal document of title than a deathbed statement. But as he had done with his previous recollection of Rachel, which interrupted his statements about the inheritances for Joseph's sons, Jacob now interrupts his statement of Machpelah's location and purchase history. Jacob names the occupants of the site, ending with the statement, "and there I buried Leah."

We can't resist contrasting Jacob's two statements about his wives. His account of Rachel's death was an emotional, seemingly involuntary revelation of deepest feelings, but his statement about Leah's burial seems mechanical, formal, devoid of affect. And perhaps that difference is what the text is trying to point out to us. The rhythm of the sentence indicates that, just as for Abraham and Sarah, his wife, and for Isaac and Rebekah, his wife, Jacob is asking his sons to complete the family burial arrangements for Jacob with Leah, his wife. We might be tempted to read this as a mark of major victory for Leah. But the level of emotion behind Jacob's words here—or, rather, the lack of emotion—may offer a deeper indication of the final outcome of the sisters' rivalry.

Leah may have won the formal title of wife, but she'd always had that since the first night in the wedding tent. Her lifelong striving sought Jacob's affection and love, but it seems from Jacob's final, detached mention of her that she never received it. Compared to the emotional connection that Leah so deeply desired, being buried next to Jacob must be cold comfort indeed.

The emotional tone of Jacob's final mention of Rachel makes

it clear how much he loved her. But, just as with Leah, Rachel likewise ends up only with something that she had from the beginning. Jacob loved Rachel unswervingly from the moment they met at the well until his final days, even after her death. That, however, was not what Rachel was striving for. She wanted children—progeny who would carry on Jacob's heritage as heirs to God's covenant. Unfortunately, as the biblical narrative will unfold, Joseph's tribes of Ephraim and Manasseh will be carried off and disappear as part of the Ten Lost Tribes, while the tribe of Rachel's other son, Benjamin (whose tribe is almost extinguished by the other tribes for its evil ways; Judg. 20:8–21:1), will ultimately lose its identity through absorption into the tribe of Judah. Rachel got love, but not the posterity she craved.

As noted in Avivah Zornberg's splendid analysis of the psychological dynamics of the Leah-Jacob-Rachel triangle, this love story is actually a love tragedy. Each sister fails to derive sufficient gratification from what she has in the relationship, and each instead yearns for what her rival has.[29] Jacob tries to make it up to his wives after their deaths—elevating Leah's status by burying her as his wife in Machpelah and elevating Rachel's status by increasing the number of tribes descending from her. But Jacob doesn't seem to understand that he can do nothing at this point to undo their lifetime of rivalry.

We can also note that the competition that engulfed Leah and Rachel throughout their married lives does not end with their deaths. As so often happens in family conflicts, their rivalry continues to play out in the lives of their children. Some of this is apparent in the biblical text. The entire final portion of Genesis, chapters 37 to 50, is the story of Rachel's son Joseph and his conflict with the sons of Leah (and to a lesser extent with the sons of Bilhah and Zilpah), which can be seen as an extension of the struggle between their mothers, Leah and Rachel.[30]

The last chapter of Genesis relates that Jacob's sons and their families bury him at Machpelah, as he had requested, and that

Joseph then assures his brothers he does not bear anger against them for selling him into slavery (Gen. 50:7–14). But the Rabbis embellish the Bible's simple story of Jacob's burial to provide important literary balance and resolution to his life. In the prior chapter of the Bible, Jacob's references to his two wives furnished the last words on the direct rivalry between Leah and Rachel. However, Jacob's entire married life with them and their handmaidens grew out of his own intense rivalry with his twin brother. We have already noted one midrashic tale of how Jacob's conflict with Esau finally ends after the death of Leah: Jacob is said to have inflicted a fatal wound on Esau while Jacob and his sons are defending against Esau's attack. Now a different midrashic tale offers a different ending for the rivalry between Jacob and Esau, an ending that is deferred until Jacob's burial.

In this midrash, Esau is not killed soon after Leah's death. Instead, he makes his final appearance later at Machpelah when Jacob's sons bring their father's body for burial there. Esau disputes the sons' right to bury Jacob in Machpelah, falsely claiming that Jacob had already used his only space in the cave when he buried Leah. Thus, the remaining burial space belongs to Esau. Jacob's sons know that Esau had earlier deeded his place in Machpelah (as well as his claims to the Promised Land and the world to come) in exchange for the other family property and wealth when Jacob and Esau divided their inheritance from Isaac. But the deed had been left back in Egypt, so the brothers interrupt Jacob's burial and send Naphtali (whom Jacob has called "a hind let loose" [a swift runner], Gen. 49:21) to bring back Esau's deed to Machpelah. When Hushim, Dan's deaf son, learns the reason for the burial delay, he becomes so enraged that he kills Esau with a single strike to the head. According to this midrash, the blow knocks Esau's eyes out of his head, and they fall onto the knees of Jacob's body, whereupon Jacob opens his eyes and smiles.[31]

We can note that this tale of Esau dying at Jacob's burial provides poetic confirmation of Rebekah's earlier concern when she urged Jacob to flee to Haran to escape Esau's murderous rage over losing the blessing: "Why should I lose both of you in one day?" (Gen. 27:45). In the midrashic legend, both brothers are, in a sense, lost on the same day—the day when Esau dies and Jacob is buried.[32]

Leah's Lessons from the Burials of Jacob, Rachel, and Leah

Throughout our story of Leah we have seen how midrash dramatizes the basic biblical narrative by emphasizing major parallels and contrasts in the lives of Leah, Rachel, and Jacob. Now we have seen how the biblical and midrashic descriptions of the three burials serve as a final recapitulation of some of these unique characters' central qualities. Because of the special roles Jacob and Rachel play in Leah's story, the implications of all three burials are part of the lessons we learn from Leah's story.

The Lessons of Jacob's Burial

The midrashic legend about Jacob's burial awards him the ultimate victory in his struggles with Esau. The Rabbis appear to have created Jacob's burial tale to make sure that we do not miss what they feel is the central point of the whole story. Of course the pious scholar Jacob must triumph over his evil other half—Esau, the hunter of the fields. After all, the Rabbis are scholars, not hunters. But this midrash says more.

The Rabbis were generally speaking to their people at times when Jews lived under the grinding oppression of superior world forces. The early commentaries identify Jacob with the people Israel, while Esau is the symbol of the military might of Rome. That is why Jacob's story closes with a burial midrash. Burial is the final scene of life, the gateway to the afterlife. The Rabbis were speaking to a people suffering in temporal weakness and national subservience. Jacob's final smile of triumph signals that all will be made right in the world to come. The power of Esau/Rome is temporary. The ultimate victory for Jacob/Israel is assured.

But our exploration of Leah's story has taught us that midrash possesses the power to excavate multiple layers concealed within a biblical narrative. The Rabbis' intention to console and affirm the people in their time of suffering is only the surface layer of Jacob's burial midrash. The scene closes with Jacob's body smiling in triumph when Esau is killed by Jacob's grandson Hushim for raising a false claim to the burial space in Machpelah. Jacob is already dead, however, and so—as has happened in so many of the major events of his life—it once again falls on others to say the words and take the actions necessary to finally vindicate him.

Many of us may remember being taught that the greatest Jewish hero of Genesis was Abraham, who was called by God to become the first Jew, and who continues to the present day as the revered first Patriarch of not only Judaism but also Christianity and Islam. So it may be surprising to learn that midrash declares that it is Jacob, not Abraham, who is the ultimate hero of Genesis.[33] Even in death, however, Jacob defies the typical ideal of heroism; his character retains paradox and contradiction. Still opposed by the physical might of his twin half, still embroiled in disputes over legal niceties, Jacob closes his story in silence, relying on others to manage his conflicts.

The Lessons of Rachel's Burial

Rachel's life similarly presents the dramatic tension of an apparently simple surface story hiding a tangle of underlying contradictions. Rachel isn't satisfied with Jacob's constant romantic love for her. Nothing but children will gratify her: "Rachel envied her sister; and Rachel said to Jacob, Give me children, or I shall die" (Gen. 30:1). Rachel is granted the children she demands, but as a consequence dies in her second childbearing. She is excluded from the family burial cave at Machpelah by virtue of Leah's position as the first of the sisters to have married Jacob (and thus perhaps his only technically legal wife), a priority that Rachel herself had helped to engineer. And yet the Bible and midrash join to point out that it is only because Rachel is not buried in Machpelah that later the Israelites on their way to exile are able to pass by her tomb, where her cries can move God to repent God's punishment of the people and pledge God's ultimate forgiveness.

To the extent that the rivalry between Leah and Rachel is a competition to produce children, Rachel's pleas for the exiles from her burial site can even be said to provide her with a special victory.

> *Thus said the Lord: A cry is heard in Ramah, lamentation, bitter weeping; Rachel weeping for her children. She refuses to be comforted for her children, who are gone. Thus said the Lord: Restrain your voice from weeping, your eyes from shedding tears; for there is a reward for your labor, declares the Lord: They shall return from the land of the enemy. (Jer. 31:14–15)*

In Jeremiah's full prophesy, God's promise for return of the exiles expressly mentions Ephraim, the symbol for the ten tribes of the Northern Kingdom. Thus, when Rachel successfully pleads for "her" children, she becomes the adoptive mother and saving force of the Ten Lost Tribes—four of Leah's tribes, two tribes each from Bilhah and Zilpah, as well as two of Rachel's own tribes, Ephraim and Manasseh.

Rachel's burial beside the people's path to exile is thus her great tragedy and her great triumph. It is emblematic of her life of paradox. She is a heroine who loses when she wins (as in her bargaining to obtain the mandrakes—an act that is condemned by the Rabbis and leads to additional children for Leah and a postponement of children for Rachel) and wins when she loses (as in her enabling Leah to marry Jacob by providing the secret signs and answering for her sister on the wedding night—an act that is praised by the Rabbis and that gives Rachel's cries the power to move God).[34]

But in another sense, neither Rachel's burial nor the story of her cries for the exiles is the final word on her life. To the extent that she can claim ultimate victory over Leah, the basis for such a claim is not found in the writings of the Rabbis but in the remembrance of the people. As previously noted, in our prayers and blessings today we traditionally place Rachel ahead of Leah, returning their status to what would have occurred but for the deception at Jacob's wedding.[35] One contemporary commentator concludes that Rachel's overwhelming popularity among all the Matriarchs is evident from her unique position in the art, literature, and most of all the hearts of the Jewish people.[36]

The Lessons of Leah's Burial

If we were to consider only the biblical text, we would have to admit that Leah is more of a supporting character than a main actor. Limited to a single, enigmatic description ("tender" eyes) and two brief lines of direct dialogue, Leah is permitted to express herself only through the names she gives her sons. The Bible, then, fails to tell her full story, which is only revealed through the imaginative interpretations and elaborations of midrash. From those two thousand years of continuing commentaries, we have recovered a treasure of revelations about what Leah may have felt emotionally and what she may have said at those most significant times in her life—the times when our understanding of human affairs convinces us that she must have experienced strong emotions and must have spoken out.

By most objective measures, Leah is the winner in her rivalry with Rachel. It is true that Rachel's son Joseph becomes the hero of the closing portion of Genesis. In the long run, however, Joseph's descendants, the tribes of Ephraim and Manasseh, disappear into exile, and the descendants of Joseph's brother, Benjamin, are absorbed into the tribe of Judah (Leah's son). Thus, all the Jews in the world who trace their lineage back to Abrahamic Jewish roots are presumed to have descended from Leah's Judah or from the priestly tribe of Levi, also Leah's son. So it is most appropriate that Leah is buried in Machpelah, for it is the resting place for the chain of Matriarchs whose line has continued to the Jews of today: Sarah, Rebekah, and Leah.

But despite all the triumph that we can read into Leah's burial in Machpelah, it is difficult to avoid the feeling that Leah's ultimate victory over her sister is in many ways a hollow one. In the biblical text, she evinces no connection with her children, except for using them as board pieces in her game of sibling rivalry. Leah hopes that her children might draw Jacob closer to her in love. Although some midrashic tales claim that Jacob does grow to love Leah after Rachel's death, that may be mere wishful thinking by commentators determined to impose a neat, happy ending on a very messy, very human story. The biblical Leah is never able to attain the one thing that she yearns and strives for throughout her lifetime—Jacob's full love. Leah feels the absence of this love all the more keenly (or perhaps she only feels it at all) because her sister Rachel so effortlessly possesses that love, without even seeking it, from the moment Jacob sees the beautiful young sister at the well.

CONCLUSION
Learning from Leah's Story

The Bible made Leah a Matriarch, but it took midrash to make her a heroine. Our examination of Leah's story with the help of the traditional rabbinic midrash and modern commentary has also rewarded us with a bonus: appreciation for the workings of the midrashic process that is so central to understanding and appreciating the richness of the Bible.

Even those Rabbis most determined to stress God's recognition and reward for the moral excellence of the Matriarchs and Patriarchs cannot ignore the adversities that mar Leah's life. And if a God of justice ought to reward goodness, the conditions of Leah's life don't seem to demonstrate a uniformly affirmative divine judgment. So instead of ignoring Leah's sorrowful struggles, midrash focuses on the fact that her hardships do not destroy her. Rather, they become the basis for her moral development. Leah learns that perseverance and adaptability can make a difference, even when a primary goal of life proves unattainable.

Both Bible and midrash recognize that Leah does not merely fade into the background in reaction to her hardships. Leah changes. She changes her character in the same way that we see Jacob changing his character, choosing new and better ways to respond to the experiences of life. But when Leah refocuses on more realistic objectives, this is far from being an act of surrender. Her ultimate victory is marked by much more than dogged perseverance or how she adjusts her hopes and goals to match a restricted reality. The essence of Leah's victory can be found in the model that she offers us of moral heroism in the face of adversity. Her most important lesson to us is that even harsh, unfair challenges need not automatically call forth equally harsh and unfair responses. Leah manages to remain faithful to her own ethical standards, even at the risk of forfeiting any chance of winning the immediate rivalry with Rachel.

Leah's story can also teach us another major lesson for our lives. Both the Bible and midrash portray God intervening repeatedly to help Leah and relieve her distress. In the view of some commentators God acts in response to Leah's previous manifestations of virtue, such as when God grants Leah fertility to end her tears of anguish at the prospect of having to marry her evil-natured cousin, Esau.

However, we can also read the narrative as showing God intervening for Leah simply because of her suffering. God acts because of Leah's deep distress at being unloved. So the model presented to us here may not relate to Leah's character so much as God's character. On this basis, the lesson is that we too should show concern for the unloved—the disadvantaged and distressed—in our society. Read in this way, Leah's story presents the Bible's universal moral command for compassion toward others.

Midrash frequently compares or contrasts Leah and Rachel. Although I have tried to focus on revealing Leah as an individual rather than only comparing her to her sister, perhaps the final assessment of Leah cannot avoid comparing the sisters. So as an ultimate test, I considered which of these two Matriarchs I would choose as a role model of ethical character for my children and grandchildren. It is clear that Leah's actions are not all admirable, but the same can be said of the other two points of this love triangle, Rachel and Jacob. The Bible and midrash generally present their heroines and heroes with all their undeniable human faults; the main players in Leah's story are no exception. But for me, those inevitable human faults that Leah displays are, paradoxically, the basis for my conclusion that hers is the ethical character I would choose.

Rachel opens Leah's story in the midrash with a magnificent act of self-sacrifice—giving Leah the secret signs and answering for her in the wedding tent to enable Leah to marry Jacob first. Rachel subsequently changes by developing her personality but not her moral character. The ethical trajectory of her life after the wedding appears to descend to an increasingly stubborn, desperate pursuit of unchanging demands. She becomes more assertive, more effective, more directive—practical qualities that I would indeed wish for my children and grandchildren, but for which I don't see a comparable moral development.

Leah, on the other hand, demonstrates a developing moral sensitivity when she adjusts her goals to the limitations of her reality and eventually stops competing with her sister in order to preserve some fundamental family harmony. I think that reading the Bible with the benefit of midrash reveals Leah's heroic character, one well worth emulating, thus securing for Leah her position as a great Matriarch.

This has been my personal search for Leah, the Lost Matriarch, and I think I have found what I was searching for—a deeper appreciation of both the existential sorrows of Leah's life and the consequent development of her moral heroism, facets hidden within the few lines the Bible allows to her.

But as is true for most searches, I have also found some very important things that I wasn't aware I was looking for. Writing this book has given me the gift of experiencing some of the penetrating analysis and creative wit of midrash, together with gaining an appreciation for the unique midrashic process as a path for engaging with the Bible.

The search for Leah's story has also provided me with other gifts. I want to acknowledge one of the most valuable of these—a sense of personal identification with the multitude of commentators, from ancient to modern, who have been pursuing this same search over these past two millennia. It is easy to be misled by the superficial differences across this wide time span, especially the development of information technology that now allows ready access to lifetimes of accumulated commentaries in books, on disks, and on the Internet. But beneath the modern technological advances, the quest remains the same. Human nature and the human condition remain the same, and the engaging but challenging biblical text remains the same. I hope that all readers of this book will feel a sense of their own special relationship and shared purpose with past and future commentators—a sense of personally participating in the midrashic process.

A few commentaries suggest that Leah, by the time of her death, eventually did receive the marital and family love she hoped for.[1] As a literary matter, we might find such a resolution to be a too-convenient invention that seems wholly unsubstantiated in the text. But now that we have explored Leah's full story of ethical behavior in the face of overwhelming challenges, we can perhaps at least join in the wish that this final midrashic tale of a happy ending for Leah—our Lost Matriarch—was a part of her life too.

ACKNOWLEDGMENTS

We often presume that writing a book is a solitary task, and for much of the time it does feel like that. But this book owes its existence to the generous sharing of talents and wisdom by many people.

My interest in commentary by the great Rabbis of the Midrash has been nurtured through fortunate opportunities for regular study with many outstanding contemporary rabbis, including Rabbi Isaac Klein, z"l, at Temple Emanu-El, Buffalo, New York, the synagogue where I grew up; Rabbi Harold Schulweis, Rabbi Ed Feinstein, and the current and previous associate rabbis at Valley Beth Shalom synagogue, Encino, California, my synagogue for over forty years; and Rabbis David Neiman, z"l, Benzion Bergman, and Chaim Seidler-Feller.

I have also been privileged to pursue university-level adult-education programs, lectures, and classes at Valley Beth Shalom synagogue (including the Hazak and Keruv programs); to study at American Jewish University (including classical Hebrew language with instructor Sarah HarShalom); and to hear the lectures and seminars generously shared with the public by the Jewish studies programs at UCLA (under the direction of Professor David Myers and his successors), Hillel at UCLA (under the direction of Rabbi Chaim Seidler-Feller), and California State University at Northridge (under the direction of Professor Jody Myers). These educational opportunities have been supplemented through the learning and camaraderie I have enjoyed in informal study groups, including Mem-Aleph Havurah and the Westside Men's Study Group (led for several years by Professor Arnold Band). I was also helped by the opportunity to explore some preliminary concepts for this book in talks to the Valley Beth Shalom synagogue's library minyan and the lecture program at VBS-Hazak.

I especially want to acknowledge the many insights and delights I have gained through the privilege of participating in the Hirshleifer-Rosett Faculty Tanakh Study Group, hosted by Rabbi Chaim Seidler-Feller and Hillel at UCLA. The group's extensive and spirited discussions in recent years during our analysis of Genesis, especially the many memorable weeks delving into the story of Dinah, opened for me many fresh possibilities in the text that have both enriched my personal understanding and also contributed to some of the interpretations appearing in this book.

Rabbi Harold and Malkah Schulweis each read several early drafts and generously shared their valuable comments, suggestions, and encouragement. Their enthusiasm and warm friendship overcame my inevitable doubts as to whether I would ever be able to make this book a reality.

My research could not have been completed without the gracious hospitality and assistance of the library staffs at American Jewish University, Valley Beth Shalom, UCLA, Los Angeles Public Library, Hebrew Union College, and the Master's College.

Of course, all the above carried me only through completion of the initial manuscript. Proceeding to publication required more. For that phase, I am deeply grateful to Rabbi Barry Schwartz, director of the Jewish Publication Society, who championed this book and helped me to refine its concepts and execution. That transformation was furthered by the many valuable critiques and suggestions from the publisher's preliminary manuscript readers, and subsequently by the skills of the professional staff of the University of Nebraska Press, especially Sabrina Stellrecht and Michele Alperin, who brought the manuscript through the copyediting process.

And I cannot express how deeply I appreciate the contributions of Carol Hupping, the managing editor of the Jewish Publication Society. With unfailing kindness and respect, she has lent her great talents and much time and effort to helping me persevere in improving and developing this book well beyond the point where I thought it was probably good enough. Carol has gone beyond editing to become the guide, coach, and collaborator for this project.

Finally, my wife, Lola, uncomplainingly put up with many years of intrusions upon normal family life that resulted from my always having the perfect excuse: working on "the book." Her understanding and support made writing this book doubly a labor of love for me.

Jerry Rabow

GLOSSARY OF NAMES
AND DEFINITIONS

Where convenient, terms and names have been briefly defined in the
text the first time they are used. The following are restatements or
expansions of those definitions.

Abraham: The Patriarch who becomes the first Jew when he
accepts God's commandment to leave his homeland and
family in order to found a great nation of descendants.
Abraham is the husband of Sarah, and the father of Ishmael, and of Isaac, who marries Rebekah and becomes the
father of Esau and Jacob.

aggadah: The stories purporting to tell the history of the
world and its ancient peoples, including the Jewish people
and its heroines and heroes.

Alter, Robert: Contemporary biblical scholar, translator, and
Torah commentator. A leading contributor to the movement of reading the Bible as literature.

Apocrypha: Ancient books written around the time of the
Hebrew Bible but not included in the canon of the Hebrew
Bible. Some apocryphal books are considered authoritative
by some Christians.

Aramean: Semitic tribes that are reported in the Bible to
repeatedly attack the Israelites.

Artson, Rabbi Bradley Shavit: Contemporary teacher, Torah
commentator, and dean of the Zeigler School of Rabbinic
Studies at the American Jewish University.

Asenath: The daughter of Poti-phera, priest of On, who
becomes Joseph's wife in Egypt. According to midrashic

legend, Asenath is actually the daughter of Dinah and Shechem, adopted by Poti-phera.

Ashkenazic: Referring to the group of Jews who originally settled in Germany and subsequently spread to Poland, Russia, and Eastern Europe. The rituals, language, laws, and customs of Ashkenazic Jews and their descendants often differ from those of the other major subgroup, Sephardic Jews (who were originally from Spain and Portugal and, after the expulsion orders of 1492 and 1497, spread to the Middle East, Turkey, Italy, and North Africa).

Bethel: A border location mentioned in the Bible. During his flight to Haran, Jacob has his famous "ladder" dream at Bethel. According to the midrashic reading of that text, the twelve stones he sets out around his sleeping area that night have miraculously fused into a single stone when he wakes the next morning.

Bible: As used in this book, the Hebrew Bible. *See* Tanakh.

Bilhah: One of the two handmaidens (in addition to Zilpah) whom Laban gives to his daughters Leah and Rachel upon their respective marriages to Jacob. According to midrash, Bilhah and Zilpah are also Laban's daughters, but by a concubine rather than his legal wife. They are the mothers of four of Jacob's twelve sons.

B'reishit: Genesis, the first book of the Hebrew Bible; it contains the story of Leah.

concubine: A woman whose status was less than that of a legal wife to her husband, but who otherwise had a marital and family relationship generally similar to that of a legal wife.

David: The second (technically the third) king of Israel, from approximately 1010 to 970 BCE. His story is told primarily in Samuel 1 and 2. A fundamental messianic doctrine, based on the book of Isaiah, holds that the Messiah will be a male descendent of David.

derash: The method of interpreting the Bible by exhaustively searching the words of the text to discover their deeper theological or moral meanings, often revealed through connections to other words or events in the Bible.

Diaspora: Commonly used to describe the condition of dispersion (scattering) of the Jewish people living outside the Jewish homeland. Jews today living outside the modern State of Israel are living in the Diaspora.

Dinah: Leah's seventh (named) child and Jacob's only daughter mentioned by name in the Bible. The extended story of her relationship with Prince Shechem is related in Genesis 34 and is the subject of much midrashic interpretation and commentary.

Eliphaz: Esau's oldest son. According to midrash, he robs Jacob on Jacob's flight to Haran.

Friedman, Richard Elliott: Contemporary Torah commentator and translator.

Hagar: The maidservant whom the barren Sarah gives to Abraham to be his concubine; the mother of Ishmael.

halakhah: Declarations of Jewish law, either from the Bible or from rabbinic pronouncement, binding on humanity in general or on Jews in particular.

Haran: The Mesopotamian city that is the biblical location of an Aramean branch of Abraham's family, including Rebekah (who marries Isaac) and her brother, Laban. Laban is the father of Leah and Rachel (who marry Rebekah's son Jacob). Haran is also referred to in the Bible as Paddan-aram (the "Aramean highway") and Aram-nahariam ("Aram between the two rivers" or "Aram on the Euphrates").

Hasidic: Referring to the popular Jewish movement called Hasidism, begun in the eighteenth century by the Ba'al Shem Tov. Hasidism was marked by an anti-intellectual emphasis on closeness to God through individual and communal joy. Individual groups of disciples (hasidim) followed a particular charismatic master (tzadik or rebbe).

Hirsch, Samson Raphael (1808–88): Renowned nineteenth-century German Orthodox rabbi and Torah commentator.

Ibn Ezra (1089–1164): Leading Hebrew-language grammarian, Torah commentator, and author.

Job: The subject of the biblical book of Job. Job, a gentile, is afflicted with terrible devastation, including illness, economic ruin, and the loss of his family in an apparent test of his fidelity to God. At the end of his story, he receives new prosperity and a new family. According to midrashic legend, his second wife is Dinah, the daughter of Jacob and Leah.

Joseph: Jacob's eleventh son (his first by Rachel), who becomes the hero of the conclusion of the book of Genesis when he predicts the great famine and becomes the viceroy of Egypt. Joseph arranges for Jacob and his family to settle in Egypt, beginning the Jews' 400 years of living there, ultimately as slaves, ending when Moses leads the Exodus.

Jubilees, book of: An early Hebrew book retelling much of the book of Genesis and the first part of the book of Exodus, often with variations from and additions to the masoretic text.

Kabbalah: The Jewish mystical tradition, which received its impetus from various esoteric writings starting in the twelfth century.

Kimchi, David (Radak) (1160–1235): Noted Hebrew grammarian, philosopher, and Torah commentator.

Laban: An Aramean, the brother of Rebekah, who tricks Jacob into marrying his daughter Leah first, rather than her sister, Rachel, Jacob's intended bride.

Lost Tribes. *See* Ten Tribes.

Machpelah: According to the Bible, Abraham purchased this burial site when Sarah died. Abraham, Sarah, Isaac, Rebekah, Jacob, and Leah are buried there.

Maimonides (Rambam) (1135–1204): Biblical interpreter and codifier, philosopher, physician, and world-renowned rabbinic authority.

Messiah: Lit., "anointed one." In Judaism, the ruler who will be presiding at the End of Days. Based on prophecies in Isaiah and on other biblical and rabbinic sources, the Messiah will be a descendant of King David (and therefore of Leah).

middah k'neged middah (meaning, "measure for measure"): The notion that God intervenes in history with ironic, poetic justice. Under this concept, perplexing events in the Bible can be explained as instances where God rewards or punishes a person in ways that reflect and repeat the essence of his or her previous good or evil deeds, or sometimes the deeds of his or her ancestors.

midrash: Commentaries on the biblical text. In this book, the term refers to commentaries contained in works that stretch from early rabbinic sources to works by contemporary Bible scholars.

mikveh: Jewish ritual bathing facility. Immersion in the *mikveh* is part of the rituals for preparing for Shabbat, conversion to Judaism, and marking the end of a wife's inaccessibility for marital relations following her monthly menstruation.

Nachmanides (Ramban) (1194–1270): Influential philosopher, author, and commentator on Bible and Talmud. Nachmanides often offers alternative interpretations to those of Maimonides.

Netziv: Acronym of Rabbi Naftali Zvi Yehuda Berlin (1816–93), head of the Volozhin Yeshivah in Russia (Belarus) and author of several works of rabbinic commentary.

Onqelos: Second-century author of the most authoritative *Targum* (Aramaic translation of the Hebrew Bible).

Oral Torah: According to Jewish tradition, the additional words of law and instruction that God spoke to Moses at the time of the giving of the Written Torah at Mount Sinai. The Oral Torah was not initially written down, but is seen as having been passed on in an oral tradition from the Rabbis to their disciples, and then to those disciples' students, etc., until eventually written as Talmud, midrash, and other commentary.

polygamy: The practice of a man being married to more than one woman at a time. Although polygamy is not banned in the Bible, and was even practiced by Jacob and others, rabbinic rulings from the Middle Ages to contemporary times prohibit the practice for Jews.

polysemous: The quality of some words in the Bible that are read as intentionally communicating double meanings.

peshat: The method of interpreting the Bible in accordance with the simple, plain (literal) meaning of the words, in their context.

Qumran: The Jewish religious community that, in the second century BCE, established the recently excavated library we now call the Dead Sea Scrolls.

Radak: *See* Kimchi, David.

Rambam: *See* Maimonides.

Ramban: *See* Nachmonides.

Rashbam (1080–1174): Bible and Talmud commentator. Rashbam was Rashi's grandson and student.

Rashi (1040–1105): Extremely influential medieval Bible and Talmud commentator. Rashi's commentaries were published in some of the earliest printed volumes of the Torah and Talmud.

Reuben: Jacob's firstborn son, born to Leah. Midrash proposes various explanations for why Reuben loses the double-inheritance privilege of the firstborn to Joseph, Rachel's son.

Ruth: The subject of the biblical book of Ruth. Ruth is a convert to Judaism who marries Boaz, a descendant of Leah. The townspeople bless her in the names of Rachel and Leah. Ruth becomes the ancestress of King David, and thus ultimately of the Messiah to come.

Sephardic: Referring to the Jews who originally settled in Spain and Portugal. *See* Ashkenazic.

Septuagint: The early (third century BCE) Jewish translation of the Hebrew Bible into Greek, for the Jewish community of Alexandria.

Shechem: The prince of the nation of Shechem, who entices/abducts/rapes (the commentaries are not in agreement) Dinah, the daughter of Jacob and Leah.

Talmud: The central compilation of early rabbinic commentary on the Bible, recorded during the period 200–600 CE. Actually, there are two distinct works of the Talmud: the Jerusalem—or Land of Israel—Talmud, completed about 400 CE, and the Babylonian Talmud, completed about 600 CE. Most commentaries over the subsequent centuries have been based on the more accessible Babylonian Talmud.

TANAKH: The Hebrew Bible, consisting of the Five Books of Moses (the Torah, from the word for "instruction"), together with the collections of nineteen later books in two other sections called the Prophets and the Writings.

Targum: Aramaic translation of the Bible. The most famous and authoritative *Targum* is by Onqelos.

Ten Tribes ("Lost Tribes"): The ten northern tribes of ancient Israel that disappeared after being conquered and scattered into captivity by the Assyrians in 722 BCE.

teraphim: Icons of pagan household gods. Rachel steals the teraphim of her father Laban when Jacob's family flees from Haran.

Torah: The Pentateuch (the Five Books of Moses), comprising the first five books of the Hebrew Bible. Informally, the term is sometimes also used to refer to the complete Hebrew Bible (the TANAKH), or to the complete Hebrew Bible together with the Oral Law, as explicated in the Talmud and midrash.

Yom Kippur: In Judaism, the solemn, annual Day of Atonement, when Jews fast and pray for forgiveness for their sins.

Zilpah: One of the two handmaidens Laban gives to his daughters Leah and Rachel upon their marriages to Jacob. *See* Bilhah.

Zornberg, Avivah Gottlieb: Contemporary Bible commentator who often combines traditional midrashic sources with modern psychological and linguistic insights.

NOTES

Preface

1. **Definition of midrash:** Neusner, *Introduction*, 223–24.
2. **Purposes of rabbinic midrash:** Kugel, *How to Read*, 148.
3. **Principle of indeterminacy:** Cherry, *Torah*, xi.
4. **Priority of the Oral Torah:** Kugel, *How to Read*, 680.

Note on the Sources

1. **Problems in translating the Hebrew Bible:** Kugel, *How to Read*, 36–37, 142; Kugel, *Bible as It Was*, 4–5.
2. **Translation sources:** The foundation sources for the *Midrash Rabbah* translations below are the Neusner translations originally published by Scholars Press as vols. 1, 2, and 3 of *Genesis Rabbah: The Judaic Commentary to the Book of Genesis—A New American Translation* (Brown Judaic Studies series, nos. 104, 105, and 106) and *Lamentations Rabbah: An Analytical Translation* (Brown Judaic Studies series, no. 193). The foundation sources for the Talmud translations below are the Neusner translations originally published by Scholars Press as *The Talmud of Babylonia: An American Translation—Tractate Berakhot* (Brown Judaic Studies series, no. 78), *The Talmud of Babylonia: An American Translation—Tractate Sanhedrin* (Brown Judaic Studies series, no. 81), and *The Talmud of Babylonia: An Academic Commentary—Tractate Megillah* (USF Academic Commentary series, no. 19).

Introduction

1. **The Messiah's descent from Leah:** Isa. 11:1.
2. **Tribes:** Currently, some African, Indian, and Asian tribes claim to be Jewish remnants of the Lost Tribes; if these claims are correct,

they could be descendants of Lost Tribes from Leah or from Jacob's other wives. However, the Ethiopian tribes recognized as Jews and granted admission by the State of Israel claim descent from Solomon's son and members of his court; if their claim is correct, they could be descendants primarily of Leah.

3. **Reading God in the Torah:** Rabbi Ed Feinstein in a lecture at Valley Beth Shalom Synagogue, Encino CA, February 15, 2012.

4. **Midrashic justifications for Jacob's actions in the birthright episode:** *Hachut Hameshulash*, 507 (citing Kimchi); Ibn Ezra, *Commentary*, 1:253; Townsend, *Midrash Tanhuma*, 148–49; Nachshoni, *Weekly Parashah*, 145. For a detailed discussion of the birthright story, see Supplement A: *Midrash on Jacob's Birthright Episode*, at www.jerryrabow.com.

5. **Commentaries concluding that Jacob's actions in the blessing episode were not justified:** Moyers, *Genesis*, 287 (quoting Hestenes); Townsend, *Midrash Tanhuma*, 172–73. For a detailed discussion of several aspects of the blessing story, see Supplement B: *Midrash on Jacob's Blessing Episode*; Supplement C: *Midrash on Jacob Leaving Home*; and Supplement D: *Midrash on the Robbery of Jacob and His Night at Bethel*, at www.jerryrabow.com.

1. Waiting for Leah

1. **History of the Western concept of romantic love:** Borscheid, *Romantic Love*, 157–68; Park, *Ways of Loving*, 1–3; Powell, *Romance*; Reddy, *History*.

2. **Why Leah did not help with the flock:** Ramban (Nachmanides), *Commentary*, 1:360–61.

3. **Rachel protected by the custom of the older sister marrying first:** Tuchman and Rappaport, *Passions*, 190.

4. **Other reasons for Rachel herding alone:** Ramban (Nachmanides), *Commentary*, 1:360–61 (Leah's sensitive eyes); Tuchman and Rappaport, *Passions*, 190–91 (citing Ramban: Leah's sensitive eyes or Rachel's better skills; and citing Chizkuni: Rachel acted out of respect for her older sister).

5. **Jacob and Rachel as the Bible's first romance:** Goldstein, *Jewish Folklore*, 77–78.

6. **Jacob's kiss:** Culi, *Torah Anthology*, 3a:43 (not a kiss on the lips); *Etz Hayim*, 170, *p'shat* n. 11 (only Jacob knew of the relationship at the time of the kiss); *Midrash Rabbah*, Gen. 70.12 (permissible kiss

between relatives); Ramban (Nachmanides), *Commentary*, 1:361 (not a kiss on the face); Rosenblatt, *After the Apple*, 103 (Rachel's lack of mutuality); Tuchman and Rappaport, *Passions*, 193–95 (romantic kiss; permissible kiss between relatives; Rachel accepted the kiss without comment or response).

7. **Rachel reminded Jacob of his mother:** Tuchman and Rappaport, *Passions*, 195 (citing R. Abraham [1186–1237, son and successor of Maimonides]).

8. **Jacob grew up in the tents:** Gen. 25:27; Jacob was Rebekah's favorite: Gen. 25:28; Jacob cooking: Gen. 25:29; Rebekah cooking: Gen. 27:9; Sarah cooking: Gen. 18:6; Rebekah commanding Jacob's participation in obtaining the blessing: Gen. 27:8.

9. **Jacob's concern for Rachel's reputation:** Ginzberg, *Legends of the Jews*, 281; *Midrash Rabbah*, Gen. 70.12; Tuchman and Rappaport, *Passions*, 196.

10. **Jacob's prophetic knowledge that Rachel would die young and not be buried in Machpelah:** Ginzberg, *Legends of the Jews*, 281; *Midrash Rabbah*, Gen. 70.12; Rashi, *Commentaries*, 1:320n11; Zornberg, *Beginning of Desire*, 208.

11. **Translation of "brother":** R. E. Friedman, *Commentary on the Torah*, 98; *Targum Onqelos*, 105.

12. **"Aramean" referring to swindler:** *Encyclopedia of Biblical Interpretation*, 44:2, Anthology Sec. 7; Weissman, *Midrash Says*, 286; and see Brown, *Brown-Driver-Briggs*, 941.

13. **Midrashic interpretations can be based on similar-sounding words:** Kugel, *How to Read*, 144.

14. **Midrashic story of Jacob's immediate proposal and conversation with Rachel at the well:** Ginzberg, *Legends of the Jews*, 282; Talmud, *Megillah* 13b; Tuchman and Rappaport, *Passions*, 198; Weissman, *Midrash Says*, 284.

15. **Midrashic efforts to exonerate Jacob from criticism:**
    (a) **In the birthright episode:** See A. Z. Friedman, *Wellsprings*, 51; *Hachut Hameshulash*, 507, 537–38 (citing Kimchi), 505 (citing Rashbam); Ibn Ezra, *Commentary*, 1:253; *Midrash Rabbah*, Gen. 63.8; Nachshoni, *Weekly Parashah*, 145–48; Townsend, *Midrash Tanhuma*, 148–49; Weissman, *Midrash Says*, 246–48.
    (b) **In the blessing episode:** See Armstrong, *In the Beginning*, 78; Attar, *Or Hachayim*, 223–25; Bialik, *Book of Legends*, 44–45; Culi, *Torah Anthology*, 2:497, 499, 510; Epstein, *Torah Temimah*, 121–22;

Hachut Hameshulash, 542 (citing Rashbam), 545 (citing Sforno); Hirsch, *Pentateuch*, 2nd ed., 1:441–44n1; Ibn Ezra, *Commentary*, 1:262; Sarna, *Commentary: Genesis*, 191–92; *Book of Jubilees*, 26:6–22, pp. 161–62; Kugel, *How to Read*, 142; *Midrash Rabbah*, Gen. 65.15, 18, 19, 67.4; Nachshoni, *Weekly Parashah*, 163; Townsend, *Midrash Tanhuma*, 154–55, 172; Talmud, *Makkot* 24a; *Targum Onqelos*, 101n12.

16. **Jacob defends his deceptions**: Ginzberg, *Legends of the Jews*, 282; *Midrash Rabbah*, Gen. 70.13.

17. **The secret signs**: Talmud, *Bava Batra* 123a; Talmud, *Megillah* 13b; Tuchman and Rappaport, *Passions*, 198; Weissman, *Midrash Says*, 285.

18. **The signs as secret words**: Tuchman and Rappaport, *Passions*, 216–17.

19. **The signs as secret touches**: Ginzberg, *Legends of the Jews*, 282 and n. 159.

20. **Toe, thumb, and ear**: These specific places are also specified for the purification of the priests. Lev. 8:23–24; Exod. 29:20.

21. **Laban following his great-uncle Abraham's hospitality tradition**: Gen. 18:2–8 (Abraham's hospitality); Gen. 22:20 (Laban's relationship to Abraham).

22. **The reasons behind Laban's greeting, embracing, and kissing Jacob**: *Midrash Rabbah*, Gen. 70.13.

23. **Laban was waiting for Jacob's wealth**: Attar, *Or Hachayim*, 247.

24. **The legend of Jacob's robbery**: Culi, *Torah Anthology*, 3a:5–6; Ginzberg, *Legends of the Jews*, 274–75; Weissman, *Midrash Says*, 273. For a detailed discussion of why Jacob was penniless when he arrived at Haran, see Supplement D: *Midrash on the Robbery of Jacob and His Night at Bethel*, at www.jerryrabow.com.

25. **Laban was testing Jacob's skills**: Attar, *Or Hachayim*, 247.

26. **Laban recognizes Jacob as a fellow deceiver**: *Etz Hayim*, 170, d'rash n. 13.

27. **Esau as Edom**: In Mal. 1:3–4, God identifies Esau as Edom.

28. **Status of the handmaidens**: Culi, *Torah Anthology*, 3a:104, 106; Ginzberg, *Legends of the Jews*, 284 and n. 167; *Midrash Rabbah*, Gen. 74.13; Rashi, *Commentaries*; 1:355–56n50; Tuchman and Rappaport, *Passions*, 214.

29. **Leah and Rachel as twins**: Culi, *Torah Anthology*, 3a:197; *Encyclopedia of Biblical Interpretation*, 44:199, Anthology Sec. 62.

30. **Relative status of Leah's and Rachel's descendants**: *Midrash Rabbah*, Gen. 70.15.

31. **Translation of *rakhot* as "tender":** R. Alter, *Genesis*, 153; King James Bible, 1611 ed., at Gen. 29:17; R. E. Friedman, *Commentary*, 99 (translation); Hirsch, *Pentateuch*, 2nd ed., 1:470n17; *Tanach* (Stone/Artscroll ed.), 69; Tuchman and Rappaport, *Passions*, 201–2. And see Brown, *Brown-Driver-Briggs*, 939–40.

32. **Leah's eyes were beautiful:** R. Alter, *Genesis*, 153n17 (soft, attractive, gentle, sweet); Bloom, *Book of J*, 108 (exquisite); *Hachut Hameshulash*, 572 (Kimchi: beautiful), 571 (Rashbam: light in color, perhaps blue); Rashbam, *Commentary*, 172 (beautiful, light in color, perhaps blue); *Targum Onqelos*, 106 (lovely); Tuchman and Rappaport, *Passions*, 201–2 (soft, gentle).

33. **Weak eyes:** For translations of *rakhot* as "weak," see Gen. 29:17 in Hertz, *Pentateuch*, 108 (translation: "weak"; commentary: "Better, *tender*, which the Targum understands in the sense of 'beautiful.'"); *Holy Scriptures*, 35 (JPS, 1917); *Torah*, 53 (JPS, 1992); *Etz Hayim*, 171 (translation: "weak," *p'shat* commentary: "This does not describe poor vision, but eyes lacking in luster or lacking in tenderness or sensitivity.").

34. **Leah's eyes were unattractive:** R. Alter, *Genesis*, 153n17 (dull, lusterless, weak); Attar, *Or Hachayim*, 248 (weak in appearance); Epstein, *Torah Temimah*, 1:130 (worn); *Etz Hayim*, 171 (*p'shat* commentary: lacking in luster or lacking in tenderness or sensitivity); Ibn Ezra, *Commentary*, 1:282 (physically weak; poor vision); Mitchell, *Genesis*, 61 (dull); Sarna, *Commentary: Genesis*, 204 (dull, lusterless). And see *New English Bible*, 30 (translation: dull-eyed).

35. **Leah's poor vision as expressing Jacob's blindness motif:** Visotzky, *Genesis of Ethics*, 164.

36. **Leah and Rachel were equally beautiful:** Ronson, *Women of the Torah*, 123; Townsend, *Midrash Tanhuma*, 186.

37. **Leah and Rachel were equally beautiful except for Leah's eyes:** Ginzberg, *Legends of the Bible*, 171; Ginzberg, *Legends of the Jews*, 283; *Book of Jubilees*, 28:5, p. 169.

38. **Consequences of Leah's unattractiveness:** Alshech, *Torat Moshe*, 134; Attar, *Or Hachayim*, 248 (as literary device).

39. **Leah's distress over her pledged marriage to Esau:** Leah learned about the marriage pledge from the townspeople. Since issues of public reputation and humiliation are important to Leah, Rachel, and Jacob, perhaps part of Leah's dismay here was due to her concern about the community's opinion of her promised husband.

40. **Leah's weak eyes resulted from her crying:** Epstein, *Torah Temimah*, 130; Ginzberg, *Legends of the Bible*, 171; Ginzberg, *Legends of the Jews*, 2nd ed., 283; *Midrash Rabbah*, Gen. 70.16; Rashi, *Commentaries*, 1:322n17; Talmud, *Bava Batra* 123a; Townsend, *Midrash Tanhuma*, 186; Zornberg, *Beginning of Desire*, 211.

41. **Leah's weak eyes refer to her inability to control feminine tears:** *Hachut Hameshulash*, 572 (citing Kimchi).

42. **The Bible doesn't generally emphasize a heroine's appearance:** Kirsch, *Moses*, 6. But see Gen. 12:11–14 and 26:6–7 for the stories of Sarah and Rebekah each being presented by her husband as his sister when they were in a foreign land because she was so beautiful that he feared for his life.

43. **Importance of a wife's beauty:** Attar, *Or Hachayim*, 249 (sustains the marital bond); *Hachut Hameshulash*, 573 (citing Kimchi: especially for the righteous, to procreate and to better serve God in joy); Talmud, *Shabbat* 25b (especially for scholars); Tuchman and Rappaport, *Passions*, 204–5 (citing Radak: desire leads to children and contentment), 205 (citing Or Hachayim: sustains the marital bond).

44. **Jacob loved Rachel for lofty reasons:** Attar, *Or Hachayim*, 249; Nachshoni, *Weekly Parashah*, 171 (for her character); Tuchman and Rappaport, *Passions*, 203 (citing Or Hachayim: emanation of her inner spiritual beauty).

45. **Leah's inner beauty:** Raver, *Listen to Her Voice*, 65.

46. **Leah's sincere prayers moved God:** *Midrash Rabbah*, Gen. 70.16; Ronson, *Women of the Torah*, 123.

47. **God intervened three times for Leah:** Townsend, *Midrash Tanhuma*, 186, 194.

48. **Rachel's marriage delayed because Jacob lacked the bride-price:** R. Alter, *Genesis*, 154n18; *Hachut Hameshulash*, 575 (citing Sforno). And see sources for the legend of Jacob's robbery cited at note 24 to chapter 1 above.

49. **Jacob chose Rachel out of fear of Esau:** Townsend, *Midrash Tanhuma*, 186; Weissman, *Midrash Says*, 288.

50. **Jacob gradually came to love Rachel:** Townsend, *Midrash Tanhuma*, 186.

51. **Jacob's attempt to specify Rachel:** *Midrash Rabbah*, Gen. 70.17; Rashi, *Commentaries*, 1:323n18.

52. **Jacob and Rachel as the Bible's first romance:** Goldstein, *Jewish Folklore*, 77–78.

53. Jacob's seven years of working for Rachel passed swiftly for him: A. Z. Friedman, *Wellsprings*, 59 (citing Abraham Joshua Heschel: because of his spiritual love); *Hachut Hameshulash*, 578 (citing Sforno: in light of her great value).

54. Jacob's seven years working for Rachel passed swiftly for him because he was blinded by love: Sforno, *Commentary*, 155n20.

55. Jacob's coarse language: Rashi, *Commentaries*, 1:324n21.

56. Jacob's impatience to sire his promised twelve sons: *Midrash Rabbah*, Gen. 70.18; Rashi, *Commentaries*, 1:324n21; Tuchman and Rappaport, *Passions*, 209 (citing Chizkuni), 209–10 (citing Sforno).

57. Jacob first married at age eighty-four: Ginzberg, *Legends of the Jews*, 282; Ronson, *Women of the Torah*, 125; Talmud, *Megillah* 17a.

58. Jacob was impatient to fulfill a husband's obligations: Attar, *Or Hachayim*, 250–51; Tuchman and Rappaport, *Passions*, 209–10.

59. Wedding deception parallels blessing deception: Rosenblatt, *After the Apple*, 90.

60. Jacob's coarse language is excused by prior fruitless conversations with Laban: Tuchman and Rappaport, *Passions*, 208–9 (citing Ramban).

61. Jacob was expressing sexual impatience: R. Alter, *Genesis*, 154n21.

2. Leah's Wedding Night

1. Distinction between *peshat* and *derash*: Benjamin Edidin Scolnic, "Traditional Methods of Bible Study," in *Etz Hayim*, 1494.

2. Drought in Haran when Jacob arrived: Weissman, *Midrash Says*, 280, 283.

3. Jacob brought water and prosperity to Haran: *Midrash Rabbah*, Gen. 70.19; Tuchman and Rappaport, *Passions*, 211.

4. Laban solicited the neighbors' help: Ginzberg, *Legends of the Bible*, 171; Ginzberg, *Legends of the Jews*, 283.

5. Neighbors were to get Jacob drunk: Nachshoni, *Weekly Parashah*, 173; Tuchman and Rappaport, *Passions*, 212; and see Brown, *Brown-Driver-Briggs*, 1059.

6. The drinking song: Bin Gorion, *Mimekor Yisrael*, 64; Ginzberg, *Legends of the Bible*, 172; Ginzberg, *Legends of the Jews*, 283; Tuchman and Rappaport, *Passions*, 212.

7. Drinking song was a warning to validate the wedding: Culi, *Torah Anthology*, 3a:52.

8. Modern reading of the Bible can presume human literary brilliance rather than divine authorship: R. Alter, *Biblical Narrative*, 10.

9. Jacob was told that wedding was held in evening darkness to accommodate the bride's modesty: Ginzberg, *Legends of the Jews*, 283.
10. Leah's wedding feast started in daylight: *Etz Hayim*, 172, *p'shat* n. 23.
11. Jacob deceived in darkness, as he had deceived Isaac: *Etz Hayim*, 172, *d'rash* n. 25.
12. Laban physically pushed Leah into the wedding tent: Attar, *Or Hachayim*, 252; Tuchman and Rappaport, *Passions*, 212 (citing Ramban).
13. Jacob deceived Isaac out of obedience to Rebekah: Attar, *Or Hachayim*, 223; Bialik, *Book of Legends*, 44; Epstein, *Torah Temimah*, 121–22; *Midrash Rabbah*, Gen. 65.15; Hirsch, *Pentateuch*, 2nd ed., 1:441-42n1; Talmud, *Makkot* 24a.
14. "Brought" (Heb.) derived from (caused to) "come": Brown, *Brown-Driver-Briggs*, 99.
15. Jacob didn't know it was Leah until the morning: Rashbam, *Commentary*, 134, 173; Tuchman and Rappaport, *Passions*, 215.
16. Who Leah was during the night: Talmud, *Megillah* 13b; Rashi, *Commentaries*, 1:324n25.
17. Rachel gave Jacob's secret signs to Leah to spare her humiliation: Rashi, *Commentaries*, 1:324n25; Talmud, *Bava Batra* 123a; Talmud, *Megillah* 13b.
18. No foreplay on Jacob's wedding night with Leah: Attar, *Or Hachayim*, 252.
19. Whether Jacob imitated Esau's voice when he deceived Isaac: Culi, *Torah Anthology*, 2:499; *Hachut Hameshulash*, 536 (citing Rashbam); Ramban (Nachmanides), *Commentary*, 1:339; Rashbam, *Commentary*, 154–55; Rymanover, *Torah Discourses*, 141–42.
20. Leah fooled Jacob by sounding like her sister: *Hachut Hameshulash*, 536 (citing Rashbam); Ramban (Nachmanides), *Commentary*, 1:339; Tuchman and Rappaport, *Passions*, 216 (citing *Torah Teminah*).
21. Rachel hid beneath the wedding bed and answered for Leah: *Midrash Rabbah*, Lam. Prologue 24, pp. 47–48; Tuchman and Rappaport, *Passions*, 216; Weissman, *Midrash Says*, 288.
22. Rachel's sacrifice enabled her to move God: *Midrash Rabbah*, Lam. Prologue 24, pp. 47–48.
23. Leah became Rachel for the wedding night: Tuchman and Rappaport, *Passions*, 215 (by deception); Zornberg, *Beginning of Desire*, 185 (by psychological transformation).

24. **Blessing episode:** For a detailed discussion of Esau's reaction to losing the blessing, see Supplement B: *Midrash on Jacob's Blessing Episode*, at www.jerryrabow.com.

25. **Jacob told Laban about his deceptions of Esau and Isaac:** *Midrash Rabbah*, Gen. 70.13; Rashi, *Commentaries*, 1:321n13.

26. **Leah's response to Jacob's complaints on the morning after her wedding:** R. Alter, *Genesis*, 155n26; Culi, *Torah Anthology*, 3a:53; Ginzberg, *Legends of the Bible*, 172; *Midrash Rabbah*, Gen. 70.19; Tuchman and Rappaport, *Passions*, 217.

27. **The wedding deception as the Bible's moral commentary on Jacob deceiving Isaac:** R. Alter, *Biblical Narrative*, 45; R. Alter, *Genesis*, 155n26.

28. **Jacob did not favor Leah because of the wedding deception:** Armstrong, *In the Beginning*, 85; **because of her failure to identify herself during their sexual relations that night:** Tuchman and Rappaport, *Passions*, 224 (citing Ramban); **and because of her harsh response the next morning:** Ronson, *Women of the Torah*, 128–29; Townsend, *Midrash Tanhuma*, 185. **Jacob showed his anger in his words toward Leah and in minimizing his marital relations with her:** Tuchman and Rappaport, *Passions*, 225 (citing Abarbanel). But see *Midrash Rabbah*, Gen. 71.2 (Jacob later favored Rachel in an attempt to equalize her position because Leah had been able to produce so many sons).

29. **Leah's hurtful words on the morning after her wedding:** Leah's verbal attack on Jacob's own history of deception seems to be a defensive, perhaps reflexive, retort to his bitter complaint to her in the midrashic story. Perhaps the essence of this conversation does not reflect poor ethical behavior by Leah, but only her deep pain after this most bizarre wedding.

30. **Jacob's mistaken belief in his bride's identity may have invalidated marital relations on Leah's wedding night:** Tuchman and Rappaport, *Passions*, 213, 218 (citing Netziv).

31. **Reuben was conceived on the first wedding night:** Culi, *Torah Anthology*, 3b:517.

32. **Laban is culpable for causing Jacob to have sexual relations with Leah while believing she was Rachel:** Culi, *Torah Anthology*, 3a:53.

33. **Jacob's mistaken belief that he was having marital intercourse with Rachel led to Leah's firstborn, Reuben, losing the birthright:** Attar, *Or Hachayim*, 251–52.

34. **Laban continues the birthright motif by citing the oldest daughter's right to marry first:** Nachshoni, *Weekly Parashah*, 171–72.

35. **Rachel spoke hurtfully to Leah during Leah's wedding week:** Berman, *Midrash Tanhuma*, 189.

3. Leah Begins Married Life

1. **Jacob loved Leah also:** Tuchman and Rappaport, *Passions*, 221 (citing Radak).

2. **Jacob loved Leah during her first exclusive week as his wife:** *Hachut Hameshulash*, 579 (citing Kimchi); Tuchman and Rappaport, *Passions*, 223 (citing *Kli Yakar*).

3. **Jacob's love will always be in terms of "also":** Zornberg, *Beginning of Desire*, 186.

4. **During her honeymoon week, Leah hoped that Jacob would come to love her:** Tuchman and Rappaport, *Passions*, 223 (citing Netziv).

5. **Jacob's love for Rachel grew after he married her:** Attar, *Or Hachayim*, 255; Tuchman and Rappaport, *Passions*, 222 (citing Or Hachayim).

6. **Jacob loved Rachel more because he had to work more for her:** Tuchman and Rappaport, *Passions*, 221 (citing Rashbam).

7. **Polygamy was legal:** Klein, *Guide*, 388–89 (polygamy for Jews was not outlawed until the rabbinic ban for Ashkenazic Jews in the eleventh century; the practice was not prohibited for Sephardic Jews living in Muslim territories until 1950).

8. **Invalidity of Rachel's marriage:** *Etz Hayim*, 173, *p'shat* n. 28.

9. **Marriage laws would be violated unless Rachel died upon entering the Holy Land:** Tuchman and Rappaport, *Passions*, 316 (citing Ramban).

10. **Jacob's greater love for Rachel, his second wife, was unnatural:** Tuchman and Rappaport, *Passions*, 221–22 (citing Ramban).

11. **If Rachel had married first, she would still have born Joseph and Benjamin:** *Midrash Rabbah*, Gen. 98.4.

12. **Jacob loved Leah, but less than Rachel:** *Hachut Hameshulash*, 580 (citing Kimchi); Nachshoni, *Weekly Parashah*, 175; Tuchman and Rappaport, *Passions*, 221 (citing Radak).

13. **Jacob can be portrayed more nobly if he didn't hate Leah:** R. Alter, *Genesis*, 155n31; Culi, *Torah Anthology*, 3a:62; Deut. 21:15; *Etz Hayim*, 1113, *p'shat* n. 15.

14. **Jacob didn't show the anger that was in his heart:** Tuchman and Rappaport, *Passions*, 226 (citing Or Hachayim).

15. Leah didn't see Jacob's anger, so she continued to hope he would come to love her more: Attar, *Or Hachayim*, 256.
16. Leah feared the public shame of divorce: Weissman, *Midrash Says*, 290.
17. Leah feared that divorce would lead to Esau claiming her: Berman, *Midrash Tanhuma*, 189.
18. Leah's tears convinced God to make her fertile so that Jacob would not divorce her: *Midrash Rabbah*, Gen. 71.2.
19. Rachel spoke hurtfully to Leah during Leah's wedding week: Berman, *Midrash Tanhuma*, 189.
20. Conception depends on God as well as the wife and husband: *Midrash Rabbah*, Gen. 71.7.
21. God was responsible for Leah's fertility: *Targum Onqelos*, 106.
22. Leah was physically unable to conceive: Ginzberg, *Legends of the Bible*, 173; Ginzberg, *Legends of the Jews*, 285; *Hachut Hameshulash*, 580 (citing Kimchi).
23. God was concerned that the community would presume that Leah's barrenness showed her lack of righteousness: Attar, *Or Hachayim*, 256.
24. God made Leah fertile so that Jacob would not divorce her: Attar, *Or Hachayim*, 256.
25. Reuben was the result of Jacob's first seminal emission: *Midrash Rabbah*, Gen. 98.4; Rashi, *Commentaries*, 1:535n3.
26. Rachel was barren from the same physical defect: Tuchman and Rappaport, *Passions*, 226–27 (citing Radak).
27. God made Rachel barren to equalize the sisters' competition for Jacob's love: Attar, *Or Hachayim*, 256.
28. Not clear if Rachel was barren naturally or due to God's active intervention: *Book of Jubilees*, 28:11–12, pp. 170–72.
29. Leah's six sons didn't change Jacob's lifelong preference for Rachel: R. Alter, *Genesis*, 288n7; Leibowitz, *Bereshit*, 539.
30. God thought that Leah's sons would cause Jacob to love her: Ginzberg, *Legends of the Jews*, 285; Ronson, *Women of the Torah*, 129; Townsend, *Midrash Tanhuma*, 185.
31. God only intended that Leah's fertility would bar divorce: Culi, *Torah Anthology*, 3a:63; *Midrash Rabbah*, Gen. 71.2.
32. Leah's name choices for her first four sons show her changing expectations: Tuchman and Rappaport, *Passions*, 228.
33. "Levi" from word for "being joined": Brown, *Brown-Driver-Briggs*, 530–31.

34. "Yehudah" from word for "giving thanks": Brown, *Brown-Driver-Briggs*, 392.

35. Leah's first two sons' names recall how Jacob was fooled during the wedding night by sight and sound, just as Jacob fooled Isaac with sight and sound: R. Alter, *Genesis*, 156n33.

36. Leah's name choices for her first sons show that the births have not made a difference in Jacob's attitude: Tuchman and Rappaport, *Passions*, 230 (citing Netziv).

37. Leah named Judah as thanks for bearing more than her one-quarter share of Jacob's twelve sons: Attar, *Or Hachayim*, 257; Culi, *Torah Anthology*, 3a:66; *Midrash Rabbah*, Gen. 71.4; Rashi, *Commentaries*, 1:328n35.

38. Leah's naming Judah was the first time a human blessed God: Talmud, *Berakhot* 7b; Tuchman and Rappaport, *Passions*, 233.

39. Judah's name signifies Leah's growing contentment: *Etz Hayim*, 174, *d'rash* n. 35.

40. Judah's name signifies Leah's desire to stop having children: Ibn Ezra, *Commentary*, 1:283–84.

41. Leah stopped bearing children because Jacob stopped having marital relations with her: R. Alter, *Genesis*, 157n35.

42. Rachel has not yet spoken in the Bible: R. Alter, *Biblical Narrative*, 187; Tuchman and Rappaport, *Passions*, 237.

43. Rachel attributed the difference between her barrenness and Leah's fertility to God rewarding Leah: Attar, *Or Hachayim*, 257.

44. Rachel envied Leah's piety: Ginzberg, *Legends of the Jews*, 285; *Midrash Rabbah*, Gen. 71.6; Rashi, *Commentaries*, 1:328n1; Tuchman and Rappaport, *Passions*, 236.

45. Dead person: The Hebrew word used in Gen. 30:1 for "dead" (*metah*) is in participle form, which can function here as an adjective phrase ("a dead person"). See Brown, *Brown-Driver-Briggs*, 559.

46. Four persons considered as dead: *Midrash Rabbah*, Gen. 71.6; Culi, *Torah Anthology*, 3a:67; Rashi, *Commentaries*, 1:328n1; Talmud, *Nedarim* 64b; Tuchman and Rappaport, *Passions*, 237–38.

47. Rachel was angry at God for forgiving Leah but punishing Rachel: Tuchman and Rappaport, *Passions*, 235 (citing Torat Hachida).

48. For sins against individuals, God's forgiveness first requires forgiveness from the injured party: Talmud, Mishnah *Yoma*, 85b.

49. Rachel felt that she needed Jacob's forgiveness: Tuchman and Rappaport, *Passions*, 236.

50. **Jacob kept Rachel sterile to avoid spoiling her beauty:** *Midrash Rabbah*, Gen. 23.2; Rashi, *Commentaries*, 1:48–49; Tuchman and Rappaport, *Passions*, 238 (citing Sha'arei Aharon), 272 (citing Netziv).

51. **Rachel's reference to death echoes Esau's statements in the birthright episode:** R. Alter, *Genesis*, 158n1.

52. **Rachel will have the children she demands, but that will make her a dead person:** R. Alter, *Genesis*, 158n2.

53. **The dynamics of the Jacob-Rachel-Leah love triangle:** Zornberg, *Beginning of Desire*, 209–10; see also Leibowitz, *Bereshit*, 334 (citing Akedat Yitzhak), and Tuchman and Rappaport, *Passions*, 237–38.

54. **Why Jacob was angry at Rachel's demands:** Attar, *Or Hachayim*, 258; *Etz Hayim*, 175, d'rash n. 2; Leibowitz, *Bereshit*, 334 (citing Radak); Ramban (Nachmanides), *Commentary*, 1:367.

55. **Further reasons for Jacob's anger at Rachel's demands:** *Hachut Hameshulash*, 583 (citing Kimchi); Ramban (Nachmanides), *Commentary*, 1:367; Tuchman and Rappaport, *Passions*, 239 (citing Radak).

56. **The righteous should pray for miracles for others:** Ramban (Nachmanides), *Commentary*, 1:366; Tuchman and Rappaport, *Passions*, 240.

57. **Unlike Isaac, Jacob already had sons, so Jacob saw the problem as Rachel's:** *Midrash Rabbah*, Gen. 71.7; Rashi, *Commentaries*, 1:328–29n2.

58. **Rachel should follow Sarah's example, since God ended Sarah's barrenness because she gave her handmaiden to Abraham:** Culi, *Torah Anthology*, 3a:68.

59. **Jacob's response will be punished when Leah's sons entreat Rachel's son Joseph:** Culi, *Torah Anthology*, 3a:69; Ginzberg, *Legends of the Bible*, 174; *Midrash Rabbah*, Gen. 71.7; Ronson, *Women of the Torah*, 136; Townsend, *Midrash Tanhuma*, 193; Tuchman and Rappaport, *Passions*, 240.

60. **Bilhah was Rachel's half sister:** Culi, *Torah Anthology*, 3a:104,106; Ginzberg, *Legends of the Jews*, 286; *Midrash Rabbah*, Gen. 74.13; Rashi, *Commentaries*, 1:355–56n50; Tuchman and Rappaport, *Passions*, 214, 220.

61. **Hagar's children would be counted as Sarah's:** *Midrash Rabbah*, Gen. 45.2; Rashi, *Commentaries*, 1:154n2.

62. **Providing Hagar would earn Sarah merit:** *Midrash Rabbah*, Gen. 71.7; Rashi, *Commentaries*, 1:154n2.

63. **Rachel provided Bilhah to earn the reward of fertility:** Culi, *Torah Anthology*, 3a:68; Rashi, *Commentaries*, 1:154n2.

64. **Hagar saw her immediate pregnancy as evidence of Sarah's lack of merit:** *Midrash Rabbah*, Gen. 45.4; Rashi, *Commentaries*, 1:156n4.

65. **Sarah caused Hagar to miscarry:** *Midrash Rabbah*, Gen. 45.5; Rashi, *Commentaries*, 1:156–57n5.

66. **Minimal difference between wife and concubine:** *Etz Hayim*, 175, p'shat n. 4.

67. **Bilhah and Zilpah became freed women and wives:** Attar, *Or Hachayim*, 258; *Hachut Hameshulash*, 586 (citing Sforno); Tuchman and Rappaport, *Passions*, 245–46.

68. **Bilhah and Zilpah and their sons never achieve equality with the families of Rachel and Leah:** Ginzberg, *Legends of the Jews*, 284 and n. 167.

69. **Status of the handmaidens:** For additional discussion of the status of Bilhah and Zilpah, see Supplement E: *Midrash on the Handmaiden-Wives*, at www.jerryrabow.com.

70. **The meaning of "Naphtali":** Ibn Ezra, *Commentary*, 1:285–86; Rashi, *Commentaries*, 1:330n8.

71. **"Naphtali" repeats the theme of wrestling in Jacob's life:** R. Alter, *Genesis*, 159n8.

72. **Leah selflessly provided Zilpah to Jacob:** *Etz Hayim*, 175–76, p'shat n. 9.

73. **Leah provided Zilpah to Jacob for other reasons:** *Book of Jubilees*, 28:20, p. 173; Ramban (Nachmanides), *Commentary*, 1:368–69; Tuchman and Rappaport, *Passions*, 250–51 (citing Ramban).

74. **Whether Zilpah was the older or the younger handmaiden:** Rashi, *Commentaries*, 1:331n10; Tuchman and Rappaport, *Passions*, 251–52.

75. **"Gad" refers to betrayal:** See use of *bagaditah* to describe betrayal of a spouse in Mal. 2:14.

76. **The meaning of "Gad":** Ginzberg, *Legends of the Jews*, 286 and n. 183; Rashi, *Commentaries*, 1:331n11; Tuchman and Rappaport, *Passions*, 253 (citing Sforno).

77. **Alternative meaning of "Gad":** Ginzberg, *Legends of the Jews*, 286 and n. 183.

4. Leah Continues the Conflict

1. **The mandrake root resembles the human shape and is believed to have fertility or aphrodisiac powers:** Culi, *Torah Anthology*, 3a:72; Preuss, *Medicine*, 462; Tuchman and Rappaport, *Passions*, 256–57.

2. *Dudaim* **linked to** *dodim*—**lovemaking:** R. Alter, *Genesis*, 160n14.

3. **The Matriarchs would not quarrel over magical plant:** Ramban (Nachmanides), *Commentary*, 1:369; Tuchman and Rappaport, *Passions*, 256–57 (citing Ramban).

4. **Reuben brought the fragrant fruit, not a magical root:** Ramban (Nachmanides), *Commentary*, 1:369; Talmud, *Sanhedrin* 99b; and see Songs 7:14.

5. **The *dudaim* was a fragrant jasmine or violet plant:** Culi, *Torah Anthology*, 3a:72; Rashi, *Commentaries*, 1:332n14.

6. **The mandrake works like any medicinal herb:** Tuchman and Rappaport, *Passions*, 256–57.

7. **Leah's sharp retort:** While Leah's harsh words to her sister in the mandrakes bargaining may provide a measure of her anguish at not being able to diminish Jacob's unceasing infatuation with Rachel, this shouldn't excuse Leah's gratuitously causing pain to Rachel.

8. **Rachel controlled Jacob's sleeping arrangements:** R. Alter, *Genesis*, 160n16.

9. **Leah and Rachel were bargaining over sexual gratification, not marital love:** *Etz Hayim*, 176, p'shat n. 15.

10. **Leah was granted six sons because of Rachel's mandrakes bargaining:** Ginzberg, *Legends of the Bible*, 175; Ginzberg, *Legends of the Jews*, 287.

11. **Leah will be buried in Machpelah because of Rachel's mandrakes bargaining:** Ginzberg, *Legends of the Bible*, 175; Ginzberg, *Legends of the Jews*, 287; *Midrash Rabbah*, Gen. 72.3; Rashi, *Commentaries*, 1:332n15.

12. **Leah went out to Jacob to save Rachel from embarrassment:** Culi, *Torah Anthology*, 3a:72–73; Tuchman and Rappaport, *Passions*, 260 (citing Netziv).

13. **Leah was rewarded for her role in the mandrakes incident:** Attar, *Or Hachayim*, 259; Ginzberg, *Legends of the Jews*, 287; Tuchman and Rappaport, *Passions*, 260 (citing Sforno).

14. **It is proper for a wife to initiate sex for the purpose of procreation:** Talmud, *Nedarim* 20b.

15. **Leah went out to assure that Rachel and Jacob would honor the bargain:** Attar, *Or Hachayim*, 259; Tuchman and Rappaport, *Passions*, 260.

16. **The Bible generally doesn't tell stories about women only:** Rabbi Bradley Shavit Artson, lecture at Valley Beth Shalom Synagogue, Encino, California, Jan. 21, 2009.

17. **God rewarded Leah for her desire to bear Jacob's sons:** *Midrash Rabbah*, Gen. 72.5; Rashi, *Commentaries*, 1:333n17.

18. **Leah "stopped bearing" because of Jacob:** The text doesn't say that Leah became "barren" (*akarah*, the word it used to describe Rachel in Gen. 29:31). Rather, it states that Leah "stopped [ceased from] bearing" (*va-ta-amod mi-ledet*, Gen. 29: 35; see Brown, *Brown-Driver-Briggs*, 764), perhaps implying only the absence of marital relations instead of infertility.

19. **Meaning of "Issachar":** Culi, *Torah Anthology*, 3a:74; *Etz Hayim*, 176–77, *p'shat* n. 16, 18; R. Alter, *Genesis*, 161n18.

20. **Meaning of "Zebulun":** Rashi, *Commentaries*, 1:333n20 (citing Onqelos).

21. **Leah's hopes after bearing six sons:** Rashi, *Commentaries*, 1:333n20.

22. **Zilpah's pregnancy went unnoticed because of her youth:** *Midrash Rabbah*, Gen. 71.9; Rashi, *Commentaries*, 1:330–31n10.

23. **Dinah was Zebulun's twin:** Culi, *Torah Anthology*, 3a:75; *Hachut Hameshulash*, 591 (citing Kimchi); Ibn Ezra, *Commentary*, 1:288; Tuchman and Rappaport, *Passions*, 265.

24. **Each of Jacob's daughter-twins married another brother, allowing the sons to avoid prohibited marriages to Canaanite women:** Culi, *Torah Anthology*, 3a:78; Weissman, *Midrash Says*, 292.

25. **Dinah began as Zebulun's twin brother:** *Hachut Hameshulash*, 591 (citing Kimchi).

26. **Leah's prayers changed Dinah's gender:** Ginzberg, *Legends of the Jews*, 287; Rashi, *Commentaries*, 1:333–34n21; Talmud, *Berakhot* 60a; Townsend, *Midrash Tanhuma*, 193–94; Tuchman and Rappaport, *Passions*, 265–66.

27. **Twelve stones fused into one stone:** *Midrash Rabbah*, Gen. 68.11; Rashi, *Commentaries*, 1:311n11.

28. **Change of gender would require a miracle:** Talmud, *Berakhot* 60a.

29. **Prayers for miracles that would suspend the natural order are generally prohibited:** Berman, *Midrash Tanhuma*, 192–93; Talmud, *Avodah Zarah* 54b.

30. **It is not ordinarily permissible to pray to change gender after it has been determined during pregnancy:** Culi, *Torah Anthology*, 3a:75; Talmud, *Berakhot* 60a.

31. **Rachel's prayers caused the miracle:** Neusner, *Talmud of the Land of Israel*, 1:340 (*Berakhot* 9:3); Tuchman and Rappaport, *Passions*, 266.

32. **All four wives' prayers caused the miracle:** Ginzberg, *Legends of the Jews*, 287.

33. **Joseph and Dinah exchanged identities in the wombs of Leah and Rachel:** Dresner, *Rachel*, 59–60.

34. **The meaning of "Dinah":** Rashi, *Commentaries*, 1:333–34n21.

5. Leah and the Family Leave Haran

1. **God "remembered" Rachel:** *Etz Hayim*, 177, *p'shat* n. 22 referencing p. 46, *p'shat* n. 1.

2. **God ended Rachel's barrenness as a reward for her having given the signs to Leah:** Culi, *Torah Anthology*, 3a:76; Rashi, *Commentaries*, 1:334n22.

3. **God was moved to emulate Leah's pity for Rachel:** *Encyclopedia of Biblical Interpretation*, 44:104, Anthology Sec. 19; and see Miles, *God*, for an approach to reading the Bible as the story of God's interdependence with humanity, and God's change and development as a result of interactions with God's creatures.

4. **Other reasons for Rachel's reward:** Berman, *Midrash Tanhuma*, 191–92; Tuchman and Rappaport, *Passions*, 269 (citing Sforno).

5. **The mandrakes episode caused God to delay ending Rachel's barrenness:** Tuchman and Rappaport, *Passions*, 269 (citing Alshich).

6. **The entire family feared that Esau might claim the women:** Ginzberg, *Legends of the Jews*, 303; *Hachut Hameshulash*, 640 (citing Kimchi); *Midrash Rabbah*, Gen. 76.9.

7. **Rachel prayed for fertility:** Tuchman and Rappaport, *Passions*, 269 (citing R. Abraham, son of Maimonides).

8. **Rachel learned that she had to pray for herself:** Tuchman and Rappaport, *Passions*, 270 (citing Ramban).

9. **Rachel's prayers were reinforced by Leah, Bilhah, and Zilpah:** Culi, *Torah Anthology*, 3a:75–76.

10. **Rachel's infertility was due to physical sterility:** Culi, *Torah Anthology*, 3a:76.

11. **Joseph ended Rachel's public disgrace from being childless:** Rashi, *Commentaries*, 1:334–35n23; Tuchman and Rappaport, *Passions*, 271 (citing Ramban).

12. **Joseph only covered over Rachel's disgrace:** Rashi, *Commentaries*, 1:334n23.

13. **Sources of Rachel's disgrace:** Tuchman and Rappaport, *Passions*, 271 (citing Alshich).

14. **Jacob made Rachel sterile to maintain her beauty and sexual availability:** Tuchman and Rappaport, *Passions*, 238 (citing Sha'arei Aharon), 272 (citing Netziv). And on the origin of that practice, see *Midrash Rabbah*, Gen. 23.2; Rashi, *Commentaries*, 1:334n23.
15. **Final years in Haran:** For additional discussion of Jacob's final years with Laban, see Supplement F: *Midrash on Jacob's Final Six Years in Haran*, at www.jerryrabow.com.
16. **Laban violated his obligation to save Jacob's bride-price for Leah and Rachel:** Sarna, *Understanding Genesis*, 200.
17. **Rachel spoke hurtfully to Leah during Leah's wedding week:** Berman, *Midrash Tanhuma*, 189.
18. **Laban seized Jacob's gifts to Rachel during the first seven years and gave them to Leah:** Berman, *Midrash Tanhuma*, 191.
19. **Leah's verbal attack on Jacob on the morning after the wedding:** R. Alter, *Genesis*, 155n26; Ginzberg, *Legends of the Bible*, 172; *Midrash Rabbah*, Gen. 70.19; Tuchman and Rappaport, *Passions*, 217.
20. **Laban wanted to keep Jacob in Haran:** Ginzberg, *Legends of the Bible*, 171; Ginzberg, *Legends of the Jews*, 283.
21. **The sisters answered jointly:** As translated in R. E. Friedman, *Commentary on the Torah*, 105.
22. **Rachel was the cause of Jacob remaining in Haran:** Rashi, *Commentaries*, 1:344n4.
23. **Other explanations for Rachel answering first:** Culi, *Torah Anthology*, 3a:92 (she first consulted with Leah); *Hachut Hameshulash*, 610 (citing Kimchi: she loved Jacob more than Leah did).
24. **Rachel's priority before Leah in the book of Ruth:** Rashi, *Commentaries*, 1:344n4.
25. **Rachel's priority before Leah in prayer:** Klein, *Guide*, 401; *Siddur Sim Shalom*, 41b.
26. **Leah previously omitted from prayers entirely:** Dresner, *Rachel*, 70.
27. **Rachel's motive for stealing the teraphim:**
    (a) **To stop Laban from worshiping idols:** *Hachut Hameshulash*, 610–11 (citing Rabbeinu Chananel); *Midrash Rabbah*, Gen. 74.5; Rashi, *Commentaries*, 1:348n19; Tuchman and Rappaport, *Passions*, 289.
    (b) **To remove uncleanliness from Laban's house:** Berman, *Midrash Tanhuma*, 198; Culi, *Torah Anthology*, 3a:94; Ginzberg, *Legends of the Jews*, 291 and n. 218.

28. **Rachel stole the teraphim to stop Laban from learning about Jacob's flight:** Berman, *Midrash Tanhuma*, 198; Culi, *Torah Anthology*, 3a:94; *Hachut Hameshulash*, 611 (citing Rashbam), 612 (citing Kimchi); Ibn Ezra, *Commentary*, 1:301; Ginzberg, *Legends of the Bible*, 178; Nachshoni, *Weekly Parashah*, 182; Ramban (Nachmanides), *Commentary*, 1:383; Tuchman and Rappaport, *Passions*, 287–88 (citing Netziv).

29. **Rachel stole the teraphim for their fertility powers:** Raver, *Listen to Her Voice*, 65.

30. **Jacob's curse of death was irrevocable, like the decree of a king:** *Midrash Rabbah*, Gen. 74.4, 74.9; Tuchman and Rappaport, *Passions*, 295.

31. **Jacob's curse did not cause Rachel's death:**
    (a) **Jacob uttered a promise, not a curse:** *Hachut Hameshulash*, 616 (citing Kimchi); Rashbam, *Commentary*, 192.
    (b) **Rachel died an ordinary childbirth death:** Ibn Ezra, *Commentary*, 1:303.
    (c) **Jacob's curse was conditional on Laban's finding the teraphim:** *Hachut Hameshulash*, 620 (Eliyahu Munk's comments on Sforno).

32. **Men considered menstrual blood highly contaminating:** Culi, *Torah Anthology*, 3a:100.

33. **Rachel wasn't menstruating because she was already pregnant with Benjamin:** R. E. Friedman, *Commentary on the Torah*, 107.

34. **Rachel deceived her father:** For a detailed discussion of Rachel's deception of her father when Laban searched for the teraphim, see Supplement G: *Midrash on Laban's Pursuit of the Family*, at www.jerryrabow.com.

35. **Bilhah and Zilpah were Laban's daughters by a concubine:** Culi, *Torah Anthology*, 3a:104, 106; *Midrash Rabbah*, Gen. 74.13; Rashi, *Commentaries*, 1:355–56n50.

36. **Laban returned to poverty when Jacob left:** Culi, *Torah Anthology*, 3a:108.

37. **Laban tried to incite Esau to attack Jacob:** Ginzberg, *Legends of the Jews*, 293–94. For a detailed discussion on Laban's final meeting with the family, see Supplement G: *Midrash on Laban's Pursuit of the Family*, at www.jerryrabow.com.

38. **Robert Alter's critique of traditional midrashic efforts to glorify the Patriarchs:** See R. Alter, *Genesis*, 154n21.

6. Leah Comes to the Promised Land

1. Jacob's failure to contact Isaac and Rebekah from Haran later punished when Joseph will similarly fail to contact Jacob from Egypt: Rashi, *Commentaries*, 1:424n34.

2. Jacob and Esau as two sides of a single personality: Cf. Soloveitchik, *Man of Faith*, 10, 85, 91, 106 (Adam I and Adam II are two aspects of the human character).

3. Jacob's return to the border of the land was again accompanied by angels: R. Alter, *Genesis*, 177n2.

4. The meanings of Mahanaim (two camps): R. Alter, *Genesis*, 177n2 (Jacob's divided treatment of his family); *Hachut Hameshulash*, 626 (citing Kimchi: the family camp and the angels' camp); Ibn Ezra, *Commentary*, 1:310 (the family camp and the angels' camp); Visotzky, *Genesis of Ethics*, 183 (the family camp and the angels' camp).

5. How Jacob divided his camp: Culi, *Torah Anthology*, 3a:120; *Hachut Hameshulash*, 641 (citing Sforno); Ibn Ezra, *Commentary*, 1:312–14); Ramban (Nachmanides), *Commentary*, 1:398; Attar, *Or Hachayim*, 276.

6. Other meanings of Mahanaim (two camps): R. Alter, *Genesis*, 178n8 (Jacob's life divided between his two wives); Visotzky, *Genesis of Ethics*, 183 (Jacob's internal conflicts and inconsistent actions).

7. Jacob's division of his family showed his preference for Rachel, and then Leah: *Etz Hayim*, 203, *d'rash* n. 1–2, *p'shat* n. 1; Ginzberg, *Legends of the Jews*, 303; Ibn Ezra, *Commentary*, 1:319; *Midrash Rabbah*, Gen. 78.8; Visotzky, *Genesis of Ethics*, 189

8. Rashi's comment on Jacob's division of his family: Rashi, *Commentaries*, 1:373n2.

9. The emotional impact on the handmaidens' sons: Visotzky, *Genesis of Ethics*, 189.

10. Jacob's parental favoritism as a source of the upcoming violence by Dinah's brothers in Shechem, as well as the later vengeful actions by Joseph's brothers at the pit: Visotzky, *Genesis of Ethics*, 189.

11. Jacob repeated the parental favoritism of his parents: Moyers, *Genesis*, 301 (comment by Burton Visotzky); Visotzky, *Genesis of Ethics*, 189.

12. Joseph was shielding Rachel from being claimed by Esau: Culi, *Torah Anthology*, 3a:148; or from being forcibly seized by him: Ginzberg, *Legends of the Jews*, 303; *Midrash Rabbah*, Gen. 78.10; Rashi, *Commentaries*, 1:374–75n7.

13. **Leah seems confident and unafraid:** Culi, *Torah Anthology*, 3a:148.

14. **A peaceable Jacob evaded Esau's vengeance:** *Etz Hayim*, 203–4, d'rash n. 4; Ginzberg, *Legends of the Bible*, 188; *Midrash Rabbah*, Gen. 78.9; *Hachut Hameshulash*, 655 (citing Kimchi). For a detailed discussion of the brothers' meeting, see Supplement H: *Midrash on the Reconciliation of Jacob and Esau*, at www.jerryrabow.com.

15. **Jacob hid Dinah from Esau:** Ronson, *Women of the Torah*, 153–54; Townsend, *Midrash Tanhuma*, 220.

16. **Jacob's hiding of Dinah continued his disregard of Esau's firstborn priorities:** *Midrash Rabbah*, Gen.76.9, 80.4; Zornberg, *Beginning of Desire*, 226.

17. **Dinah could have reformed Esau:** Townsend, *Midrash Tanhuma*, 220; Weissman, *Midrash Says*, 325.

18. **Jacob was wrong to have withheld Dinah from Esau:** Townsend, *Midrash Tanhuma*, 220.

19. **Dinah "went out" just as Leah "went out":** Rashi, *Commentaries*, 1:382–83n1.

20. **Dinah is likewise criticized for initiating sexual activity:** Epstein, *Torah Temimah*, 146; Neusner, *Talmud of the Land of Israel*, 31:94 (*Sanhedrin* 2:6).

21. **Midrash does not strongly condemn Leah for "going out":** See discussion of the mandrakes incident in chapter 4, above.

22. **Dinah was at fault for additional improprieties:** Attar, *Or Hachayim*, 283; *Midrash Rabbah*, Gen. 80.5.

23. **Leah held responsible for Dinah's actions:** *Midrash Rabbah*, Gen. 80.5; Townsend, *Midrash Tanhuma*, 217–19.

24. **Dinah shows how daughters repeat their mothers' errors:** *Midrash Rabbah*, Gen. 80.1; Rashi, *Commentaries*, 1:382–83n1; Townsend, *Midrash Tanhuma*, 217.

25. **To "come in to" indicates sexual relations without love, but not necessarily rape:** R. E. Friedman, *Commentary on the Torah*, see 115–16n.

26. **"Grabbed her" or "took hold of her" connote violence:** Brown, *Brown-Driver-Briggs*, 305.

27. **The harsh language here indicates that Dinah was a victim of rape:** Attar, *Or Hachayim*, 283; Culi, *Torah Anthology*, 3a:166; Bass, "No Means No," 87.

28. **Dinah's brothers' revenge may have been justified even if there were no rape:** R. E. Friedman, *Commentary on the Torah*, see 115–16n.

29. **Shechem's true emotions:** *Hachut Hameshulash,* 665 (citing Kimchi: he was only trying to placate her); Townsend, *Midrash Tanhuma,* 221 (he came to love her).

30. **Dinah as the doubly violated token in a political game:** Aschkenasy, *Woman at the Window,* 58.

31. **Jacob's failure to react:** Armstrong, *In the Beginning,* 95 (because Dinah was the daughter of Leah); Townsend, *Midrash Tanhuma,* 217, 219 (because women are to blame if they suffer because of being gadabouts).

32. **Dinah's brothers reacted while Jacob remained silent:** Armstrong, *In the Beginning,* 97–98.

33. **Leah was alive at the time of Dinah's encounter with Shechem:** Raver, *Listen to Her Voice,* 71.

34. **Simeon and Levi acted as true brothers:** *Hachut Hameshulash,* 668 (citing Kimchi); *Midrash Rabbah,* Gen. 80.10; Rashi, *Commentaries,* 1:387n25.

35. **Why Dinah remained at Shechem's palace:** Frymer-Kensky, *Reading the Women,* 189; Raver, *Listen to Her Voice,* 71; Visotzky, *Genesis of Ethics,* 196–97.

36. **Dinah warned her family of Shechem's intended attack:** Ginzberg, *Legends of the Jews,* 309; Weissman, *Midrash Says,* 328.

37. **Dinah had to be forced to return home:** *Midrash Rabbah,* Gen. 80.11.

38. **Simeon had to promise to marry Dinah:** *Midrash Rabbah,* Gen. 80.11; Culi, *Torah Anthology,* 3a:78.

39. **Dinah as Zebulun's twin:** Weissman, *Midrash Says,* 292.

40. **Dinah as the mother of Simeon's son:** *Midrash Rabbah,* Gen. 80.11.

41. **Dinah as the mother of Shechem's son:** *Hachut Hameshulash,* 670 (citing Kimchi).

42. **The legend of Joseph marrying the daughter of Dinah and Shechem:** *Etz Hayim,* 255, d'rash n. 45; Ginzberg, *Legends of the Bible,* 232; Ginzberg, *Legends of the Jews,* 347–49; Bin Gorion, *Mimekor Yisrael,* 1:71–72; Weissman, *Midrash Says,* 292.

43. **Circumcision as a fitting revenge for Shechem's rape:** Biale, *Eros and the Jews,* 23.

44. **Morality of the brothers' negotiations:** Attar, *Or Hachayim,* 284–85 (with wisdom); Ramban (Nachmanides), *Commentary,* 1:416 (with subtlety); *Targum Onqelos,* 120 (with wisdom); Rashi, *Commentaries,* 1:384n13 (with cleverness; with wisdom). See also Brown, *Brown-Driver-Briggs,* 599 (smooth, polished), 941 (with deceit or treachery).

45. The brothers' response as continuation of the theme of deceit appearing in the blessing and wedding episodes: R. Alter, *Genesis*, 191n13.

46. The brothers' revenge was justified: Rashi, *Commentaries*, 1:384n13.

47. The brothers' revenge as a model of appropriate response in Diaspora: Hirsch, *Pentateuch*, 2nd ed., 1:523–24n25.

48. Dinah later married Job: Culi, *Torah Anthology*, 3a:163; Ginzberg, *Legends of the Bible*, 266; *Midrash Rabbah*, Gen. 57.4, 76.9.

49. Why the entire kingdom of Shechem deserved punishment: Attar, *Or Hachayim*, 286–88 (the people participated in Dinah's abduction or imprisonment); Rambam (Maimonides), *Mishneh Torah*, bk. 14, p. 234 (Kings and Wars 9.14: the people failed to control their rulers); Ramban (Nachmanides), *Commentary*, 1:419 (the people must have been wicked); Weissman, *Midrash Says*, 327 (the people failed to control their rulers); and see Ramban (Nachmanides), *Commentary*, 1:416 (the brothers' violence was unplanned and just got out of hand).

7. Deaths of Rachel, Leah, and Jacob

1. Midrashic discussions about Rachel's death and burial:

   (a) Burial on the road necessary for later redemption of the exiles: Bialik, *Book of Legends*, 50; Culi, *Torah Anthology*, 3a:197; *Midrash Rabbah*, Gen. 82.10; Rashi, *Commentaries*, 1:528n7; Ronson, *Women of the Torah*, 161.

   (b) Death at the border necessary to avoid illegality of her marriage in the Holy Land: Culi, *Torah Anthology*, 3a:195–96; Rashi, *Commentaries*, 1:360n5; Ronson, *Women of the Torah*, 160 (citing Ramban); Tuchman and Rappaport, *Passions*, 316 (citing Ramban).

   (c) Burial outside Machpelah resulted from Rachel's bargain over the mandrakes: *Midrash Rabbah*, Gen. 72.3; Rashi, *Commentaries*, 1:332n15.

   (d) Death due to either Jacob's inadvertent curse or his delay in tithing: Zornberg, *Beginning of Desire*, 374.

   (e) For a detailed discussion of Rachel's death: See Supplement I: *Midrash on the Death of Rachel*, at www.jerryrabow.com.

2. The Jacob-Leah-Rachel love triangle simplified by Rachel's death: Zornberg, *Beginning of Desire*, 212.

3. Leah as the wife and Rachel as the mistress: Rosenblatt, *After the Apple*, 92.

4. **Fusing of the twelve stones at Bethel:** *Midrash Rabbah*, Gen. 68.11 (signifying unity of the twelve tribes); Rashi, *Commentaries*, 1:311n11 (text references to the stone[s] change from plural to singular); Weissman, *Midrash Says*, 276.

5. **The sisters' ages at their deaths:** Ginzberg, *Legends of the Jews*, 358 and n. 307.

6. **Jacob came to love Leah:** *Book of Jubilees*, 36:23–24, p. 214; *Midrash Rabbah*, Gen. 71:2.

7. **Reuben acted in order to validate Leah's marriage:** *Hachut Hameshulash*, 685 (citing Kimchi).

8. **Jacob ceased marital relations with Bilhah:** *Book of Jubilees*, 33:1–16, pp. 197–99.

9. **Reuben making a political claim:** R. Alter, *Genesis*, 200n22.

10. **Reuben did not have sexual relations with Bilhah:** Culi, *Torah Anthology*, 3a:198; Epstein, *Torah Temimah*, 150; *Midrash Rabbah*, Gen. 98.4; Rashi, *Commentaries*, 1:396n22; Talmud, *Shabbat* 55b; Weissman, *Midrash Says*, 336.

11. **The family mourned Leah:** Ginzberg, *Legends of the Jews*, 320.

12. **Esau's attack on Jacob's family:** Ginzberg, *Legends of the Bible*, 192; Ginzberg, *Legends of the Jews*, 320–22; Weissman, *Midrash Says*, 323–24.

13. **The sun healed Jacob's strained thigh:** Ginzberg, *Legends of the Jews*, 302; *Hachut Hameshulash*, 651 (citing Kimchi).

14. **Esau's sons became subservient to Jacob's sons:** Ginzberg, *Legends of the Jews*, 321–22.

15. **How Jacob and Esau divided their inheritance from Isaac:** Ginzberg, *Legends of the Jews*, 320 and n. 316.

16. **How Jacob became entitled to bury Leah in Machpelah:** Ginzberg, *Legends of the Jews*, 316.

17. **Jacob preferred the younger Ephraim over Manasseh because of Ephraim's greater destiny:** Rashi, *Commentaries*, 1:532n19.

18. **Jacob was Isaac's intended firstborn:** *Midrash Rabbah*, Gen. 63.8; Nachshoni, *Weekly Parashah*, 136; Sforno, *Commentary*, 131n20; Weissman, *Midrash Says*, 241.

19. **Joseph was Jacob's intended firstborn:** Bialik, *Book of Legends*, 47; Culi, *Torah Anthology*, 3b:517–18.

20. **Jacob apologized to Joseph for Rachel's hasty burial on the road:** Leibowitz, *Bereshit*, 538–39; Rashi, *Commentaries*, 1:528n7.

21. **Jacob justified Rachel's burial by her later role in arguing for the exiles:** Rashi, *Commentaries*, 1:528n7; Tuchman and Rappaport, *Passions*, 337.

22. Jacob justified Rachel's burial by the practical circumstances: Tuchman and Rappaport, *Passions*, 336 (citing Ramban).

23. Jacob's grief establishes the standard for husbands: Talmud, *Sanhedrin* 22b.

24. The extent of Jacob's grieving for Rachel: R. Alter, *Genesis*, 288n7; Leibowitz, *Bereshit*, 539.

25. Jacob's concern that Leah's status will eclipse Rachel's: Attar, *Or Hachayim*, 399–400; Hirsch, *Pentateuch*, 2nd ed., 1:647–48n7.

26. Jacob adopted Joseph's sons to increase Rachel's legacy: R. Alter, *Genesis*, 288n7; Hirsch, *Pentateuch*, 2nd ed., 1:647–48n7.

27. Machpelah has resumed its importance as a revered Jewish site: *Encyclopaedia Judaica*, 2nd ed., s.v. "Machpelah, Cave of."

28. The importance of Rachel's burial location: Bialik, *Book of Legends*, 50; Culi, *Torah Anthology*, 3a:197; Jer. 31:14–16; *Midrash Rabbah*, Gen. 82.10; Rashi, *Commentaries*, 1:528n7; Ronson, *Women of the Torah*, 161.

29. The psychological underpinnings of the rivalry between Leah and Rachel: Zornberg, *Beginning of Desire*, 209–10.

30. The Leah-Rachel rivalry continued through Joseph and his brothers: See Berman, *Midrash Tanhuma*, 271–73; Bialik, *Book of Legends*, 55–56; *Midrash Rabbah*, Gen. 93.7. For a detailed discussion of how the family conflict continued among Jacob's children, see Supplement J: *Midrash on the Leah-Rachel Rivalry Continuing through Joseph and His Brothers*, at www.jerryrabow.com.

31. Esau was killed at Jacob's burial: Ginzberg, *Legends of the Bible*, 262; Ginzberg, *Legends of the Jews*, 414.

32. Esau's death at Jacob's burial fulfilled Rebekah's prophetic concern: Bialik, *Book of Legends*, 57; Talmud, *Sotah* 13a.

33. Jacob is the ultimate hero of Genesis: Berman, *Midrash Tanhuma*, 167.

34. Rachel's sacrifice on Leah's wedding night gave her the power to move God: *Midrash Rabbah*, Lam. Prologue 24.

35. Rachel generally receives priority today: See discussion in chapter 5 text at note 25.

36. Rachel is beloved by the people: Dresner, *Rachel*, x–xi.

Conclusion

1. Leah was eventually appreciated and loved: *Book of Jubilees*, 36:22–24, p. 214; *Midrash Rabbah*, Gen. 71.2.

BIBLIOGRAPHY

Akenson, Donald Harman. *Surpassing Wonder: The Invention of the Bible and the Talmuds*. New York: Harcourt, Brace, 1998.

Alshech, Rabbi Moshe ben Chayim (Hakadosh). *Torat Moshe: Commentary on the Torah*. Vol. 1. Translated by Eliyahu Munk. Jerusalem: Rubin Mass, 1988.

Alter, Robert. *The Art of the Biblical Narrative*. New York: Basic Books, 1981.

———. *Genesis: Translation and Commentary*. New York: W. W. Norton, 1996.

Alter, Yehudah Leib, of Ger. *The Language of Truth: The Torah Commentary of the Sefat Emet*. Translated by Arthur Green. Philadelphia: Jewish Publication Society, 1998.

Anton, Maggie. *Rashi's Daughters: Book One—Joheved*. Glendale CA: Banot, 2005.

Armstrong, Karen. *In the Beginning: A New Interpretation of Genesis*. New York: Alfred A. Knopf, 1996.

Aschkenasy, Nehama. *Woman at the Window: Biblical Tales of Oppression and Escape*. Detroit: Wayne State University Press, 1998.

Attar, Chayim ben. *Or Hachayim: Commentary on the Torah*. Vol. 1. Translated by Eliyahu Munk. New York: Lambda, 1999.

Bass, Lia. "No Means No." In *The Women's Torah Commentary*. Edited by Elyse Goldstein. Woodstock VT: Jewish Lights, 2000.

Berman, Samuel A. *Midrash Tanhuma-Yelammedenu*. Hoboken NJ: KTAV, 1996.

Biale, David. *Eros and the Jews: From Biblical Israel to Contemporary America*. New York: Basic Books, 1992.

Bialik, H. N., and Y. H. Ravnitzky. *The Book of Legends*. New York: Schocken, 1992.

Bin Gorion, Micha Joseph, comp. *Mimekor Yisrael, Classical Jewish Folktales.* 3 vols. Bloomington: Indiana University Press, 1976.

Bloom, Harold. *The Book of J.* Biblical text translated by David Rosenberg. New York: Vintage, 1990.

Book of Jubilees. Translated by R. H. Charles. 1902. Jerusalem: Makor, 1971. Also available online at http://www.piney.com/ApocJubilee Book.html.

Borscheid, Peter. "Romantic Love or Material Interest: Choosing Partners in Nineteenth-Century Germany." *Journal of Family History* 11, no. 2 (1986): 157–68. Abstracted at jfh.sagepub.com/content/11/2 /157.abstract.

Braude, William G. "Pirke de-Rabbi Eliezer." In *Tanna debe Eliyyahu: The Lore of the School of Elijah.* Translated by Israel J. Kapstein. Philadelphia: Jewish Publication Society, 1981.

Brown, Francis, S. R. Driver, and Charles A. Briggs. *The Brown-Driver-Briggs Hebrew and English Lexicon.* Peabody MA: Henrickson, 1906, 2000.

Cherry, Shai. *Torah through Time.* Philadelphia: Jewish Publication Society, 2007.

Cohen, Rev. A. *Everyman's Talmud.* New York: Dutton, 1949.

Culi, Yaakov. *The Torah Anthology (Me'am Lo'ez).* Vols. 2, 3a, and 3b. Translated by Aryeh Kaplan. New York: Maznaim, 1977.

Diamant, Anita. *The Red Tent.* New York: Picador USA, 1997.

Dresner, Samuel H. *Rachel.* Minneapolis: Fortress, 1994.

Encyclopedia of Biblical Interpretation. New York: American Biblical Encyclopedia Society, 1959.

Epstein, Boruch Halevi. *The Essential Torah Temimah.* Vol. 1. Translated by Shraga Silverstein. New York: Feldheim, 1989.

Etz Hayim Torah and Commentary. Edited by David Lieber. *P'shat* commentary edited by Chaim Potok. *D'rash* commentary edited by Harold Kushner. New York: Jewish Publication Society, 2001.

Fields, Harvey J. *A Torah Commentary for Our Times.* New York: UAHC Press, 1990, 1993.

Fox, Everett. *The Five Books of Moses.* New York: Schocken, 1995.

Frank, Adam. "Conservative or Orthodox?" *Voices of Conservative/ Masorti Judaism* 6, no. 2 (Winter 2012/2013).

Friedman, Alexander Zusia. *Wellsprings of Torah.* New York: Judaica Press, 1969.

Friedman, Richard Elliott. *Commentary on the Torah: With a New English Translation.* New York: HarperCollins, 2001.

——. *Who Wrote the Bible?* New York: Summit, 1987.

Frymer-Kensky, Tikva. *Reading the Women of the Bible.* New York: Schocken, 2002.

Ganzfried, Solomon. *Code of Jewish Law.* New York: Hebrew Publishing Co., 1961.

Ginzberg, Louis. *Legends of the Bible.* Philadelphia: Jewish Publication Society, 1909, 1956.

——. *Legends of the Jews.* 2nd ed. Philadelphia: Jewish Publication Society, 2003; computer ed. Varda Books, 2003.

Goldstein, David. *Jewish Folklore and Legend.* New York: Hamlyn, 1980.

Hachut Hameshulash: Commentaries on the Torah by Rabbeinu Chananel, Rabbi Sh'muel ben Meir (Rash'bam), Rabbi David Kimchi (R'dak), Rabbi Ovadiah Seforno. Translated by Eliyahu Munk. Vols. 2 and 3. Brooklyn NY: Lambda, 2003.

Hammer, Jill. *Sisters at Sinai: New Tales of Biblical Women.* Philadelphia: Jewish Publication Society, 2001.

Hertz, J. H., *The Pentateuch and Haftorahs.* 2nd ed. London: Soncino, 1960.

Hirsch, Samson Raphael. *The Pentateuch.* 2nd ed. Translated by Isaac Levy. New York: Judaica Press, 1971.

Holy Scriptures. Philadelphia: Jewish Publication Society, 1917.

Hyman, Naomi M. *Biblical Women in the Midrash: A Sourcebook.* Northvale NJ: Jason Aronson, 1997.

Ibn Ezra (Abraham ben Meir). *Ibn Ezra's Commentary on the Pentateuch.* Vol. 1. Translated by H. Norman Strickman and Arthur M. Silver. New York: Menorah, 1988.

The Jewish Study Bible: Jewish Publication Society Tanakh Translation. Edited by Adele Berlin and Marc Zvi Brettler; Michael Fishbane, consulting editor. New York: Oxford University Press, 2004.

King James Bible, 1611 edition. http://www.kingjamesbibleonline.org.

Kirsch, Jonathan. *The Harlot by the Side of the Road.* New York: Ballantine, 1997.

——. *Moses, A Life.* New York: Ballantine, 1998.

Klein, Isaac. *A Guide to Jewish Religious Practice.* New York: Jewish Theological Seminary, 1979.

Kugel, James L. *The Bible as It Was.* Cambridge MA: Belknap/Harvard University, 1997.

————. *How to Read the Bible*. New York: Free Press, 2007.

Labowitz, Shoni. *God, Sex and Women of the Bible: Discovering Our Sensual, Spiritual Selves*. New York: Simon & Schuster, 1998.

Lamm, Maurice. *The Jewish Way in Love and Marriage*. San Francisco: Harper Row, 1980.

Leibowitz, Nehama. *Studies in Bereshit (Genesis)*. 4th rev. ed. Jerusalem: World Zionist Organization, 1981.

Midrash Rabbah. Brooklyn: Judaica Press/Soncino Press, 1983. CD-ROM version: New York: Davka /Judaica Press, 1995.

Miles, Jack. *God: A Biography*. New York: Alfred A. Knopf, 1995.

Mitchell, Stephen. *Genesis: A New Translation of the Classic Biblical Stories*. New York: HarperCollins, 1996.

Moyers, Bill. *Genesis: A Living Conversation*. New York: Doubleday, 1996.

Nachshoni, Yehuda. *Studies in the Weekly Parashah*. Vol. 1. New York: Mesorah, 1988.

Neusner, Jacob. *Introduction to Rabbinic Literature*. New York: Doubleday, 1994.

————. *Genesis Rabbah: The Judaic Commentary on Genesis—A New American Translation*. Vol. 1, *Parashiyyot One through Thirty-Three. Genesis 1:1–8:14*. Brown Judaic Studies, no. 104. Atlanta: Scholars Press, 1985.

————. *Genesis Rabbah: The Judaic Commentary on Genesis—A New American Translation*. Vol. 2, *Parashiyyot Thirty-Four through Sixty-Seven. Genesis 8:15–28:9*. Brown Judaic Studies, no. 105. Atlanta: Scholars Press, 1985.

————. *Genesis Rabbah: The Judaic Commentary on Genesis—A New American Translation*. Vol. 3, *Parashiyyot Sixty-Eight through One Hundred. Genesis 28:10–50:26*. Brown Judaic Studies, no. 106. Atlanta: Scholars Press), 1985.

————. *Lamentations Rabbah: An Analytical Translation*. Brown Judaic Studies, no. 193. Atlanta: Scholars Press, 1989.

————. *The Talmud of Babylonia: An Academic Commentary—Tractate Megillah*. USF Academic Commentary Series, no. 19. Atlanta: Scholars Press, 1995.

————. *The Talmud of Babylonia: An American Translation—Tractate Berakhot*. Brown Judaic Studies, no. 78. Chico: Scholars Press, 1984.

————. *The Talmud of Babylonia: An American Translation—Tractate Sanhedrin*. Brown Judaic Studies, no. 81. Chico: Scholars Press, 1984.

Neusner, Jacob, ed. *Talmud of the Land of Israel*. Chicago: University of Chicago Press, 1989.

New English Bible, Oxford Study Edition. New York: Oxford University Press, 1970, 1976.

Park, James. *New Ways of Loving: How Authenticity Transforms Relationships*. 6th ed. Minneapolis: Existential Books, 2007. Excerpted at http://www.tc.umn.edu/~parkx032/NWL1.html.

Plaut, W. Gunther. *The Torah: A Modern Commentary*. New York: Union of American Hebrew Congregations, 1974, 1983.

Powell, Kimberly. *Romance through the Ages: Customs of Love, Marriage & Dating*. Quoted at http://genealogy.about.com/cs/timelines /a/romance_history.htm.

Preuss, Julius. *Biblical and Talmudic Medicine*. Translated and edited by Fred Rosner. New York: Jason Aaronson, 1978, 1993.

Rabow, Jerry. *50 Jewish Messiahs*. Jerusalem: Gefen, 2002.

Rambam (Maimonides). *The Code of Maimonides (Mishneh Torah)*. Book 14. Translated by Abraham M. Hershman. New Haven: Yale University Press, 1949.

Ramban (Nachmanides). *Commentary on the Torah*. Vol. 1. Translated by Charles B. Chavel. New York: Shilo, 1971.

Rashbam (Rabbi Samuel Ben Meir). *Rabbi Samuel Ben Meir's Commentary on Genesis: An Annotated Translation*. Translated by Martin I. Lockshin. Lewiston NY: Edward Mellen, 1989.

Rashi. *The Torah with Rashi's Commentaries*. Vol. 1. Artscroll/Saperstein Edition. Brooklyn NY: Mesorah, 1995.

Raver, Miki. *Listen to Her Voice: Women of the Hebrew Bible*. San Francisco: Chronicle, 1998.

Reddy, William M. *The History of Romantic Love*. http://www.duke.edu /~wmr/romantic%20love.htm.

Ronson, Barbara L. Thaw. *The Women of the Torah: Commentaries from the Talmud, Midrash, and Kabbalah*. Northvale NJ: Jason Aronson, 1999.

Rosen, Norma. *Biblical Women Unbound*. Philadelphia: Jewish Publication Society, 1996.

Rosenblatt, Naomi Harris. *After the Apple: Women in the Bible*. New York: Miramax, 2005.

Rymanover, Menahem Mendel. *The Torah Discourses of the Holy Tzaddik Reb Menachem Mendel of Rimanov, 1745–1815*. Translated by Dov Levine. Hoboken NJ: KTAV, 1996.

Sarna, Nahum M. *The JPS Torah Commentary: Genesis*. Philadelphia: Jewish Publication Society, 1989.

———. *Understanding Genesis*. New York: Jewish Theological Seminary/McGraw-Hill, 1966.

Schiffman, Lawrence, ed. *Texts and Traditions*. Hoboken: KTAV, 1998.

Sforno. *Commentary on the Torah*. Translated by Raphael Pelcovitz. Brooklyn NY: Mesorah, 1987, 1997.

Siddur Sim Shalom for Shabbat and Festivals. New York: Rabbinical Assembly, 1998.

Soloveitchik, Joseph B. *The Lonely Man of Faith*. Northvale NJ: Jason Aronson, 1965.

Soranus (of Ephesus). *Gynecology*. Translated by Owsei Temkin. Baltimore: Johns Hopkins Press, 1956.

Steinsaltz, Adin. *The Talmud: The Steinsaltz Edition—A Reference Guide*. Vol. 1. New York: Random House, 1989.

Talmud (Soncino). CD-ROM version. New York: Davka/Judaica Press, 1991.

Tanach. Edited by Nosson Scherman. Stone Edition. Brooklyn NY: Mesorah, 1996.

Targum Onqelos to Genesis. Translated by Bernard Grossfeld. Wilmington DE: Michael Glazier, 1988.

Torah: A Women's Commentary. Edited by Tamara Cohn Eskenazi and Andrea L. Weiss. New York: URJ Press, 2007.

Torah: The Five Books of Moses. 3rd ed. Philadelphia: Jewish Publication Society, 1962, 1992.

Townsend, John T., trans. *Midrash Tanhuma*. Hoboken NJ: KTAV, 1989.

Tuchman, Shera Aranoff, and Sandra E. Rappaport. *The Passions of the Matriarchs*. Jersey City NJ: KTAV, 2004.

Visotzky, Burton. *The Genesis of Ethics*. New York: Crown, 1996.

Weissman, R. Moshe. *The Midrash Says: The Book of Beraishis*. Brooklyn NY: Benei Yakov, 1980.

Zohar. Vol. 2. Translated by Daniel C. Matt. Stanford CA: Stanford University Press, 2004.

Zornberg, Avivah Gottlieb. *The Beginning of Desire: Reflections on Genesis*. New York: Doubleday, 1995.

INDEX

Isaac, 172; and Abraham, 6, 86; birth of, 86, 88; death of, 137–38, 172; Jacob obtaining blessing from, 8, 30, 32, 50, 53, 57–59, 61, 77, 97, 130, 159, 172; and Rebekah, 6, 125

Ishmael, ix, 6, 7, 29, 63, 88, 90

Issachar, 107, 110

Jacob: and anger toward Rachel, 82–83, 85–86, 87; bequest by, 167, 173–74, 177; Bilhah and Zilpah given as wives to, 10, 29–30, 87–88, 90–95, 97, 110; and blindness motif, 31, 32–33, 40; Canaan-to-Haran flight by, 8, 17, 30, 40, 84, 124–25, 130, 139, 141, 180–81; curse of, 130–31; death and burial of, 14, 105, 173–82; as deceiver and trickster, 23, 24, 27, 38, 39, 58, 159; divisions marking life of, 139–40; Esau's birthright obtained by, 7, 23, 30, 84, 173; Esau's confrontation with upon return to Canaan, 137–38, 139–41, 142–43; feelings toward Leah of, 61, 72–73, 76, 77–78, 161, 171, 185; Haran-to-Canaan return by, 113, 123, 124, 130, 137, 138, 139, 180–81; as Laban's "brother," 21–22, 27, 50–51; Laban's initial meeting with, 25–28; labor for Laban by, 9–10, 26–27, 37, 39–40, 48, 67, 69, 119, 123–24, 126, 132; and Leah's death, 171, 173, 178; Leah's yearning for love from, 36, 77, 99, 111, 115, 119, 178, 185; and love for

Rachel, 9, 10, 18, 23, 34–35, 37, 39–40, 47, 67–71, 73, 76, 85, 98, 127, 143, 173, 178–79; and marriage negotiations with Laban, 36–39; moral and psychological profiles of, 6, 9, 18–19; and morning-after talk with Laban, 57–60; and morning-after talk with Leah, 60–62, 211n29; name of, 7–8; passivity of, 153–54, 170; and prophecies, 19, 41, 78, 84, 97, 113, 114, 133, 139–40, 166–67, 196; and Rachel's death, 166–67, 168, 175–78; Rachel's first kiss from, 17–18, 53; Rachel's initial meeting with, 14, 17–24; and Rebekah, 8, 19, 40, 97, 153, 180–81; righteousness of, 8, 39, 69–70, 123, 158; and rivalry with Esau, 6–7, 8, 134, 138, 180; sexual impatience of, 41–42, 51, 54, 63, 75; and sexual realtions with Leah, 53–54, 62, 75, 80, 104, 109; and sexual relations with Rachel, 68, 103–4; and Shechem-Dinah episode, 152–54; obtaining Isaac's blessing, 7, 8, 30, 32, 50, 53, 57–59, 61, 77, 97, 130, 159, 172; tears of, 18–20; wealth of, 126–27, 133; and wedding-night hoax, 9–10, 47–54, 60–62, 63, 125–26, 159

Jeremiah, 183

Jewish people, 55, 67–68; oppression of, 181; and Promised Land, 55–56, 160; and violence, 160

Jewish Publication Society, xv

Job, 160, 198

Joseph, 31, 71, 87, 142, 143, 198; birth of, 120–23; Jacob's bequest to, 167, 173–74, 177; naming of, 122, 123, 134; as savior of Jews, 10, 166, 177; selling into slavery of, 180; wife of, 157–158

Jubilees, book of, 75, 94, 168–69, 198

Judah, 10, 63–64, 171; naming of, 77, 78, 79, 134; tribe of, 1, 31, 177, 179, 184

Judaism: conversion to, 159; laws of, 24, 62, 69, 119, 197 (under *halakhah*); and miracles, 129; Rachel's precedence in, 127–28, 184

Judith, ix

justice: biblical concept of, 87; divine, 49–50, 59, 61, 146, 148; measure-for-measure, 4–5, 20, 24, 49–50, 58–59, 61, 87, 148, 199

Kabbalah, 198

Kimchi, David (Radak), 198

Kugel, James, xiii, 21

Laban, 15, 62, 198; as deceiver and trickster, 21–22, 23, 39, 47, 51; and Esau, 28, 133; handmaidens given to daughters by, 29–30, 94–95; initial meeting with Jacob, 25–28; Jacob as "brother" of, 21–22, 27; Jacob's labor for, 9–10, 26–27, 37, 48, 69, 119, 123–24, 126, 132; Jacob's morning-after talk with, 57–60; Leah's and Rachel's feelings for, 125, 126; marriage negotiations with Jacob, 36–39; as personification of evil, 28; stealing of teraphim from, 128–31; and wedding feast, 45–48; and wedding-night hoax, 9–10, 47–48, 49, 50, 51, 63, 125–26, 159

Leah: age of, 15–16, 42, 134; barrenness and infertility of, 109, 148, 154, 218n18; Bible's treatment of, 2–3, 9, 10, 28–36, 42, 103, 105, 170, 184, 187; birth of daughter by, 111–17, 167; birth of sons by, 1, 76–80, 87, 107–11; burial at Machpelah of, 2, 14, 20, 105, 163, 172–73, 178, 179, 184–85; change and self-transformation of, 79, 162, 187–88, 189; death of, 154, 170–71, 178; and Dinah-Shechem episode, 154; and Esau, 34, 73, 143, 154, 207n39; eyes of, 31–32, 33–34; and feelings about Laban, 125, 126; fertility of, 74–75, 119; God and, 2, 11, 35–36, 74–75, 82, 108–9, 120, 143, 188; importance of, 1–4, 188–89; and mandrakes incident, 101–7, 163, 217n7; as Matriarch, x, 2, 98, 128, 163, 187, 189–90; moral heroism and character of, 3, 35–36, 43, 99, 117–18, 135, 162, 188, 189; overcoming of adversity by, 98–99, 187, 188; physical appearance of, 11, 32, 42, 134; prophetic knowledge by, 114; righteousness of, 115, 120; Zilpah given as handmaiden to, 29–30, 94–95

Also by Jerry Rabow

Digital Photography Tutor

Guide to Jewish Mourning and Condolence

50 Jewish Messiahs